GLOBAL TELEVISION AND
THE POLITICS OF
THE SEOUL OLYMPICS

POLITICS IN ASIA AND THE PACIFIC
Interdisciplinary Perspectives

Haruhiro Fukui
Series Editor

Global Television and the Politics of the Seoul Olympics,
James F. Larson and Heung-Soo Park

Japan's Foreign Aid: Power and Policy in a New Era,
edited by Bruce M. Koppel and Robert M. Orr, Jr.

Popular Protest and Political Culture in Modern China: Learning from 1989,
edited by Jeffrey N. Wasserstrom and Elizabeth J. Perry

Southeast Asia in the New International Era, Clark D. Neher

FORTHCOMING

China Under Reform: A Preliminary Reassessment, Lowell Dittmer

Japan's Land Policy and Its Global Impact, Shigeko N. Fukai

Mass Politics in the PRC: State and Society in Contemporary China,
Alan P.L. Liu

Nationalism in Contemporary Japan, Bruce Stronach

Comparative Politics of Asia, Sue Ellen M. Charlton

Popular Protest and Political Culture in Modern China,
Second Edition, edited by Jeffrey N. Wasserstrom
and Elizabeth J. Perry

Southeast Asia in the New International Era, Second Edition,
Clark D. Neher

GLOBAL TELEVISION AND THE POLITICS OF THE SEOUL OLYMPICS

James F. Larson

NATIONAL UNIVERSITY OF SINGAPORE

Heung-Soo Park

YONSEI UNIVERSITY

Westview Press

BOULDER • SAN FRANCISCO • OXFORD

070.444
L334g
1993

Politics in Asia and the Pacific: Interdisciplinary Perspectives

Copyright © 1993 by Westview Press, Inc.

Published in 1993 in the United States of America by Westview Press, Inc., 5500 Central Avenue, Boulder, Colorado 80301-2877, and in the United Kingdom by Westview Press, 36 Lonsdale Road, Summertown, Oxford OX2 7EW

Library of Congress Cataloging-in-Publication Data
Larson, James F.
  Global television and the politics of the Seoul Olympics / James
F. Larson, Heung-Soo Park.
    p.   cm. — (Politics in Asia and the Pacific)
  Includes bibliographical references and index.
  ISBN 0-8133-1693-6.—ISBN 0-8133-1694-4 (pbk.)
  1. Television and sports—Korea (South).   2. Sports and state—
Korea (South).   3. Olympic Games (24th : 1988 : Seoul, Korea).
4. Television and politics—Korea (South).   5. Korea (South)—Foreign
relations.   I. Park, Heung-Soo.   II. Title.   III. Series.
GV742.3.L37   1993
070.4'49796'095195—dc20   93-24871
                                                                               CIP

Printed and bound in the United States of America

      The paper used in this publication meets the requirements
(∞)   of the American National Standard for Permanence of Paper
      for Printed Library Materials Z39.48-1984.

10   9   8   7   6   5   4   3   2   1

Contents

Tables and Figures

Foreword

On September 17, 1988, more than one billion people worldwide watched the Olympic Opening Ceremony, telecast from Seoul. This was the largest television audience in history. Other aspects of this mega-event include the $407 million sale of television rights to the Olympics, with NBC making up the largest single part of this record-setting total. *Global Television and the Politics of the Seoul Olympics* provides an inside look at what went on during the 16 days of athletic competition, and the several years leading up to this mega-event.

One sees that where sports stop and television broadcasting begins is not a clear line of distinction, nor is the boundary of Olympic broadcasting with politics always so clear. For example, on June 29, 1987, the man who would become President of Korea made a declaration in which he stated that sweeping democratic reforms would be implemented in his nation. This after a long tradition of military dictatorships in Korea during the several decades of the cold war. His declaration was undoubtedly necessitated by the approaching Olympics and the threat of demonstrations by students and others.

The televising of the Olympics provided a window with the world for Korea. Over 10,000 accredited broadcast personnel were in Seoul in September 1988. How they reported the Olympics, and depicted the nation in which the Olympics took place, made this news event "The Broadcast Olympics." The 1988 Olympics affected the television system in Korea, leading to a major upgrading of the nation's telecommunication infrastructure (a similar impact has occurred in other nations; for example, Mexico's television system went to color broadcasting at the time of the 1968 Olympics).

Television also influenced the Olympics. Seoul has a 13-hour time difference with New York. Thus, for prime-time (8 PM to 11 PM) broadcasts in the United States, the Olympics events were scheduled so that final events (especially for those sports most popular in the United States) were held in the morning. Further, a special daylight savings time was implemented in Korea, so as to get the Olympic events more closely synchronized with New York time.

This book helps us understand that a lot goes on at the Olympics in addition to the sports events. It is very well written by its co-authors, the leading American communication scholar on Korea and the leading Korean scholar of communication. *Global Television and the Politics of the Seoul Olympics* will be of interest to students of media events, to those concerned with international communication, and to those who wish to understand how media institutions shape the messages that they produce.

It is a classy treatment of a major world event, written in a way that is insightful and involving. I commend it to you.

Everett M. Rogers
University of New Mexico

Preface

Much of the scholarly attention to Asia in recent decades involves efforts to explain its remarkable economic dynamism. Another subject of growing interest, as the existence of this new series attests, is contemporary politics in the region. However, the relationship between politics and economics has evolved differently in each country around the region. In some nations, such as Taiwan or South Korea, rapid economic growth was accompanied by political liberalization. In others, such as the Philippines, the move toward political openness preceded the economic takeoff. Another example, Singapore, has experienced economic dynamism while continuing authoritarian political leadership that rejects some fundamental tenets of liberal democracy.

Part of the explanation for such differences among nations undoubtedly lies in the cultural diversity of the vast Asian region. However, a convincing interpretation must augment considerations of economics, politics, and culture with issues posed by the arrival of the information age in Asia. The global revolution in telecommunications affected many nations in Asia during the 1980s. One political consequence was that the scrutiny of global television and uses of the new media became factors in such occurrences as the "people power" revolution in the Philippines, the events in Beijing's Tiananmen Square in 1989, and political liberalization in Taiwan and South Korea.

In the Korean case, the new role of communications and the media in politics was accentuated by the world's largest regularly planned television and media event—the Seoul Olympics. This book places those Games—by most measures, among the most successful in modern Olympic history—in the context of both South Korea's own telecommunications revolution and the contemporaneous evolution of global television. Both the local and the global treatment are necessary to explain South Korea's political transformation, though they can be neatly separated only for purposes of discussion and analysis. From the inception of our research, it was apparent that the Olympic project was inseparable from the political situation in South Korea. Conversely, given the integral role of television and other media in the Olympics, South Korean politics were becoming enmeshed with international political concerns and the impending global scrutiny of television.

In this light, our study illustrates a conceptual difficulty that confronts students of political communication with increasing frequency. It can quickly be grasped by posing the question of whether Roh Tae Woo's now-famous June 29 declaration of 1987 was an act of foreign or domestic policy. Clearly, it was both. In communication terms, he addressed not only a nationwide television audience in South Korea but also an international audience through the global news media. Politically, his declaration not only addressed some of the core issues that separated opposition groups and the ruling party at home but also sent strong and reassuring messages to constituencies throughout the world about South Korea's commitment to successfully host the Olympics.

The June 29 declaration is but one of several aspects of the Korean case that demonstrate how profoundly the media have changed contemporary politics. Another example is the manner in which the media themselves increasingly become actors in the political process. This occurred during the Seoul Olympics when NBC Television sparked controversy and helped ignite a public wave of anti-American sentiment in Korea.

This book was begun in 1985 as a collaborative attempt to observe and document the process of planning, producing, and broadcasting the world's largest regularly planned media event. Even then, at mid-decade, the amount of effort and attention given to the forthcoming Seoul Asian Games and Olympics made it apparent that they could not be treated simply as media events.

Our study asks what the Seoul Olympics—both as an event and as a long-term national effort—contributed to political, economic, and cultural change in South Korea. (That tremendous change has occurred in all three of these spheres is beyond question.) Politically, they were a central tool of South Korea's successful Northern policy and a factor in liberalization at home. Economically, they coincided with the rise of the nation's electronics and telecommunications industry to the position of leading exporter and most strategic economic sector. Culturally, they were pivotal in opening up new perspectives on the outside world, particularly for younger generations of Koreans.

Certainly, political, economic, and cultural change would have occurred in South Korea in the absence of the Seoul Olympics, partly as a result of the nation's five-year economic and social development plans.

However, our study suggests that the Games were an important catalyst, principally because they have become such a large television and media-centered phenomenon.

The book stresses a political communication interpretation of the Seoul Olympics at multiple levels. On a global scale, the Olympic Games were a massive exercise in image politics for Korea, utilizing television along with other media. The paramount goal was to update and improve South Korea's national image. On this count, we present findings that are necessarily partial, rather than definitive: Although global television expanded and matured during the 1980s, researchers are still in the early stages of learning how to assess such massive exposure. Nevertheless, our findings suggest that a new and largely positive image of Korea was conveyed by television and the other media. By implication and based on some limited survey research by other scholars, there can be little doubt that public perceptions of the nation also shifted, especially in the former Socialist bloc nations.

At a national level, the Seoul Olympics were a political project with numerous political consequences. The decision to bid for the Olympics originated with a relatively small number of high government and sports officials while Park Chung Hee was still president. As our study illustrates, the top-down, authoritarian character of Korean politics in the 1970s and 1980s largely explained how the Games could be used as a project to mobilize an entire nation. Furthermore, Korean leaders were well aware of the historical precedent of the 1964 Tokyo Olympics, which many thought had boosted Japan's economic growth. They understood that the Olympics would have tremendous publicity value in their international propaganda battle with North Korea. Even so, they could hardly have imagined the degree to which the rapid evolution of global television during the 1980s would magnify the eventual scope and impact of the Games.

Another level of politics intrinsic to the modern Olympics are the politics of the global telecast. These entail such elements as the negotiation of broadcast rights, corporate sponsorship, accreditation for journalists, and the construction, planning, and control of broadcasting facilities for the Games. Our perspective is that such preparations center on considerations of control, with the ultimate object, in the case at hand, being the messages that embodied the meaning of the Seoul Olympics, along with the scope and duration of their dissemination around the world.

Finally, our study addresses questions of Olympic television and media policy. These have asserted themselves with increasing urgency as television and telecommunications have continued their rapid global development. The policy questions touch important interests of many constituencies, from the International Olympic Committee (IOC) and its Radio and Television Commission to sports bodies, national Olympic committees, and broadcasting organizations and unions. Ultimately, they involve issues about the institutions and the process through which Olympic television policy is carried out. The universalistic aims of the modern Olympic movement dictate a process that is inclusive—not limited, for example, to the IOC and the dominant commercial broadcasting organizations. It seems appropriate that the Seoul Olympics, having achieved nearly universal participation, should also help to bring the question of Olympic television and media policy into clearer focus. For such a policy lays down the ground rules for the political process through which the contemporary Olympic spectacle is shaped.

James F. Larson
Heung-Soo Park

Acknowledgments

The authors of this book first met in 1985 when Professor Larson was a Visiting Fulbright Scholar at Yonsei University. Their acquaintance grew into a longer-term collaboration during which many individuals and organizations provided support for the research reported here. Indeed, so many helped that the mention of a few entails the risk of omitting others. Therefore, the authors wish to first acknowledge those many others—not named here or cited on later pages—whose assistance contributed in some way to this book.

Fellow communication faculty members at Yonsei participated with research, counsel, and support through the entire project. They are Professors Choe Chungho, Suh Chung Woo, Oh In-Hwan, Lee Sang Hwe, and Kim Young Seok. Professors Lee and Kim conducted a nationwide survey before and after the 1986 Asian Games, the results of which were subsequently presented at two international conferences on the Olympics, the media, and cultural exchange. Professor Jae Won Lee of Cleveland State University spent the fall of 1988 as a Fulbright Scholar in Yonsei's Department of Mass Communication, worked with the authors on the early stages and design of the present research, and conducted participant-observation research during the Olympics.

The larger community of scholars in communications and other fields, both in Korea and internationally, also stimulated the present research. In 1987, Professor Kang Shin Pyo of Hanyang University and his University of Chicago colleague Professor John MacAloon organized the "International Conference on the Olympics and East/West and South/North Cultural Exchange in the World System." The same year, Professor Thomas McPhail and colleagues at the University of Calgary hosted a conference on "The Olympic Movement and the Mass Media," occasioned by the 1988 Olympic Winter Games. The Seoul Olympic Organizing Committee sponsored both the "World Academic Conference of the Seoul Olympiad," which preceded the Games in 1988, and the "Seoul Olympiad Anniversary Conference" in 1989. Professor Heung-Soo Park served on the executive committee for the first meeting and as secretary-general for the second. These gatherings marked a significant increase in scholarly activities associated with the Olympics. In particular, they brought together a group of scholars who were centrally concerned with television and the other media, as well as the media's role in cultural exchange. In May 1990, research on television coverage of the Seoul Olympic opening ceremony was the basis of a major panel presentation for the international symposium on "Sport ... the Third Millenium," organized by Professor Fernand Landry and his colleagues at Laval University in Quebec City, Canada.

The research for this book was endorsed and supported in many ways by the Seoul Olympic Organizing Committee (SLOOC), through its president, Park Seh-Jik, and by Kim Un-Yong, South Korea's member of the International Olympic Committee (IOC), and many other individuals. Among them were Cho Sung Min, director-general for broadcasting, and Lee Jae Hong, press spokesman for SLOOC, who also served as its representative on the IOC Press Commission.

The host broadcaster, KBS/SORTO, also provided essential cooperation and information. Its director, Lee Jung-Suk, gave generously of his own time and also arranged for observation and data-gathering in the International Broadcast Center and interviews with key staff members of the host broadcasting organization, including Hwang Kil-Woong.

The Goldstar Electronics Company, Ltd., through its president, Koo Cha Hak, provided an in-kind grant of videocassette recorders to the University of Washington School of Communications; this allowed extensive off-the-air videotaping in Seattle, resulting in a research archive of more than 250 hours of U.S. network, Canadian, and Soviet coverage of Korea and the Olympic Games. The SKC Company, Ltd., through its president, Lee Gi Dong, provided all the videotape used in that project. Professor Nancy Rivenburgh of the University of Washington School of Communications, then a doctoral student, supervised videotaping of Olympic television coverage in Seattle and used the archive for her doctoral dissertation.

As an important outgrowth of the academic conferences held in Seoul, the authors began a collaboration with Professor Miquel de Moragas, communication scholar and director of the Centre d'Estudis Olimpics at the Autonomous University of Barcelona. With him, Professor Larson and his colleague Nancy Rivenburgh served on the central research team for the project on "Global Television and the Olympic Games: The Experience of Barcelona 1992." Professor Park directed the Korean component of that research.

One legacy of the Seoul Olympics lies in the effort to broaden the relationship between the Olympic movement and the scholarly community worldwide. It is hoped that the publication of this volume will illustrate in a small way the convergence of multidisciplinary research interests that occurred in Seoul, thanks to the efforts of many individuals. The authors' goal is to lay out one perspective, a politics- and communication-centered one, through which future generations of scholars may achieve a better understanding of the Olympics and related global phenomena.

1

The Seoul Olympics as
a Critical Case Study

During much of September 1988, the eyes of the world focused through television and other media on South Korea, as its capital, Seoul, hosted the Games of the Twenty-fourth Olympiad. Not since the Korean War nearly four decades earlier had such massive worldwide attention centered on the Korean peninsula. Nor had prior events opened such a wide "window on the world" for citizens of a nation that had long ago been known as the "Hermit Kingdom." For most of the present century, Korea had endured either Japanese colonialism or a predominantly military relationship with other nations as a cold war flash point. Both the world focus of attention and the new perspectives afforded the Korean public are essential to an understanding of the broad political, cultural, and economic import of the Seoul Olympics. Neither can be adequately understood without careful attention to the central role of the media, especially television, in the modern Olympic movement. That much seemed clearly implied, whether intentionally or not, in the choice of an official slogan for the Games. It was, after all, global television that most effectively brought "the world to Seoul" and "Seoul to the world."[1]

By all measures, the Seoul Olympics were the largest planned television event in history to that date. In an era of increasingly global communications, that distinction alone is hardly remarkable. The Summer Olympics perennially serve as an important showcase for the international television industry, allowing it to field-test the latest in audiovisual, telecommunications, and computer technologies. A growing body of scholarship acknowledges that the Games are a paradigm for the study of media events and communication processes in a world knit more closely together by electronic communications.[2] The Olympics are a prominent illustration of

1

a general point made by Kenneth Boulding: "Communication is a phenomenon of outstanding importance in social systems. It becomes increasingly important as we move through time in both biological and societal evolution."[3] Others have made similar observations from many different intellectual perspectives. They range from cultural studies approaches to "super media" and sociological analyses of the effects of the new electronic media to "cultural indicators" research and various studies of the "postindustrial" or "information society."[4]

The Olympics also hold a special position in the realm of politics. Within the world political structure, they are both "actor and stage," to borrow Richard Espy's metaphor, and they embody the three basic forces of nationalism, internationalism, and transnationalism.[5] In the drama that unfolded around the Seoul Olympics, Korea became both actor and stage in a highly distinctive manner. The 1988 Summer Olympics were, in reality, a decade-long pan-national project that was the exception rather than the rule in the modern Olympics. The massive effort can be explained, in part, by Korea's status as a developing nation. During the 1970s the government of President Park Chung Hee had been forced to abandon a bid to host the Asian Games for lack of adequate resources. By contrast, the period of preparation for the Seoul Olympics coincided with rapid economic growth and South Korea's transformation into an industrialized nation.

Beyond the preceding considerations of television and politics, the larger import of the Twenty-fourth Olympiad becomes apparent only through its unique relationship to four contemporaneous transformations taking place internationally and in Korea during the 1980s. First, the Games occurred during the communications revolution of the late twentieth century, epitomized for many by television but encompassing the whole range of information and telecommunications technologies. The changes in communication were highly visible in such areas as business and commerce, the media themselves, diplomacy, war and other crises, and international sport, including the Olympics. The Armed Forces Korea Network (AFKN), a broadcasting service to U.S. military troops, made the Seoul Olympics the first in history during which virtually the entire population of the host country could view the full telecast of another nation over its own airwaves.[6] Moreover, South Korea's own communications revolution featured extremely rapid development, especially during the 1980s, of a modern telecommunications infrastructure. Along with transportation, such an infrastructure has become a prerequisite for successfully hosting the modern Olympics. South Korea's efforts not only met the requirements for the Seoul Olympic Games but also helped set the stage for accelerated movement toward developing an information society in Korea.

The second transformation was the breakdown of the cold war consensus that had provided both an underpinning and a frame of reference for many countries of the East and West, the North and South. Korea's status as a noncombatant nation in World War II, whose division by outside powers marked an early and defining moment in the cold war,[7] decisively shaped its approach to the Seoul Olympics—hence, the poignancy and power of the opening ceremony theme, "Toward One World, Beyond All Barriers." From the very first discussions in 1978 of a possible bid for the Olympics, the Games were viewed by South Korean leaders as an instrument of foreign policy through which the central political problem of national division might be addressed. Initially, they were seen as a means to counter North Korean propaganda and to help terminate the state of confrontation with the North.[8] Closer to 1988, the Olympics became an important vehicle for the pursuit of South Korea's *Nordpolitik,* or Northern policy.

As the cold war waned, a third transformation took place within South Korea during the 1980s. The nation moved from the heavy-handed military dictatorships of the cold war era toward a more liberal, democratic system of government. The Fifth Republic under President Chun Doo Hwan was the last of these dictatorships, and it became widely and somewhat derisively known among Koreans as the "Sports Republic" because of both the Olympics and the introduction of professional sports in Korea. The International Olympic Committee (IOC) awarded the Games to Seoul in September 1981, in the wake of a staged military coup led by General Chun and only fifteen months after the tragic and bloody Kwangju prodemocracy uprising of May 1980. The timing virtually ensured that the success or failure of the Twenty-fourth Olympiad would be inextricably linked to political change in South Korea. For many Koreans, the Olympics were tainted from the beginning by an association with the Chun regime. On the other hand, those who wanted to use the Games as a vehicle for sustaining the military government would be disappointed. Indeed, the prospective and actual international scrutiny generated by the Olympics was a decisive factor in the resolution of political tension that occurred with the "June 29 declaration" in 1987. Even that resolution was, in important respects, simply an agreement to postpone public inquiry into Kwangju and the activities of President Chun's Fifth Republic until after the nation successfully hosted the Olympics.

Finally, the Seoul Games coincided with an important transformation of the Olympic movement that marked its "coming of age" as a transnational organization and actor. The change primarily involved questions of financing and how to achieve universal participation. It led many to credit IOC President Juan Antonio Samaranch with restoring health to the Olympic movement and placing it on a businesslike footing. The introduction of

The Olympic Program (TOP) to coordinate global corporate sponsorship gave the International Olympic Committee a second major source of income to supplement television rights revenues. Meanwhile, the overall relationship of the Olympics to television and other media continued to evolve, and the movement achieved virtually global scope. To accomplish this, Samaranch played an active role in negotiations to ensure full participation by Socialist bloc nations and, until the very last minute, to seek the participation of North Korea.

The import of these changes in communication and politics extends far beyond the Olympic movement per se or the Seoul Olympics in particular. However, the changes do help to explain both the broad context and the relevance of the present study. In this volume, we make the important assumption that an understanding of the contemporary Olympics as sport or as politics requires a grasp of the essential new role played by global television and other media in the Olympic movement. However commonly this may be acknowledged, there is not a single book yet published that focuses directly and exclusively on the Olympics as a political communication phenomenon, centered around and driven by television. Through this study, we seek to fill that gap and indicate an agenda for future research on the Olympics, the media, and communication.

By adopting such a perspective, we have followed a long tradition of research on the role of communication and the media in human societies, and we interpret the Olympics as largely a media-constructed reality. Walter Lippmann articulated this perspective in his study of public opinion and the news when he observed that

> the news is not a mirror of social conditions, but the report of an aspect that has obtruded itself. The news does not tell you how the seed is germinating in the ground, but it may tell you when the first sprout breaks through the surface. It may even tell you what somebody says is happening to the seed under ground. It may tell you that the sprout did not come up at the time it was expected. The more points, then, at which any happening can be fixed, objectified, measured, named, the more points there are at which news can occur.[9]

In a similar manner, the modern Olympics are constructed every four years and at points in between based on events and processes that break through to the surface of global attention, based largely on the activities of television and the other media. Moreover, because the Olympics move to a new host city every four years, they provide a compelling opportunity to study the process through which human communication, via the media and other means, is constructed and reconstructed. Although the Seoul experience offered a single empirical case, it raised, at multiple levels, several central questions for media and communication theory. To what extent do communications media shape society and vice versa? Are the media an instrument of dominance or of pluralism in societies? Do the media contribute more to unity, stability, and integration—acting as a centrifugal force—or to change, fragmentation, diversity, and mobility—as a centripetal force? How is power over the media allocated among various actors and interests?[10] The intended theoretical import of this study pertains to international political communication and especially relationships among transnational actors, states, the media, public opinion, and policy processes in an era of globalization. Chapter 2 sets forth the theoretical approach of the study in greater detail.

The remainder of this chapter establishes more completely the critical nature of this study. It does so through an extended discussion of the Seoul Olympics in terms of (1) their size and scope as a media spectacle, (2) the revolution in global communications, (3) political changes within Korea and around the world, and (4) changes in the Olympic movement.

The Scope of Seoul as a Media Event

The scope of Olympic television and other mediated communication can only be approximated by a combination of measures. The Games involve more nations and broadcast organizations than any other event; they also showcase the latest in television and telecommunications technology and attract the largest international viewing audience. Indeed, while viewers around the globe gather by their television sets to follow the Games, the television and press contingents form a global village of a different sort in the host city, with the International Broadcast Center (IBC) and Main Press Center (MPC) serving as a modern village square.[11] In these media centers, as around the world, television screens form the focal point for the Olympic experience. All this is financed largely through television rights fees and television-dependent global sponsorship revenues, the two major sources of income on which the Olympics depend. The Winter Games, although smaller than the Summer Olympics, are also a major global media event.

The Seoul Olympics set new records by all these measures, several of which will be analyzed in later chapters. Here, it will be sufficient to summarize the scale of the Seoul Olympics as a media event, in terms of the hours of television broadcast, the size of audiences, and the viewing patterns around the world.

A total of 160 nations aired some of 10,500 hours of television from Seoul, with major countries broadcasting between 150 and 200 hours of coverage (or an average of 10 to 12 hours per day) during the Olympics. The total multistation television output from the Seoul Olympics was highest in the following countries:

Hong Kong	686 hours
Republic of Korea	608
United Kingdom	461
Malaysia	435
Mexico	414
Brazil	396

Single-channel coverage was highest on TVE 2 in Spain, which aired 270 hours of mostly live broadcasts. Other stations that aired more than 200 hours of coverage included RAI 2 (Italy), TSI (Switzerland), Imevision (Mexico), KBS 2 (Korea), ATV Gold (Hong Kong), RTM II and TV 3 (Malaysia), and BBC 1 (United Kingdom). NBC's coverage in the United states totaled more than 177 hours, averaging 9.3 hours per day for 19 days, including the preview and review programs.[12]

The average number of broadcast hours per country was 65.6 worldwide, but in key markets, the average was nearly double that with 115.5 hours. By comparison, 64 nations carried a total of 3,500 hours of television coverage of the Calgary Winter Games in 1988, for an average of 54.7 hours per country.[13] Table 1.1 shows the cumulative television audiences for the Seoul Olympics and the Calgary Winter Games by major world regions, expressed in terms of gross impacts.[14] The 10.4 billion figure for gross cumulative viewers of the Seoul Olympics was exceeded, at the time, only by that of 1986 World Cup Soccer, which was telecast in 166 nations and estimated to have more than 13.5 billion gross cumulative viewers.[15] The 1988 Calgary Winter Games had an estimated cumulative viewership of approximately 6.6 billion. Here, it is of crucial importance to note that the quantitative estimate of gross viewership for the Seoul Olympics only takes into account the 16-day telecast of the Games per se, from opening through closing ceremonies. In other words, it is an event-centered estimate that would dramatically underestimate television coverage of *Korea* generated by the Seoul Olympics. Taking the example of NBC Television in the United States, these estimates ignore audiences for "The Today Show," the network's morning talk program, which was broadcast from Seoul for the entire week preceding the Games. But even accounting for that in the case of NBC, the figures would severely underestimate the network's attention to Korea over a much longer period of time. It becomes clear that a fundamental issue in thinking about the overall extent of Korea's exposure to the world through global television is the question of focusing on an event rather than a process. Although the Olympics as an event provided a focal point and impetus for a worldwide outpouring of publicity about Korea, an accurate sense of the full extent of such publicity can only be gained by conceiving of the Olympic communication as a process measured in years.

Table 1.1 Cumulative television audiences by region for the 1988 Olympic Games (gross impacts)

	Winter Games		Summer Games		Total	
	Millions	%	Millions	%	Millions	%
Worldwide cumulatives						
Total	6,560	100.0	10,400	100.0	16,960	100.0
Average/day	410		650		n/a	
By region						
Western Europe	1,855	28.3	2,340	22.5	4,195	24.7
Eastern Europe	1,685	25.7	2,390	23.0	4,075	24.0
North America and Caribbean	920	14.0	1,260	12.1	2,180	12.9
Central and South America	230	3.5	540	5.2	770	4.5
Africa	195	3.0	440	4.2	635	3.7
Asia	1,610	24.5	3,120	30.0	4,730	27.9
Middle East	50	0.8	200	1.9	250	1.5
Oceania	15	0.2	110	1.1	125	0.7

Source: Sponsorship Research International (Division of ISL Marketing Research Department), 1989.

A study of 1988 Olympic Games audiences in the United States, United Kingdom, France, and Brazil showed that an average of 90.5 percent of all adults viewed some part of the Olympic telecast. Viewership was highest in Brazil, where the Olympics achieved a 94.5 percent penetration, and lowest in France, with 88.1 percent. (An industrial action that lasted for more than one week of the Games period in France was responsible for decreased viewership there.) The same study showed the average number of hours of Olympic television viewed in those countries:[16]

United Kingdom	26.1 hours
Brazil	24.1
United States	17.6
France	8.9

The opening ceremony perennially attracts the largest global audience of any single Olympic event. It is also of great importance to commercial broadcasters and their advertisers because it leads into the Olympic telecast, helps set the tone for what follows, and is therefore thought to influence the size of the audience for the complete Olympic telecast. In the context of the present research, the opening ceremony is also important because it is where Olympic athletes can accomplish what John MacAloon called their "central mission ... to appear as a nation among nations on the largest world stage. Full recognition as a sovereign nation in the modern world now requires two performances: membership in the United Nations and marching in the Olympic opening ceremony."[17] Of course, the host nation is on center stage, and the Seoul Olympic opening ceremony provided an unprecedented opportunity for Korea to present itself to the world as a nation and culture.

International Sports and Leisure (ISL) Marketing audited the opening ceremony audiences in 20 countries and used these audited figures to project the worldwide audience for both live and delayed telecasts of the Seoul and Calgary opening ceremonies. This procedure yielded an estimated international audience of 460 million viewers for the Seoul opening ceremony, compared with 270 million viewers for Calgary's. However, these are considered minimum *audience* levels, especially in the case of Seoul. Indeed, the host broadcaster for the 1988 Olympics, KBS/SORTO, estimated the worldwide audience for the Seoul Olympic opening ceremony at more than 1 billion viewers. The ISL Marketing report qualified its estimates:

> These estimates ignore certain key factors such as the relative distribution of potential viewers by time zone (broadcast time being a major influence on viewing), and the fact that the sample countries over-represent developed markets. As TV ratings in less-developed countries tend to be higher than in the industrials (reflecting both a greater propensity to view and less channel choice), the Opening Ceremony estimates ... should be treated as **minimum** numbers. This is particularly true for the Summer Games.[18]

Taken together, the measures of worldwide broadcast hours and audience attention leave little doubt about the massive scale of the Seoul Olympics as a television spectacle. Moreover, the effects of the unprecedented global focus on South Korea must be considered against the historical context of sporadic and low levels of media attention to that nation in the years preceding the Olympic Games.

Olympic Communication in a Global Television Era

Beginning in 1994 with the Seventeenth Olympic Winter Games, the Winter and Summer Olympics will alternate every two years.[19] This change is one more formal confirmation that the Olympics have evolved into much more than two major athletic "events." For the host city as well as for the Olympic movement and its various constituencies around the world, they are now an ongoing, long-term process, as acknowledged by Fundamental Principle Number 7 in the most recent revision of the Olympic Charter, which states that "The activity of the Olympic movement is permanent and universal. It reaches its peak with the bringing together of the athletes of the world at the great sport festival, the Olympic Games."[20]

The change to a new Olympic calendar, discussed in more detail later in this volume, was a direct result of the expanding importance of global television and associated commercial sponsorship activities. The increasingly continuous nature of Olympic coverage by television and other media underscores the need to situate the Seoul Olympics within several long-term trends that reflect the emergence of global television more generally.

A key point is to understand that this reference to *global television*,[21] like references to *television and other media*, denotes a complex of interrelated communication technologies rather than a single technology or medium. Two major changes under way in these communications technologies are (1) the continued dramatic increases in computing power and decreases in its cost, which create powerful pressures for decentralization, and (2) the advances in satellite, cellular, and fiber-optic technologies for conveying various kinds of information. These have been termed the *microcosm* and *telecosm*, respectively.[22] In the television industry, they are illustrated by such developments as the computerized newsroom, high-definition television, and digital recording and production techniques.

Furthermore, the term *global television,* as used throughout this book, encompasses more than technologies. It involves economics, organizational routines, patterns of ownership and control, politics, and ideological factors.[23] In short, the three broad dimensions of global television presented here are technology, ownership and economics, and cultural and social considerations. The emphasis of this study on global television is deliberate for its rapid evolution in the 1970s and 1980s established new parameters for intercultural communication.[24] Indeed, individual chapters of this book are intended, at a descriptive level, to document the pervasive nature and scope of that influence. The following discussion outlines the arrival of the global television era internationally as well as in Korea itself.

In retrospect, it is clear that the emergence of global television took place in three stages, each approximately a decade long. In the first, during the 1960s, television viewing increased in the industrialized economies of the world, but the normal activities of the new medium were far from global in scope. The communication satellite, a key element in the infrastructure for worldwide television, was still relatively new and costly. To use an example from U.S. television, this meant that network news organizations relied on videotapes sent to New York by plane for much of their coverage of the Vietnam War.

The second stage spanned the 1970s, a decade in which the technologies for truly global television were largely put in place. The number of na-

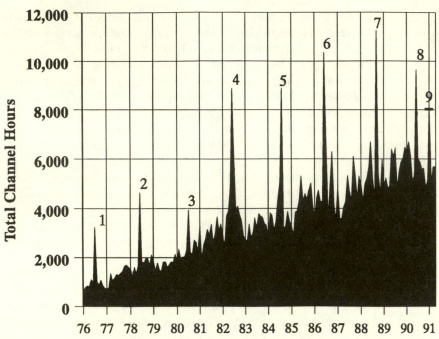

FIGURE 1.1   Intelsat occasional-use video, channel hours.

Note: The numbers within the figure refer to the following significant events—1. Olympics (Canada), 2. World Cup (Argentina), 3. Olympics (USSR), 4. World Cup (Spain), 5. Olympics (United States), 6. World Cup (Mexico), 7. Olympics (Korea), 8. World Cup (Italy), 9. Crisis in the Gulf.

Source: Intelsat, Washington, D.C., 1991.

tions possessing an Intelsat earth station or access to a nearby earth station through terrestrial links more than doubled, increasing from 43 in 1972 to 110 in 1981.[25] Electronic newsgathering (ENG) equipment also became steadily more computerized and portable. Television audiences in the industrialized nations became accustomed to the live or nearly instantaneous broadcasting of news and sports events from different parts of the world. In one tragic example, Olympic sport was transformed into a major focus of television news when terrorists attacked the athletes' village during the 1972 Munich Olympics.

Finally, the 1980s were a decade of global networking, epitomized for many by Ted Turner's Cable News Network (CNN) in the United States. The new networks drew on continued advances in television technologies, including the use of transportable earth stations for satellite newsgathering, which had become the fastest growing segment of Intelsat's international television business by 1990.[26] Figure 1.1 shows the growth in occasional-use television through the Intelsat system from 1976 through 1991. It provides a graphic measure of how sporting events like the Olympics and World Cup Soccer or news events like the crisis in the Persian Gulf generate peak periods of worldwide television traffic.

By early 1992, CNN was the largest global television network, with a total of sixteen foreign bureaus plus eight in the United States. It had also opened an overseas channel, CNN International, to supplement the original channel and its companion, Headline News. The introduction of CNN International was partly a response to competition in Asia from the STAR-TV system—a joint venture of the British Broadcasting Corporation (BBC) and Hong Kong businessman Li Kashing—and the prospect of competition in Europe from the European Broadcast Union (EBU) news channel.

An important goal of CNN International was to provide a more international service and perspective to subscribers around the world, less tied to a U.S. or North American view of world events. As its global reach expanded, the network had confronted, with increasing frequency, a dilemma over the use of a U.S. perspective rather than a broader international orientation in its treatment of events around the world. CNN coverage of the Persian Gulf crisis in 1990 and 1991 illustrated the dilemma as it provided viewers worldwide a glimpse of what international television networks can offer. When war broke out in the gulf, television systems in Asia, Europe, and doubtless other parts of the world as well found themselves with no option but to rebroadcast CNN coverage, using simultaneous translation. Not surprisingly, there was widespread criticism of the strong U.S. perspective in this coverage. The international reliance on a single, U.S.-based network for Gulf War coverage gave impetus to European and Asian discussions of alternative global television networks. More recently, following the establishment of the STAR-TV system, BBC officials claimed its news channel offered more analysis, more authoritative opinion, and a broader worldview than CNN.[27]

The 1980s were not only a decade of networking but also a period during which millions more people around the world acquired the capability to receive television signals. The number of television studios, repeater stations, and television sets in the world more than doubled between the 1976 Montreal Olympics and the Games in Seoul. In 1976, the number of television sets in the world totaled an estimated 300 million, most of which were monochrome. By 1988, that number had increased to more than 750 million, approximately half of which were color sets.[28] As with the diffusion of other new technologies, the spread of television occurred first and most rapidly in the industrialized nations. However, the decreasing cost of television receivers and the availability of small, lightweight, battery-operated sets suggests that television will soon be as universally available as the transistor radio.

Table 1.2   Worldwide audiences for selected television events

	TV Viewers (millions)
Sports Events	
Seoul Olympic opening ceremony, 1988[a]	1,000+
World Cup final match, 1986	652
Olympic Games opening ceremony, 1984	522
World Cup final match, 1982	450
Wimbledon final, 1985	350
Olympic Games opening ceremony, 1980	300
Other Events	
First moon landing, 1969	490
British royal wedding, 1981	420

[a]Seoul Olympic Organizing Committee and KBS/SORTO estimates.

Source: ISL Marketing, "The Communication Potential of Perimeter Board Advertising," paper (Lucerne, Switzerland: ISL Marketing, 1987).

As shown in Table 1.2, the spread of television around the world is accompanied by an increase in the size of the global audience for certain televised events. On September 17, 1988, an international audience estimated at more than 1 billion viewers tuned in for the Olympic opening ceremony telecast from Seoul; the majority of them were viewing simultaneously, and they constituted the largest global television audience to that point in history. MacAloon highlighted the unprecedented global attention made possible by television and suggested that "if this single social fact could be adequately interpreted—that is, interpreted in a way which does not reduce its global intercultural complexities to the perspective of one region or civilization—then we would have a far more compelling understanding of the contemporary 'world system' than we do now."[29]

The large worldwide viewership for events like the Seoul Olympic opening ceremony reflects the generally increased public reliance on television for entertainment and information. However, the formation of such mass audiences is dictated by more than simply new media technologies. Indeed, these audiences exist in the face of a widely acknowledged trend toward more fragmented and specialized audiences, facilitated by the appearance of new technologies for gathering, storing, and disseminating information in many forms, including video.

Whether through massive global attention, as in the Olympic opening ceremony, or in widespread and more specialized uses, television is changing the sociocultural environment of most nations of the world. It is, as advertisers have long known, an intrusive medium that becomes part of the fabric of each society. As observed by Elihu Katz and Daniel Dayan, television viewing is an activity in which large numbers of people routinely "disconnect themselves from their everyday concerns, enter into a protected 'time out', and allow themselves to be transported symbolically elsewhere.''[30] Although viewers may, at times, use television for entertainment or escape, there are also occasions when they turn to television with a sense of purpose, in order to establish a connection with other human beings in their nation or the world. The viewing of news broadcasts is an example of this more purposeful activity. In the United States, Great Britain, and most other industrialized nations, television has replaced newspapers as the public's preferred source of news about international affairs, and all evidence indicates this trend will spread through nearly every nation of the world.

As television technology and air travel make visual newsgathering more commonplace, the economics and structure of the media industries change apace.[31] Thus, the increased public reliance on television is partly a function of its ever-more-pervasive availability. However, it also derives, in important measure, from the inherent capacity of television to convey reports *visually, simultaneously,* and *repetitively.*

The visual immediacy of television is recognized by government officials and representatives of the media as a major consideration in the changing relationship of the media to foreign policy and diplomacy. Television is thought to personalize politics, to the benefit of such individuals as former U.S. President Ronald Reagan or Soviet leader Mikhail Gorbachev. Likewise, British television coverage of the Ethiopian famine in 1984, rebroadcast in the United States and many other nations, was credited with inducing a widespread response in Western countries. Another salient example of the changes wrought by television's visual immediacy is its role in airline hijackings, bombings, and other examples of terrorism. Michael O'Neill noted that television is a dominant medium in terrorist incidents not only because it is capable of transmitting experience in living, visual form but also because it can repeat these visual experiences at will.[32]

Just as television is becoming the main source of news and public affairs information around the world, its instantaneous presentation and selective repetition of visual information makes it the central medium in conveying the Olympic experience. In both cases—public reliance on television for news and use of television to participate in the Olympics—television assumes a more prominent role in intercultural and international communication. Indeed, depending on one's perspective, it either adds depth and dimension to the information available "on the scene" of an occurrence or renders information about other nations and cultures of the world more superficial by editing and offering it in bits and pieces. This criticism is frequently directed at U.S.-style commercial television.

In any consideration of global television generally or Olympic television in particular, the commercial character of the medium must be reckoned with. The money paid by international broadcasters for rights to televise events like the Olympics and the dramatically increased importance of those funds in financing international sporting events indicate television's commercial underpinnings. Revenues from the sale of television rights to the Seoul Olympics totaled $407,125,000 U.S. dollars.[33] Approximately 75 percent of this amount came from the U.S. broadcaster, NBC Television, continuing a pattern of dominance established in earlier Olympic games. The trend toward increased revenues from television rights, with all of its ramifications for the Olympics, began in the early 1970s. Figure 1.2 shows the increase as reflected in the rights payments made by the U.S. Olympic broadcaster. When the amounts shown in the figure are converted to 1960 dollars to eliminate the effect of inflation, they still show the same steady growth over the years.[34] Moreover, the larger rights fees are accompanied by higher expectations of host broadcasting organizations and an overall increase in the amount of money, planning, and time required to accommodate the needs of international broadcasters and the global audience. More importantly, this trend was a major influence on the modern Olympic movement, leading to several adjustments in its financing, especially following the 1984 Los Angeles Olympics.

Another indication of the growing prominence of global television and its commercial character is the more pronounced role of commercial sponsorship in financing international sport, especially since 1984. An industry study estimated that the total worldwide expenditure on sports sponsorship in 1989 was $5 billion.[35] According to that estimate, such spending had more than doubled since 1984. Using another measure, the number of international sports events grew from 315 to 660 between 1977 and 1986.[36] The concurrent expansion of television around the world is viewed by industry experts as the major catalyst in the rapid increase in commercial sponsorship by large transnational corporations in Japan, the United States, and Europe. A related impetus is the desire of certain major transnational firms to improve their corporate images or to create "global brands." In 1988, Landor Associates, an image management consultancy, surveyed consumers in the United States, Japan, and Western Europe, the world's three leading consumer markets. They found that the 10 most powerful corporate or consumer brand names in the world were, in descending order, Coca-Cola, IBM, Sony, Porsche, McDonald's, Disney, Honda, Toyota, Seiko, and BMW. The survey identified the 40 brand names that registered most strongly with consumers in all three markets. Of those, 17 belonged to U.S. corporations, 14 to European companies, and 9 to the Japanese.[37]

By way of comparison, a 1985 survey by ISL Marketing in the United States, West Germany, Portugal, and Singapore revealed that an average of four out of five respondents immediately recognized and identified the Olympic symbol of five interlocking rings. Furthermore, the symbol had a

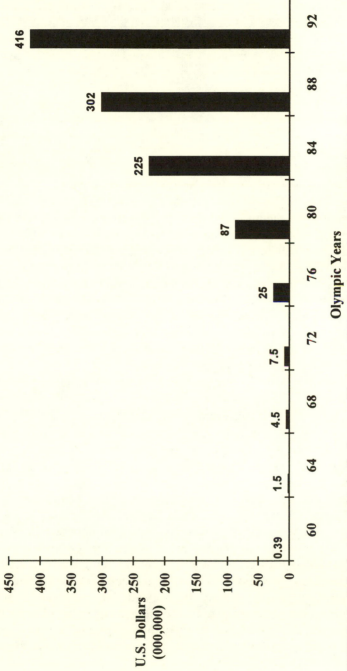

FIGURE 1.2   U.S. television rights for the Summer Olympics, 1960–1992. *Source:* International Olympic Committee.

TABLE 1.3   Consumer association of terms with the Olympic Games (in percentages)

	United States	Federal Republic of Germany	Portugal	Singapore
"International co-operation/ brotherhood"	68	82	82	67
"Worldwide appeal"	58	94	41	42
"Political interference/ boycotts"	31	68	25	11
"Most important sports event"	53	82	79	43

Source: ISL Marketing, *TOP—The Consumer View: An International Research Survey into Sponsorship of the Olympic Games* (Lucerne, Switzerland: ISL Marketing, 1985).

high level of spontaneous and aided identification in comparison with the logos and symbols of corporations like Adidas, Coca-Cola, Kodak, McDonald's, and Shell. The survey also probed a variety of consumer attitudes toward the Olympic symbol and Olympic sponsorship as a whole. From 64 percent to 71 percent of consumers in each of the markets agreed that the presence of the symbol on a package signified that the product was endorsed by the organizers of the Olympic Games. Using a prompt card that listed various positive and negative statements, consumers were asked which of the statements they most associated with the Olympic Games. Some of the results are given in Table 1.3.

For a handful of large transnational corporations, Olympic sponsorship represents an exceptional opportunity to commercially exploit an association between their corporate or brand images, on the one hand, and the ideals or characteristics of the Olympics, on the other. From a marketing communications perspective, the development of a brand image is important because a strong brand offers competitive advantage. Typically, companies that own major brands invest large sums of money in marketing communications aimed at inculcating a certain brand image in the minds of target consumers. Hence, companies consider that they own the brand images that exist in the collective mind of consumers. Accordingly, the value of a brand name is expressed in marketing terminology as *brand equity*. In practice, the exploitable commercial potential of Olympic sponsorship hinges on such matters as the match between a corporation's image goals and the goals of the Olympics, exclusivity of sponsorship within product categories, and, ultimately, the integrity of certain Olympic symbols. However, the "less-is-more" principle in sponsorship suggests that excessive commercial use of symbols may actually decrease their value over time.

The International Olympic Committee and other parties in the Olympic movement also have a strongly vested interest in the associations and meanings attached to the Games. The Olympic Charter declares all of the most central symbols of the Olympic movement to be the IOC's property. These include the Olympic flag, symbol (five interlocking rings), motto (*Citius, Altius, Fortius*), flame, torch, and the entire ceremonial. Olympic emblems like that of the Seoul Games, shown in Figure 1.3, which combine the Olympic rings with another distinctive sign, are approved and regulated by the IOC. In addition, the Olympic Charter prohibits all forms of advertising in and around venues, ensuring that Olympic rather than commercial symbols will appear in television and photographic coverage of the games.[38]

Finally, the host city and nation have a great deal at stake in the integrity and value of Olympic symbols. The Olympic emblem epitomizes the effort to benefit from an association between the Olympics and the nation. The choice and display of an Olympic mascot may also aid the association. The Seoul mascot, Hodori, is shown in Figure 1.4. Especially for Korea, association with the Olympics and its key symbols meant that it had passed an important threshold—along with other developed nations that had hosted the Games, it, too, would proudly take its place in the world.

The corporate, IOC, and national concern with visual images underscores just how central global television and other media have become to the modern Olympics and how much is at stake. The whole question of commercial sponsorship and marketing communications considerations in the Olympics will be discussed at length in Chapter 4.

The Olympics and Change Within Korea

More than any recent Olympiad, the Seoul Olympics posed an immense challenge for an entire nation. In this respect, they inevitably evoke comparisons with the 1964 Tokyo Olympics, which proclaimed Japan's rejoining the world community following World War II. However, Japan was not a developing country as Korea was in 1981 when Seoul was awarded the Olympics. Nor had its economy been devastated at the end of the war. For Japan, the Tokyo Olympics were much more a declaration that it was reentering the world system as a respectable member of the international community after the ignominy of defeat. It is noteworthy that the Olympics in Rome and Munich served the same purpose for the other two Axis powers in World War II.

Perhaps the most important point of the historical parallel between the Seoul and Tokyo Olympics can be found by examining the manner in which two different East Asian nations drew strength from the Olympics

GAMES OF THE XXIVTH OLYMPIAD SEOUL 1988

FIGURE 1.3   Seoul Olympic emblem.

FIGURE 1.4   Seoul Olympic mascot, Hodori.

and used them to expand the scope and health of their respective economies. In the Korean case, such analysis requires particular attention to
those East Asian cultural traditions—for example, mass campaigns and
mass mobilization of a populace—that might help explain the extraordinary impetus the Olympics seemed to provide to the country's overall economic growth, as happened in Japan a quarter century earlier.

As noted previously, the two main infrastructural elements required to
host the modern Olympics, beyond the sports venues themselves, are
transportation and telecommunications. During the 1980s, Korea embarked on a comprehensive and ambitious program to modernize its communications infrastructures. Consequently, it was no coincidence that in
the Olympic year, 1988, South Korea established by law a major new government institute called the Korea Information Society Development Institute (KISDI). Although that institute was only one of several research and
development (R&D) institutes working with and under the Ministry of
Communications, its creation suggests the magnitude of the effort. In principle, the institute was called upon to pursue a broad and ambitious range
of policy research aimed at building an information society, which would
benefit Korea's public, its industry, the government, and the nation's relations with the rest of the world.[39]

For several reasons, it is extremely difficult to quantify the contribution
that Olympic-related investments in these areas make to national development. First, such indirect investments as the Olympic Freeway, completion
of the Seoul subway system, or the expansion of Kimpo International Airport were already part of the Five-year Economic and Social Development
Plan, which was drafted before the Olympic Games were awarded to
Seoul. Second, the use of Olympic-related facilities or investments following the Games must be considered: In the case of Seoul, post-Games use of
facilities was a major consideration from the earliest planning, beginning
in 1982. Third, the overall impact on the national economy must be estimated not only in terms of direct investment in infrastructures needed for
the Olympic Games but also in terms of additional demand that might be
generated in related economic sectors.[40] For Korea, these industries included, among others, tourism, craftworks, sports and leisure, and electronics.

Taking such considerations into account, the Seoul Olympics were a
surplus-generating event in purely economic terms. However, the analysis
in several chapters of this volume is broader, exploring questions about
the political, social, and economic relationship of the Games to Korea's national development. An important question is the degree to which Olympics projects tapped national pride or in other ways added impetus to ongoing developments. Furthermore, in keeping with its overall focus, the
study concentrates on telecommunications and those information indus-

tries whose growth most directly impinges upon political communication processes. By the 1980s, electronics and telecommunications had emerged as a major thrust of Korea's industrial planning.

When the Olympics were awarded to Seoul in 1981, Korea was not only a developing nation but also one whose long division was both a tragic aspect of the cold war and a major challenge for the Olympic movement, coming on the heels of the U.S.-led boycott of the 1980 Moscow Games. Consequently, the import of the Seoul Olympics encompassed delicate negotiations with the North regarding hosting arrangements, the broad effort to ensure participation by all other Socialist bloc nations, the development of new relationships with surrounding regional powers, and South Korea's arrival as a major player in the economic and political system of a post–cold war world. Moreover, these external challenges occurred along with wrenching processes of political, social, and economic change within South Korea itself.

The response of the Korean people to Seoul's selection as Olympic host city can only be fully understood against the harsh reality of the country's ongoing adjustment to a newly installed military dictatorship. Most Koreans realized that the IOC decision gave legitimacy to the military regime, and this realization made the Olympics a bittersweet experience for many of them. The "Korean economic miracle" had been achieved under centralized, military-controlled governments, but by the 1980s public dissatisfaction with the continuing influence of the military was widespread. The political upheaval in Korea involved three major forces: university students, labor, and the military. The first two groups spearheaded the nation's political opposition.[41] The political struggle was over democratization, through which the country sought to remove the worst aspects of the legacy of the military dictatorships that had governed Korea during most of the cold war period.

From a political communication standpoint, the national commitment to host the Seoul Olympics played a key role in this process of democratization and the ongoing resolution of tensions between the competing opposition groups and the ruling party, dominated by the military. As touched upon earlier, the resolution of political tensions within Korea did not take place in isolation from global media forces. In exploring the relationship between the IOC actions in awarding the Games to Seoul and helping it to prepare them, on the one hand, and the processes of change in South Korea, on the other, it is only for narrative convenience that the international and the domestic changes are discussed separately. For example, during early 1987, when discontent with the military government of President Chun Doo Hwan had reached a critical level, Roh Tae Woo, then chair of the ruling Democratic Justice Party and its designated presidential candidate, issued his now-famous June 29 declaration, accepting direct presidential elections and virtually all other opposition demands. It is widely accepted that it was the prospect of massive international media attention surrounding the Seoul Olympics that led to the June 29 declaration.

One set of social changes in South Korea during the 1980s were concomitant with the nation's rapid economic growth over the previous twenty years. These included the urbanization of a formerly agricultural population; the breakdown of the traditional, Confucian sense of community; the phenomenal growth of the Christian religion in the Republic of Korea; and an enormous demographic shift toward a younger median age in the population brought about by the post–Korean War baby boom.[42]

On the other hand, there were, albeit at a different level, social changes more directly linked to the hosting of the Olympics per se. One of the most highly visible changes was the development and popularization of Olympic sports in Korea, some of which had previously been little noticed. Television and the other media played a major role in this process. Also, through a long-running series of public campaigns during the years leading up to the Olympics, the citizens of Seoul and other cities were instructed on topics ranging from proper behavior toward foreign guests, to queuing up for buses and taxis and other aspects of public etiquette according to international or Western standards. Many of the efforts were targeted at institutions, such as restaurants and hotels of all types, that were held to new and higher hygienic standards.

In any analysis of the economic and social impact of the Seoul Olympics, an interesting question arises regarding the effect on urbanization, particularly growth in Seoul. The essentially national proportions of the 1988 Olympics can be fully appreciated only in light of Seoul's special status as a capital city. It is home to fully one-quarter of South Korea's population, all major government agencies, all top schools from elementary through university level, and industry headquarters. Seoul has historically acted like a magnet, drawing individuals and families toward the nation's center of political power and toward educational and career opportunities. For Koreans, the Olympic slogan—"The World to Seoul, Seoul to the World"—carried with it all these connotations but also a measure of concern about the city's unbridled growth. The government of Korea had perennially noted and studied the deleterious effects of concentrated population growth in Seoul and had formulated plans to deal with the problem, in part by decentralizing certain government functions and offices. In that historical context, the impact on Seoul's urban growth of the attention it received as the Olympic host city is a question of some importance.

As noted at the beginning of this section, the Olympics posed a challenge not just for the city of Seoul but also for the entire nation. Here, a word is in order about the character of Korean nationalism, considering that the major cultural manifestations of nationalism encompass physical symbols, rituals, personages, and discourses.[43] Physical symbols included the Seoul Olympic emblem, the tiger cub mascot Hodori, and the Korean flag, all of which were ubiquitously displayed throughout Korea during the years and months leading up to the Olympics, reaching a peak during the Games. Rituals included the Olympic torch relay and the singing of the Korean national anthem during the Olympic opening ceremony and in a longer "fantasia" version for orchestra and choir during a major section of the cultural performance in that ceremony. The political transformation taking place in South Korea placed people like President Chun Doo Hwan and his successor, Roh Tae Woo, on center stage in relation to the Olympics and how Korea as a nation would be officially represented at the Games. Without question, such cultural manifestations of nationalism played an important role in Korea during the 1980s, along with books and other written discourse that presented Korean national identity in narrative fashion. This volume focuses on the character of Korean nationalism as it appeared in television and the other media during the Seoul Olympic experience.

The nature of Korean nationalism in the period leading up to and through the Seoul Olympics is inseparable from the harsh political realities of national division and the contrasting governmental regimes in North and South Korea. All parties concerned viewed the 1988 Olympics in relation to the central political problem of national division and the question of reunification. The South Korean government, the Seoul Olympic Organizing Committee, and IOC made a series of proposals and negotiated with North Korea until the last possible moment in an effort to share the Olympics by allowing the North to host several events. However, the idea of a full cohosting of the 1988 Games was never seriously entertained; such an arrangement would have departed from the precedent of choosing a single host city. These issues will be dealt with in Chapters 6 and 7.

The Olympics and Korea's International Relations

Whatever else may be said about these Olympics, a fundamental reality is that they took place in a nation whose division was one of the early and defining moments of the cold war. This reality shaped not only Korea's approach to the Olympics but also how other nations and the various constituencies in the Olympic movement viewed the Twenty-fourth Olympiad. Domestically, the country's division automatically made reunification the central political question in Korea during the post–World War II era. Internationally, it meant that South Korea was effectively cut off from relations with the Soviet Union, China, most of Eastern Europe, and other Socialist nations during the entire cold war period.

Without question, the most striking and crucially important changes in foreign policy were directed at China, the Soviet Union, and the other So-

cialist nations as South Korea made the Seoul Olympics the principal instrument of its Nordpolitik. This was the policy of opening up to the Socialist nations in an effort to draw North Korea into the international
system and ultimately into closer relations with South Korea, in pursuit of
the cherished goal of national reunification. Indeed, the efforts by South
Korea and representatives of the Olympic movement to negotiate
cohosting of several events of the 1988 Games is an important part of
Olympic history. Although national reunification remains a goal and the
foremost problem of Korean politics today, the success of the Northern
policy on other fronts is now a matter of historical record. In the wake of
the Seoul Olympics, Hungary, several other Eastern European nations,
and eventually the Soviet Union and China established official diplomatic
relations with South Korea.

Mediated communication, much of it through television, is closely
linked in one way or another to most of the significant social, economic,
and political changes associated with the Seoul Olympiad. Within Korea,
as on the international level, the number of spectators physically in the
stands for the Olympic ceremonies and competition pales before the number who experienced the Seoul Olympics as a media-constructed event.

Within the East Asian region, Korea symbolically and emphatically
threw off any vestiges of the Japanese colonial period by winning more
medals than its former colonizer and by choosing 1936 Olympic marathon
gold medalist and national hero Sohn Kee Chung to carry the torch into
the main stadium at the Seoul opening ceremony. Sohn had been forced to
compete in the Berlin Olympics under the Japanese flag and with a Japanese name. Korea also asserted itself vis-à-vis mainland China, most visi-
bly in an intense table tennis rivalry that began in the Asian Games and
continued through the Olympics.

The regional picture is not complete without a word about the Olympics and South Korea's relations with its longtime patron and partner, the
United States. The Games seemed to hold the promise of updating and
dramatically improving Korea's image in the United States, its largest export market. However, the actual benefits of Olympics-related television
and associated publicity in the United States were conditioned, to some
degree, by the prior patterns in both U.S. media coverage of Korea and its
policies toward that nation.

During the 1970s and 1980s, mainstream U.S. media coverage of Korea
had been sporadic and was dominated by treatments of student protests,
other political violence, or state visits and statements by U.S. presidents.[44]
Moreover, the Seoul Olympics occurred during an important and rocky
period of transition in Korean-U.S. relations. The eight years preceding the
1988 Olympics witnessed growing public expressions of anti-American-

ism in South Korea. The decade had begun in Korea with political turmoil and the national tragedy of the Kwangju prodemocracy movement, in which it is estimated that several hundred to several thousand people were killed. Just over eight months later, newly inaugurated U.S. President Ronald Reagan hosted Korean President Chun Doo Hwan as the first major foreign head of state to visit the White House, despite the fact that Chun was an army general who had seized power in a staged military coup and was widely viewed in Korea as responsible for the Kwangju deaths. In this manner, Kwangju and the U.S. response to it became a watershed in the extent and expression of anti-American sentiment in South Korea. As the Seoul Olympics were held, beginning on September 17, 1988, Reagan was completing his second term in office, the United States was preparing to elect a new president, and in South Korea, the climate was ripe for a public outburst of anti-American sentiment. It was against this backdrop that the surge of anti-American press and public comment took place during the Seoul Olympics, although the proximate causes were things like the disorderly behavior of U.S. athletes marching in the opening ceremony and the widespread perception that NBC Television was biased in its reporting of the "boxing incident," in which a Korean staff member entered the ring and punched a referee and the losing Korean boxer staged a sit-in in the ring.

Seoul in the Olympic Movement and the Olympic Movement in Seoul

As briefly noted earlier, the 1988 Games marked the coming of age of the Olympic movement as a transnational organization and actor. This maturation can be seen in the financing of the movement, its new relationship with television and the other media, its achievement of a virtually a global scope, and its new, more active political role.

Some analysts have argued that in the post–cold war world, "culture areas" and transnational organizations will play a more important role than geographical regions and nation-states did in the recent past.[45] Already, the idea that not all important international relations take place strictly between states is generally accepted. The Olympics are a paradigm of such interaction and, hence, an important object of study in the effort to develop a theory of transnational practices.[46]

The Seoul Games marked the beginning of a new, more thoroughly commercial era for the Olympic movement. With the introduction of TOP, corporate sponsorship was planned and executed on a global scale for the first time in Olympic history. The introduction of this program, described in detail in Chapter 4, was a response to a perceived crisis of overde-pendence on television rights revenues, which came to a climax with the 1984 Los Angeles Olympics. Those games made an initial profit of $222 million, which had increased to a surplus pool of $235 million by the time the Los Angeles Olympic Organizing Committee (LAOOC) was dissolved in February 1986.[47] Corporate sponsorship contributed to this financial success, but such activity relied heavily on the large U.S. market, leading some to nickname the Los Angeles Olympics the "Hamburger Games," in a reference to the prominent sponsorship role of the McDonald's Corpora-tion. However, this triumph of free enterprise enraged some members of the IOC and its president, Juan Antonio Samaranch, who did not think a proper portion of the profit was returned to the Olympic movement.[48]

Even before the 1984 Olympics, the IOC had become very concerned about its financial situation and heavy dependence on television money. In 1986, Samaranch himself described the problem: "Until now there has only been one important source of money for us: TV money. That is too danger-ous for the Olympic movement. We are trying to get hold of other sources of money."[49]

The IOC's solution to this problem was to exert more control over com-mercial sponsorship activities, especially those of the large, worldwide sponsors of the Games. It retained ISL Marketing, a Swiss-based company, to administer The Olympic Program. The general notion behind TOP was that ISL, acting as agent for the International Olympic Committee, would buy from the 164 national Olympic committees around the world the rights to the Olympic symbols and then sell them to a selected group of sponsors, such as Kodak, Visa, or Coca-Cola.

The significance of this development can only be appreciated in histor-ical perspective. In his speech on taking office as IOC president, Avery Brundage made the following comment, which would become a recurrent theme during his tenure as IOC chairman from 1952 to 1972.

> Today the Olympic Games have captured the imagination of the world. Ev-ery newspaper, even in the most remote country, has been filled with Olym-pic stories. It is the same with radio, no matter what the language. In the United States more than fifty million people witnessed and listened to a television program staged by Bob Hope and Bing Crosby for the benefit of the United States Olympic Committee. Everyone wants a connection with the Olympic Games. We must be careful and keep our proper balance, re-membering that we are concerned only with sport and not with politics or business. At the same time, we must prevent others from exploiting our prestige for their own personal purpose. Our sole strength is our indepen-dence and our high ideals. We have no money and we have no army. To protect ourselves against those who wish to take advantage, we must keep

our motives pure and honest and clear and we will retain the respect of all.[50]

With the introduction of TOP, the IOC began selling to corporate sponsors precisely the same "connection with the Olympic Games" that Brundage had warned against allowing businesses to use. When Samaranch became president in 1980, the IOC reportedly had cash reserves of only $230,000, a figure that increased to $76.1 million by September 1989.[51] By contrast, from 1989 to 1992, the IOC's income is expected to be $1.84 billion, with about half coming from television rights and the remainder from marketing, sponsorship, and other sources, according to IOC Information Director Michele Verdier.[52] In 1989, Samaranch said, "The only problem I see with commercialism is that the money generated by sports must go back to the sport. The more money there is around the world for sports, the better it will be for the athletes."[53]

In several ways, the Seoul Olympics also ushered in a new working relationship between the media and Olympic organizations. For one thing, the 10,360 accredited broadcast personnel in Seoul to cover the Olympics probably marked an upper limit for the number that can be accommodated for such an event,[54] as noted in the final report of the host broadcaster to the IOC Television Commission.[55] To coordinate the planning and production of the global telecast, an Olympic Broadcast Advisory Committee (OBAC) was formed, consisting of about twenty people representing the IOC Television Commission and major rightsholding networks or broadcast unions. They met once during the Asian Games in 1986, twice in 1987, and twice in 1988.[56]

With Seoul, the Olympic movement was also seeking to recover some semblance of full international participation. This was in keeping with its universalist aims following the cold war era boycotts led by the United States in 1980 and the Soviet Union in 1984. Such universal participation is not only required for the achievement of Olympic ideals but is also a practical necessity if the Olympic movement is to be effective as a transnational actor and organization. Those multinational corporations with global reach are also the ones capable of building and promoting global brands and becoming worldwide sponsors of the Games through TOP. The consequences for Olympic universalism of the broad new role of global corporations in the Games is a major theme of this study.

The Seoul Olympics also showed the new prominence of the Olympic movement in the international political arena. The movement engaged in a prolonged effort, together with the South Korean hosts, to ensure participation by Socialist bloc nations and to negotiate the cohosting of certain Olympic events by North Korea. However, the achievement of near-universal participation in the Seoul Games also posed a problem, as noted by IOC President Samaranch: "The size of the Olympic Games is reaching a peak where we cannot go higher."[57]

The purpose of this opening chapter was to establish the critical nature of the Seoul Olympics as a case study with broad relevance in theoretical as well as practical and policy terms. Chapter 2 outlines in some detail a theoretical approach to the Olympics that focuses centrally on their character as a television and media spectacle, the politics of which involve questions about who will control the production and dissemination of those messages that become the essence or meaning of the Olympics. Subsequent chapters take up each of the major themes of the study. Throughout, there is an effort to examine the Seoul Olympics from three perspectives: (1) in relation to the global transformations in communications and politics, (2) in light of those changes as experienced in Korea, and (3) in terms of their place within the Olympic movement and their import for the study of the Barcelona Games and other Olympics in the future.

Notes

1. "The World to Seoul, Seoul to the World" was the official slogan of the 1988 Olympics. It was suggested by a citizen of Seoul in a competition to determine the slogan that best captured the meaning of the 1988 Games. The slogan became very popular and was one of the most ubiquitous phrases displayed around South Korea in the years and months preceding the Olympics.

2. Daniel Dayan and Elihu Katz, *Media Events: The Live Broadcasting of History* (Cambridge, Mass.: Harvard University Press, 1992), and Michael R. Real, *Super Media: A Cultural Studies Approach* (Newbury Park, Calif.: Sage Publications, 1989).

3. Kenneth E. Boulding, *The World as a Total System* (Beverly Hills, Calif.: Sage Publications, 1985), p. 133.

4. Real, *Super Media*, Joshua Meyrowitz, *No Sense of Place: The Impact of Electronic Media on Social Behavior* (New York: Oxford University Press, 1985); George Gerbner, "Cultural Indicators: The Third Voice," in George Gerbner, Larry P. Gross, and William H. Melody, eds., *Communications Technology and Social Policy* (New York: John Wiley & Sons, 1973), pp. 555–573.

5. Richard Espy, *The Politics of the Olympic Games* (Berkeley: University of California Press, 1979), pp. 17–18 and 12–16.

6. Technically, the Olympics are awarded to a host *city*. However, as noted, they were truly a pan-national experience for South Korea. AFKN shared some of NBC's space in the International Broadcast Center and broadcast all of NBC's coverage throughout Korea, with the exception of commercials (which are routinely excised from the programming aired by AFKN).

7. For background on Korea and the origins of the cold war, see Bruce Cumings, *The Origins of the Korean War* (Princeton, N.J.: Princeton University Press, 1981).

8. Park Seh-Jik, *The Seoul Olympics: The Inside Story* (London: Bellew Publishing, 1991).

9. Walter Lippmann, *Public Opinion* (New York: Free Press, 1965), p. 216.

10. Denis McQuail, "Is Media Theory Adequate to the Challenge of New Communications Technologies?" in Marjorie Ferguson, ed., *New Communication Technologies and the Public Interest* (Beverly Hills, Calif.: Sage Publications, 1986), pp. 1–17.

11. Professor Lee Jae-won made this observation based on his own participant-observation research in the MPC during the Seoul Olympics.

12. ISL Marketing Research Department, *TOP: The Olympic Program*, handbook ed. 2.90 (Lucerne, Switzerland: ISL Marketing, 1989), p. 5.8.

13. Ibid., pp. 1.1, 5.1.

14. Gross impacts (or gross cumulative viewers) are conventionally referred to in advertising media planning terminology as *gross impressions*. They measure the total number of exposures to a program or advertising vehicle. The measure incorporates duplication because individuals are counted each time they view a particular Olympic program or segment.

15. ISL Marketing estimated that World Cup Soccer in 1986, telecast in 166 countries, attracted 13,506,689,000 gross cumulative viewers. See ISL Marketing, *TOP*, p. 5.5.

16. Ibid., p. 5.3.

17. John J. MacAloon, "Missing Stories: American Politics and Olympic Discourse," *Gannett Center Journal* 1 (Fall 1987): p. 121.

18. ISL Marketing, *TOP*, p. 5.14.

19. International Olympic Committee, *Olympic Charter 1991* (Lausanne, Switzerland: International Oympic Committee, December 1990), p. 37.

20. Ibid. p. 7.

21. James F. Larson, *Global Television and Foreign Policy*, Headline Series 283 (New York: Foreign Policy Association, 1988).

22. George Gilder, "Into the Telecosm," *Harvard Business Review* 69 (March-April 1991): pp. 150–161.

23. See also Anthony Smith, *The Age of Behemoths: The Globalization of Mass Media Firms*, a Twentieth Century Fund Paper (New York: Priority Press Publications, 1991).

24. For a discussion of the evolution of commercial television news, see James F. Larson, *Television's Window on the World: International Affairs Coverage on the U.S. Networks* (Norwood, N.J.: Ablex, 1984).

25. Ibid.

26. Intelsat, *Intelsat Report 1990–91* (Washington, D.C.: International Telecommunications Satellite Organization), p. 10.

27. William A. Henry III, "History as It Happens," *Time* (January 6, 1992): pp. 24–27.

28. Joe Roizen, "Olympic Update from Seoul," *TELEGEN (A Television Industry Report)*, September 7, 1987.

29. John J. MacAloon, "Encountering Our Others: Social Science and Olympic Sport" (Paper delivered at the First International Conference on the Olympics and East/West and South/North Cultural Exchange in the World System, Seoul, Korea, August 1987), p. 7.

30. Elihu Katz and Daniel Dayan, "Media Events: On the Experience of Not Being There," *Religion* 15 (1985): p. 305.

31. Ben H. Bagdikian, "The Lords of the Global Village," *The Nation* (June 12, 1989): pp. 805–820.

32. Michael J. O'Neill, *Terrorist Spectaculars: Should TV Coverage Be Curbed?* a Twentieth Century Fund Paper (New York: Priority Press Publications, 1986).

33. Seoul Olympic Organizing Committee, "Report on Television Broadcasting Operations for the Games of the XXIVTH Olympiad," April 1989.

34. John McMillan, "Bidding for Olympic Broadcast Rights: The Competition *Before* the Competition," *Negotiation Journal* (July 1991): p. 256.

35. Mintel, *Mintel Report on Sponsorship 1990* (London: Mintel, 1990).

36. "Sponsorship—Marketing's Fourth Medium—Now Worth $2.5 Billion a Year," PR Newswire (New York), June 22, 1987.

37. Landor Associates, "The First Annual Landor Imagepower Survey," PR Newswire (New York), November 14, 1988.

38. International Olympic Committee, *Olympic Charter 1984* (Lausanne, Switzerland: International Olympic Committee, 1984), pp. 7, 8.

39. Note that KISDI is one of three R&D institutes and a larger number of other organizations that fall under the purview of the Ministry of Communications. The other R&D institutes are the Electronics and Telecommunications Research Institute (ETRI) and the National Computerization Agency (NCA).

40. Kim Jong-gie, Rhee Sang-woo, Yu Jae-cheon, Koo Kwang-mo, and Hong Jong-duck, *Impact of the Seoul Olympic Games on National Development* (Seoul: Korea Development Institute, May 1989), pp. 38–61.

41. Park Heung-Soo, "A Perspective on Korea: Trends and Issues After the General Election," October 1988.

42. Ibid.

43. Harumi Befu, "Dimensions of Cultural Nationalism," in *Toward One World Beyond All Barriers*, Proceedings of the Seoul Olympiad Anniversary Conference, vol. 1) (Seoul, Korea: Poong Nam Publishing, 1990), pp. 160–180.

44. James F. Larson, "Quiet Diplomacy in a Television Era: The Media and U.S. Policy Toward the Republic of Korea," *Political Communication and Persuasion* 7 (1990): pp. 73–95.

45. Michael Vlahos, "Culture and Foreign Policy," *Foreign Policy* 82 (Spring 1991): pp. 59–78.

46. Leslie Sklair, *Sociology of the Global System* (Baltimore, Md.: The Johns Hopkins University Press, 1991).

47. Bill Shaikin, *Sport and Politics: The Olympics and the Los Angeles Games* (New York: Praeger Publishers, 1988), p. 67.

48. Stephen Aris, "The Great Olympic Soap Sell," *Financial Times*, June 11, 1988, weekend sect., p. 1.

49. Ibid.

50. Remarks by President Avery Brundage when accepting the keys of office from ex-president J. Sigfrid Edstrom at dinner given by the city of Lausanne, August 14, 1952, in *The Speeches of President Avery Brundage 1952 to 1968* (Lausanne, Switzerland: International Olympic Committee, n.d.), p. 7.

51. Randy Harvey, "Money Games: Samaranch's Legacy Will Be Greening of the Olympics," *Los Angeles Times*, September 10, 1989, pt. 3, p. 2.

52. "Olympic Games: IOC Strikes Gold," *The Independent*, September 15, 1990, p. 52.

53. William D. Murray, "Sports News," United Press International, February 20, 1989.

54. That figure includes 4,156 personnel who worked for the host broadcaster, KBS, with assistance from MBC, the other major Korean network.

55. Seoul Olympic Organizing Committee, "Report on Television Broadcasting."

56. Ibid.

57. Murray, "Sports News."

2

Constructing the Global Television Spectacle: A Theoretical Framework

The spectacular changes in the media and practices of worldwide communication, more than any other development, suggest the requirements for theoretical models to explain the contemporary Olympics. They do not imply a deterministic approach, in which new media technologies are thought to shape fresh social, cultural, and political realities at all levels, from the local to the global. Rather, they suggest that a set of questions perennially central to media theory must be focused on the Olympic phenomenon. How much do societies control and shape the media versus the degree to which new media technologies influence society? Which groups and interests characteristically exercise power over and through the media? What does it mean that such phenomena now operate in the Olympics at the global as well as the national and local levels?

As recounted in the opening chapter, global television established itself during the 1970s, matured further in the 1980s, and over these two decades, became a principal catalyst in international relations generally, including sport and the Olympic movement. Although the influence of television in politics is a relatively recent development, the relationship of politics to the Olympics, both ancient and modern, has a much longer history. Accordingly, one goal of this chapter is to set forth a general theoretical approach that is rich in both political and communication import. Certainly, television and the other media are essential to a convincing interpretation of the political, social, and economic change that occurred in Korea, East Asia, and the world around the time of the Seoul Olympics.

The model presented in this chapter builds primarily on scholarly work in two general areas: politics and sport, and the media and politics. It draws on an important stream of research in political communication to suggest a framework for understanding the Olympics as a media-constructed reality on multiple levels, including the planetary one. The approach assumes that the Olympics are both a paradigmatic media event and also a longer-term communication process. It is intended to be of use for the study of transnational actors and practices, as well as their effects in a still-emerging global system and world order.

The Study of Sport and Politics

The study of the relationship between sport and politics has a long history, traceable in the Western world to the ruminations of early philosophers about the ancient Olympics. The relationship is also a very large topic, the breadth of which is suggested in the following observation by John Hoberman.

> Sport is a latently political issue in any society, since the cultural themes which inhere in a sport culture are potentially ideological in a political sense. This latent political content becomes more evident when one considers some major polarities which bear on sport and the political world: amateurism versus professionalism, individualism versus collectivism, male supremacy versus feminism, nationalism versus internationalism, sensationalism versus (moral-political) hygienism (e.g., boxing). All of these thematic conflicts belong to the world of sport, and all are of ideological significance in a larger sense.[1]

Within the general subject of sport and politics, certain themes of greatest relevance to the present study can be summarized in relation to the three structural levels inherent in both the Olympic movement and the global system: national, international, and transnational. These three levels correspond to three basic forces at work in the world and within the Olympic movement: nationalism, internationalism, and transnationalism. This formulation draws most immediately on Espy's work,[2] but it is at least partially articulated in many other analyses.[3] It provides an organizational framework for the following discussion.

Sport and Nation

The intrinsically political nature of the modern Olympics derives, in part, from their structure, which is built around the nation-state.

The Olympic Games are structured in terms of nation-states: the athlete is a representative of a nation-state, the national Olympic committees are organized by nation-state boundaries; international sports federations are composed of national federations that are organized by nation-state boundaries; the International Olympic Committee (IOC) is the umbrella organization for the other sport organizations within the context of the Olympic Games and other Olympic-sanctioned events; and IOC members themselves are considered as ambassadors to nation-state areas. Within this context the nation-state is the primary actor in the Games, albeit acting through the sport organizations.[4]

Partly as a consequence of this structure, the nemesis of nationalism has plagued the modern Olympics since their inception in 1896. In addition to the formal structures already described, the design of Olympic ceremonies highlights nationalistic symbolism. In the opening ceremony, athletes enter nation by nation, the head of state of the Olympic host is accorded special honor, and the national anthem of the host city is played. In each medal ceremony, the winners' names and countries are announced, the national flags of the three medalists are raised, and the national anthem of the winner's country is played.

However, the ceremonial practices or formal structures prescribed or encouraged by the International Olympic Committee are not the only factors responsible for problems caused by nationalism in the Games. The media and the participating nations themselves also play an important role. Weeks and months before the Games begin, it is common for the narrative in mainstream news media around the world to stress the question of which country will "win" the Games or where particular nations will place. In nations both large and small, winning athletes are frequently treated as national heroes.[5]

The present research offers a valuable opportunity to explore the nature of Korean nationalism and how it may have been affected by the massive international interaction occasioned by the Seoul Olympics. Korea possesses a distinctive and relatively homogenous language and culture,[6] the history of which stretches back approximately 5,000 years. In keeping with this heritage, the Korean people share a unique notion of nationhood, as embodied in the words *Uri Nara*, which literally mean "our country" or "our nation."[7]

The pursuit of national pride and national prestige through Olympic success has become a hallmark of the modern Games. Pride is largely a domestic phenomenon, experienced within a nation by its citizens; prestige is an outward product, a quality that the successful nation accrues in the eyes of citizens of other countries.

The pursuit of national prestige often takes the form of overall improvement in a nation's sports program, with the goal of better performance in international competition. As briefly noted earlier, the number of Olympic medals won is frequently construed as an important indicator of the strength of a nation. During the cold war years, attainment of national prestige through sporting success was a frequent goal of the Soviet Union and Eastern European countries.[8] Today, the major actors on the international scene attach increased importance to sport and especially to the Olympic Games, as participation grows and television so dramatically augments the number of spectators involved. Because such great importance is attributed to the Olympics by governments, athletes, and spectators alike, prestige is inherent in the event.[9]

During the 1980s, South Korea undertook a massive effort to improve its sports programs, leading to an impressive total of 12 Olympic gold medals in Seoul and placing Korea fourth among competing nations, behind the USSR, East Germany, and the United States. Korea's overall total of 33 Olympic medals placed it sixth among all competitors. The manner in which the Seoul Olympics helped to generate national prestige and pride is explored in several chapters of this volume, along with the question of when either or both might have spilled over into excessive nationalism.

National pride, as experienced by a nation's citizens, relates to one of the underlying reasons why sport and the concerns of politics (government, policymaking, social order, and control) impinge on one another. Sport creates politically useful social resources.[10] It is widely seen as "character-building" and as an agent of socialization, although political scientists have paid far too little attention to its important role in political socialization.[11]

Most liberal pluralist theories of culture, the state, and civil society view sport as a set of voluntary social and cultural practices that allow for periodic releases from the tensions of everyday existence. Sport is consensual and is not seen as a formal part of the state system. On the other hand, the most common Marxist approach to sport is based on the view that all forms of cultural and political expression are superstructural elements of existence that directly reflect class interests and the material forces and relations that define capitalism as a mode of production. For the lower classes, sport supposedly provides a false sense of escape and functions as a compensatory mechanism for an alienated existence.[12] In similar fashion, the "bread and circuses" or "opiate of the masses" theories suggest that sport can be used to divert the energies of the masses away from problems of the political and social system. However, such approaches are countered by those who claim that sport can just as easily raise political consciousness.[13] The Seoul Olympics posed the question of which of these general approaches to sport and the state can best describe Korea's massive, government-led effort to successfully host the games and the participation of the Korean people in that effort.

From the moment Seoul was awarded the Olympics, the Korean government embarked on a systematic and well-funded program to broaden and strengthen the athletic prowess of the nation. The goal of this effort extended far beyond the training of athletes and teams for Olympic competition; among other things, it led to a rapid expansion of the televised sports calendar within Korea. Although the more pervasive nature of televised sports did not meet with universal public approval in the years preceding the Olympics, one result was the development of a new generation of Korean sports heroes who took their place alongside Olympic marathon gold medalist Sohn Kee Chung and other former Olympic athletes. This study will examine the buildup of South Korea's sports program with an eye toward the media's role in generating public support for the effort.

Political actors have long recognized the usefulness of association with winners, as demonstrated in the ritual of a U.S. president calling to congratulate the winning Superbowl team. Likewise, numerous national leaders have used sport as an instrument of foreign policy and diplomacy, as in the case of the U.S.- and Soviet-led boycotts of the 1980 and 1984 Olympics or the "ping-pong diplomacy" pursued by China with the United States in the early 1970s. As discussed in Chapter 1, a succession of South Korean presidents, from President Park Chung Hee through Chun Doo Hwan and Roh Tae Woo, sought to associate themselves with the idea of a successful Olympics as a national project. In so doing, they were simultaneously pursuing national reunification and waging a propaganda battle with the North, on the one hand, and seeking increased legitimacy for their own military-based governments, on the other. The powers of their presidential incumbency offered many advantages, but theirs were not the only attempts to benefit from association with the Olympics. Opposition politicians and such factions as the church, students, and labor also sought to appropriate Olympic meanings in the political struggle taking place in Korea amid rapid economic and social changes.

Sport and International Relations

International sport and international politics have, as Wallace Irwin noted, engaged in a perpetual interaction that can be traced back to the days of Plato. During an age of chronic strife among the Greek city-states, Plato gave the following advice concerning gymnastic contests in his ideal state: "Only the warlike sort of them are to be practiced and to have prizes of victory; and those which are not military are to be given up."[14] Plato's thinking was a clear precursor of that surrounding the modern Olympics, in which many states seek to use the Games in pursuit of foreign policy objectives. The Republic of Korea would prove to be no exception.

The effectiveness of sport as a foreign policy tool derives from its essential or perceived neutrality. As Espy noted, "The political import of sport is only what is imputed, so it can be used for a variety of foreign policy purposes without necessarily entailing overt political significance. Sport can provide a malleable foreign policy tool indicating various shades of political significance depending on the intent, and the perceived intent, of the parties concerned."[15] The use of sport by South Korea to pursue its northern policy of opening up to Socialist bloc nations and drawing North Korea into the international system offers an instructive example. An exciting table tennis rivalry between athletes from South Korea and mainland China sent important signals and provided a significant opening between the two nations at the time of the Asian Games. Following the 1988 Olympics, even competition between athletes from North and South Korea became an important part of the diplomatic process between the two nations as soccer teams played in both Seoul and Pyongyang.

In foreign policy terms, sport may be perceived as neutral and its meanings imputed, but in broader terms, it is often associated with internationalism. Sport may be seen as a force for internationalism or, in a slight variation, as part of the environment for interstate relations. In the latter view, international sports condition what would otherwise be an anarchic political system in which each state simply seeks to maximize its military or economic power without regard to other factors. The Olympic Charter itself may be read as an argument for such a view. Its first fundamental principle states, in part, that "The Aims of the Olympic Movement are: ... to educate young people through sport in a spirit of better understanding between each other and of friendship, thereby helping to build a more peaceful world, [and] to spread the Olympic principles throughout the world, thereby creating international goodwill."[16]

Paradoxically, the modern Olympic movement calls upon the ideal capacity of sport to transcend divisions of religion, class, race, or nationality, while at the same time, the competition intensifies the diametrically opposed political impulse of patriotism.[17] Internationalistic ideals became the thematic centerpiece of the Seoul Olympics, resounding in the opening ceremony theme of "Toward One World, Beyond All Barriers" and in the Olympic slogan, "Peace, Harmony, Progress," which was visually represented in the Seoul Olympic emblem. On the other hand, the Seoul Games unquestionably evoked among the Korean people a great surge of national pride and patriotism.

Transnationalism

It is only in the latter half of the twentieth century that sport and politics have become such important transnational phenomena. As discussed in the opening chapter, the growth of the international sports calendar, the emergence of global television, and the rise of corporate sponsorship of sport were parallel and integrally related developments. Today, televised international sport can and should be studied as an important feature of world society, with a crucial part of such a study focusing on transnational practices.[18] Moreover, the Olympics are of obvious importance as a paradigm case.

As critical theorists have noted, the unprecedented growth in the scale and scope of electronic media, here referred to as the arrival of the global television era, has greatly increased the opportunities for hegemonic control on a global scale in the cultural-ideological sphere. However, the argument that globally televised sport is hegemonic is not an open-and-shut case. In discussing different frameworks for assessing media events, Dayan and Katz noted that

> the entire genre of media events deals with the relationships among elites, broadcasters and audience. As we have tried to show throughout, this is not simply a linear relationship, but one which is circular and systemic, as much contractual as hegemonic. Nevertheless, the reverence with which media events are presented, the moments of equality and communitas which they propose, are undoubtedly reinforcing of the existing power structure, even if they open delicate, potentially subversive questions concerning alternative arrangements for the operation of power and the nature of stratification.[19]

In his extension of critical theory, Leslie Sklair suggested that the capacity for distribution of central messages on a scale not known before is doing nothing less than forging a "qualitatively new relationship between culture and ideology. ... All those who argue that it is the medium not the message that characterizes this revolution are, in my view, entirely wrong. The fact that a greater variety of messages may be broadcast on a vastly greater scale does not alter the fact that the central messages are still and more powerfully those of the capitalist global system."[20]

However, although the Olympics and other media events or processes may be establishment sponsored, some of them do invite change. As Dayan and Katz observed, "Critical theory would have a hard time explaining the role of the media in the Eastern European revolutions of 1989, or in the overthrow of the Shah in Iran, given his control over the media."[21] Their conceptualization would suggest that both audiences and the media have the power to make an event succeed or fail or to be misread. Chapter 8 explores the interaction between these two groups during the boxing incident, which ignited a wave of anti-American sentiment that swept the Korean public during the Seoul Olympics and was a major unplanned outcome of the Games.

Sport and the Moral Order

The question of the moral basis of sport pertains to each of the foregoing structural levels of the Olympics and the international system, as well as to the forces of nationalism, internationalism, and transnationalism that are at work within and among them. Questions of morality and sport are easily as profound and pervasive as those of morality and politics. In Hoberman's analysis of sport, politics, and the moral order,[22] the core doctrine of the Olympic movement is an *amoral universalism* that strives for global participation, even at the expense of rudimentary moral standards. Moreover, he adduced a considerable amount of historical evidence to show that the worlds of sport and politics coexist and that each may impinge upon the other in a destructive manner. The most notable example was the global silence that greeted the Tlatelolco massacre, in which hundreds of university students were killed just days before the 1968 Mexico City Olympics. As Hoberman put it, "When faced with the prospect of renouncing the gratification provided by the Olympic spectacle, the 'world conscience' became quiescent."[23]

Hoberman echoed Espy's analysis of the political nature of sport and the Olympics in particular, except that his study was couched in explicitly moral terms. The political problems of sport, he noted, derive from a double moral burden borne by the Olympic festival:

> First, the sport festival confers prestige—and, implicitly, a kind of moral legitimacy—on its host. For enormous numbers of people, the sports festival is a genuine expression of the fellowship of man. Second, the sport festival removes participants, at least symbolically, from that "real" world of deadly conflict and moral transgression in which innocence is always at risk. It is the power to spread this innocence and "good will"—virtue in its public, disembodied and anonymous form—which makes the sport festival an appealing vehicle for political propaganda."[24]

Although focusing his critique around the amoral universalism of the Olympic movement, Hoberman acknowledged its positive potential to channel aggressive impulses in the international arena into nonwarlike forms of competition and to promote mutual tolerance between people from different cultures.

Another way of putting these considerations is to question whether sport is inherently divisive. The Seoul Olympics posed this question in a tangible and profound manner, hosted as they were in the capital city of a nation divided for the duration of the cold war. Given that the division of the nation could not be undone, the real question posed by the Seoul Olympics was whether they could, in some meaningful sense, be instrumental in breaking down barriers. In a paper entitled, "A Proposal for a New Olympeace Movement," presented at a conference in August 1987, scholar Hong Kai suggested holding an unofficial world citizens' Olympic Games in the middle of the demilitarized zone (DMZ) separating North and South Korea. His proposal called for clearing away the minefields in a 2- to 4-square kilometer area under the foothills of Diamond Mountain near the Sea of Japan, so that ordinary people could come together to enjoy theater, music, poetry, and dance while discussing the state of the world. The symbolic significance of his proposal drew from both the status of the DMZ as one of the world's most prominent military walls or dividing lines and the sacred character of Korea's Diamond Mountain, a peak that has been likened by a prominent Korean intellectual to Mt. Olympus in Greece.[25]

The Media and International Politics

Scholarly concern with the media and international politics goes back a long way. For the purposes at hand, it is helpful to date its development in the United States, at least in terms of concerted and institutionalized effort, from approximately the World War II era. At that time, concerns about Nazi propaganda were a major force in bringing together social scientists from such areas as sociology, social psychology, and political science, leading eventually to the emergence of communication research as a field of study. Harold Laswell's model of the communication process—who says what to whom through which channel with what effect—is easily the most widely known and discussed of the transmission models that came to dominate North American scholarship during the post–World War II period. In retrospect, it is easy to understand how such a linear, mechanistic model, with its emphasis on the persuasive effects of communication, would be preferred during a period of history shaped by fears of wartime propaganda. However, there is a long-standing tension between such transmission models and an alternative, ritual perspective on the communication process.

As James Carey noted, "If the archetypal case of communication under a transmission view is the extension of messages across geography for the purpose of control, the archetypal case under a ritual view is the sacred ceremony that draws persons together in fellowship and commonality."[26] Thought of as transmission, communication tends to be one-way; as ritual, it involves sharing and interaction. Both views of communication have religious origins, but even those offer a clear contrast. The transmission approach draws from the evangelistic impulse to extend the kingdom of God on earth, but ritual models relate more to meditation, communion, and sharing.

Both transmission and ritual perspectives on communication should prove useful in understanding the contemporary Olympics. A common assumption in employing both views is that the Olympics constitute a media-constructed reality. This assumption or epistemological stance characterized the early twentieth-century work of Walter Lippmann, who wrote, "The world that we have to deal with politically is out of reach, out of sight, out of mind. It has to be explored, reported, and imagined."[27] This assumption that the political world is constructed applies just as clearly near the close of the century as it did at the outset. Moreover, the approach assumes a greater cogency given the increasing volume of televised messages that are being sent and received around the world. The net effect of the emergence of a global television era is to make the reported world that Lippmann spoke of more pervasively visual in character, with direct implications for the "pictures in our heads" that each human being creates to deal with the world outside. Were Lippmann writing today, he might well reformulate his analysis to call attention to the world outside, the television pictures, and the pictures in our heads.

Early Concern with Media Images
and Foreign Policy

One strain from propaganda research and other early communication research is of particular interest here: those scholarly efforts aimed at elucidating the relationships between the media, foreign policy, and public opinion. A better theoretical model of those relationships should help to explain how and why the Seoul Olympics were simultaneously the primary vehicle for South Korea's Northern policy of opening up relations with Socialist bloc nations and the source of new frictions with that nation's longtime ally, the United States.

Although transmission models were prevalent, the field of communication research as it developed following World War II in the United States, Europe, and other parts of the world, including Korea, was very eclectic and cross-disciplinary in nature. Research on media and foreign policy in particular attracted increased interest from representatives of several scholarly disciplines. This is illustrated in a volume edited by Herbert Kelman, which included contributions on national and international images and the various social-psychological processes that occur when nationals and governments interact.[28] In choosing national and international images as organizing concepts for the book, the contributors drew directly on the prior work of Boulding,[29] who set forth a broad conception of image as the "subjective knowledge structure" of an individual or organization. His theory accorded a central role to values and culture and, as he characterized it, "might well be called an organic theory of knowledge. Its most fundamental proposition is that knowledge is what somebody or something knows, and that without a knower, knowledge is an absurdity."[30]

He further noted that "the basic bond of any society, culture, subculture or organization is a 'public image,' that is, an image the essential characteristics of which are shared by the individuals participating in the group."[31] Such a concept of image as subjective knowledge is equally useful in understanding the Olympic movement, Korea as a nation and culture, or other nations involved in the Games. Moreover, as Boulding noted, public images almost invariably produce "transcripts," that is, more or less permanent records that can be handed down from generation to generation. These transcripts change in nature with advances in communication technologies.[32] Those of greatest interest in the present study are the visual images of televised evoked by the Seoul Olympics, along with the written words conveyed by the print media. Generally, the concept of image becomes a more cogent and broadly applicable theoretical construct with the increased ubiquity of moving, visual, televised pictures all around the world. This is, in part, because image is most frequently conceptualized as being somehow analogous to visual experience.[33]

As early as 1941, Lasswell stressed the importance of the relationship between mediated communication, seen as a series of "attention frames," and policy. His "World Attention Survey" analyzed references to symbols of nations in the press of other countries. He shared with Walter Lippmann and others the working assumption that people and nations cannot respond to an environment that is not brought to their notice. Furthermore, they shared the same basic analytical perspective, linking the three elements of media coverage, public interpretation of such coverage, and policy or action. Lippmann stressed the "map-making" function of the press. At the center of his analysis was the contention that "the analyst of public opinion must begin ... by recognizing the triangular relationship between the scene of action, the human picture of that scene, and the human response to that picture working itself out upon the scene of action."[34]

When the "human response to that picture" takes the form of foreign policy, one is dealing with the media–public opinion–foreign policy relationship. Bernard Cohen recognized as much and applied Lippmann's framework in *The Press and Foreign Policy*,[35] the first book to systematically explore the relationship between the media and the foreign policy process. His basic premise and point of departure was Lippmann's analysis of the map-making power of the press. Among students of political communication today, Cohen's work is well known and frequently cited as the first explicit statement of the agenda-setting hypothesis that stimulated so much research during the 1970s and 1980s. He observed that the press "may not be successful much of the time in telling people what to think, but it is stunningly successful in telling its readers what to think *about*."[36]

Conceptual Issues in the Media–Foreign Policy Relationship

Cohen analyzed the press as observer, participant, and catalyst in relation to the foreign policy process—three roles that are not mutually exclusive but that do circumscribe the structural relationship of the media and foreign policy. His conceptual approach provides a useful framework for assessing the changes that have occurred in the media–public opinion–foreign policy nexus with the advent of global television.

Television amplifies the observer role of the media in foreign policy as its broad, immediate, and visual reach extends all around the world, expanding the geopolitical scope of the policy process. Indications of this development include the growing number of television channels and receivers, along with the increased gathering and sharing of visual news and other programming by television organizations, as discussed in Chapter 1. Indeed, such transnational processes have already made it difficult, for certain purposes, to even use the term *foreign* policy. Accordingly, a first major difficulty with the existing scholarly literature on the media and foreign policy is that the mass media are frequently conceptualized, along with elections and organized interest groups, as an intervening variable between domestic social forces and foreign policy decisions.[37]

Like other researchers of his era, Cohen assumed that most television news was assembled from wire service reports, making it virtually indistinguishable from newspaper news, and that newsgathering and editing processes in radio and television were broadly similar to those in newspapers. Today, television's gathering and editing processes are acknowledged to be so influenced by the visual component of the broadcast as to suggest a decisive difference from print media.[38] Hence, a second conceptual difficulty with the existing work on the media and foreign policy is that it has not yet adequately come to grips with television as a visual medium.

Television has also made the media a more direct and active participant in the foreign policy process. In 1963, Cohen identified "the massive central issue" in debates among scholars, politicians, and journalists on the role of media in foreign policy as the competing demands for privacy in diplomacy and negotiation, on the one hand, and openness and publicity in news reporting, on the other.[39] Today, the public nature of the policy process is nearly universally acknowledged, and the central issue is the relative influence of the media versus policymakers in shaping the public policy dialogue. Moreover, with increasing use of satellite space bridges to link television journalists with diplomats, as shown in events like the Persian Gulf War, the media appear to function more often as a "third protagonist" in international affairs.[40] This merging of diplomatic and reporting roles is a third conceptual difficulty in the study of media and foreign policy.

The media's role as a catalyst in foreign policy involves a set of questions about the public's relationship to both media coverage and policy. The democratic model assumes that the media transmit politically significant information that is then used by the public and policymakers as part of the overall policy process. Several current approaches to the role of media as a catalyst in foreign policy incorporate a general hypothesis variously referred to as *marginalization* or *indexing*.[41] The hypothesis states that the media "index" the range of voices and viewpoints in the news according to the range of views expressed in mainstream government debate about a given topic, thereby "marginalizing" opposition or alternative views by leaving them on the fringes of media coverage. It implies that the range of voices in the news will vary widely from one issue area to another, narrowing in areas like foreign affairs that may appear more distant and inscrutable even to interested or attentive publics. Notably, this model is based on the assumption of a cultural norm on how the news media should operate, as Lance Bennett carefully observed: "The proposed norm is this: Culturally speaking, it is generally reasonable for journalists to grant government officials a privileged voice in the news, unless the range of official debate on a given topic excludes or 'marginalizes' stable majority opinion in society, and unless official actions raise doubts about political propriety."[42] This suggested norm for the U.S. political culture in turn points toward a broader conceptual issue. The conduct of contemporary foreign policy is increasingly characterized by the interaction or interpenetration of particular cultures with more global cultural processes. To be generally useful, theoretical approaches must come to grips with the role of culture in the media–foreign policy relationship, with equal attention to global and national cultures.

A final conceptual challenge is presented by the nature of the events, processes, or issue areas in relation to which one examines media and foreign policy. Most scholars of the post–World War II era have underscored to the need for study across a range of issue areas. However, the advent of the global television era has brought with it an increase in the number of planned "media events," of which the Olympics are only one example. Conceptually, this poses the difficulty of distinguishing events from the media or vice versa. Daniel Boorstin called attention to this problem in his polemic *The Image*, noting an increase in what he called "pseudo-events," such as televised debates, presidential press conferences, or certain sporting events.[43] Other scholars have since addressed the question of media-centered or media-focused events—those that are staged primarily for the media—versus events that originate independently of the media.[44] The work of Dayan and Katz,[45] who studied various media events as a new genre of broadcasting, is of particular relevance to the present research and is treated in some detail in the following section.

Taking such considerations into account and building upon Cohen's work,[46] Bennett proposed a "debate-accountability theory" of the media and foreign policy.[47] His was a media-centric view of foreign policy, at the core of which were journalists, policy officials, and publics. "The interactions of journalists and officials result in images of events and news accounts of policy options that in turn affect public opinion and broader patterns of participation, which feed back into the legitimacy and, occasionally, the selection of policy options."[48] The goal of such a theory is to explain important differences in three domains of policy related activities: "1) the production of news images based on the interactions of journalists and officials, 2) the effects of those news images on patterns of public opinion and participation, and 3) the policy constraints resulting directly from news coverage and indirectly from its impact on opinion and participation."[49]

Understanding the Seoul Olympics as Communication, Television, and Control

This book amplifies an emerging theme of a broad range of scholarship on the Olympics: the attempt to understand the role of global television and associated media technologies in constructing Olympic sport and spectacle and in turn being influenced by them. However, the book differs from other approaches by applying a political communication framework that is also useful in examining the changing relationship of media to politics and to the policy process more generally. It extends a long research tradition on the social construction of reality that, in recent decades, has gained wide currency in studies of the news media and political communication.[50] As already noted, the attractiveness of contemporary approaches that treat the news as political narrative and constructed reality is partly a function of the increased ubiquity of media messages about international affairs, especially the intrusive visual images of television and the corresponding lack of "extramedia" data.[51] Propaganda models also become useful because they involve predominant rather than incidental messages.[52]

Key assumptions underlying the theme presented here are that communication is a fundamental social process; that its importance increases with biological, social, and technological evolution; and that the modern world is characterized by an environment increasingly saturated with television images. The approach presents a three-dimensional view of the Olympics as (1) a communication event and process, (2) an event and process driven by global television, and (3) an event and process in which control of media messages is a central political concern.

This three-pronged approach places the modern Olympics at the intersection of theoretical concern with communication, the media, and politics. As the Seoul Olympics resoundingly demonstrated, these areas of inquiry are being knit together in ways that require better understanding.

The Olympics as a Communication Event and Process

During the 1970s and 1980s, Elihu Katz and Daniel Dayan published a series of articles dealing with media events, which they took to include such occurrences as the Olympic Games, Anwar el-Sadat's visit to Jerusalem, and the funeral of John F. Kennedy. Their work was synthesized in *Media Events: The Live Broadcasting of History*,[53] in which they argued that media events constitute a new narrative genre that taps the unique potential of the electronic media to command global and simultaneous attention. Their definition of media events as a genre included the following elements.[54]

1. They are interruptions of routine. During a media event, regular broadcasting schedules are suspended or preempted, which helps to transform daily life into something special.
2. The interruption is monopolistic. Most television channels switch away from their regularly scheduled programming, forming a consensus about the importance of the event.
3. The happening is live. The events are transmitted as they occur, in real time.
4. The events are typically organized outside the media. Such events take place outside the studio, in what broadcasters refer to as "remote locations," and are not usually initiated by broadcasting organizations.
5. The events are preplanned. They are announced and advertised in advance by broadcasters.
6. Media events are presented with reverence and ceremony. The journalistic commentators who preside over such events suspend their critical stance and treat their subject with a degree of reverence or even awe.
7. The events celebrate reconciliation rather than conflict. This is a key difference from daily news accounts.
8. They electrify very large audiences. Such events enthrall audiences of a nation, several nations, or the world.

9. They are hegemonic. On the whole, they celebrate establishment initiatives.
10. They are proclaimed historic. Even recurrent events like the Olympics are presented as uniquely historic.
11. There is a norm of viewing. During a media event, people tell each other that they should put other things aside to view.
12. Viewers celebrate the event. Viewers most frequently gather before the television set in groups, rather than alone.
13. They promote societal integration and renewal of loyalty to a society.

Although Dayan and Katz spoke of media events as *interruptions* of routine, they clearly acknowledged a period of time preceding such events during which they are announced and advertised. That time span may be lengthy: The Los Angeles Olympics were heralded for more than four years. Dayan and Katz's focus on events as interruptions, bounded in time, was tempered in one other important respect. In discussing the effects of media events, they distinguished between effects that take place *inside* the event and those that take place *outside.* The former are the mutual influences of the organizers, broadcasters, and audiences, and they take place during a media event. The latter may take place before, during, or after an event and include effects that relate to such societal institutions as public opinion, political institutions, diplomacy, the family, leisure, religion, public ceremony, and collective memory. Noting that only a few events have been studied empirically to ascertain these effects, Dayan and Katz characterized their own discussion of possible effects as a set of interlocking hypotheses.[55]

One goal of our study is to add to the available empirical evidence. The Seoul Olympics are depicted both as a media event and also as a longer-term communication process in which the event became a point of reference for politics, within Korea and internationally. The emphasis on long-term processes is also stronger than might be preferred by Dayan and Katz, for at least two reasons. One is the increasingly continuous nature of the Olympic phenomenon, as discussed in Chapter 1. In other words, Olympic television and other communication is itself becoming less exclusively centered on the sixteen days of athletic competition. The second reason is the focus of our research on broad questions about the role of the media in political, social, and economic changes taking place within and outside Korea. The IOC awarded the Games to Seoul in 1981, and much of this book deals with the important role of communication, especially television and the newer media, during the seven years of preparation for the Games. As it pertains to the important question of how the Seoul Olympics affected Korea's image around the world, the conceptual approach suggests that no adequate answer can be based solely on a sixteen- or twenty-day period of massive television coverage. Instead, it builds on the distinction made by Karl Deutsch and Richard Merritt in their analysis of the kinds of events occurring in the real world that might impinge on image formation and change. They distinguished between spectacular events, cumulative events, and shifts in the policy of governments or mass media.[56] Their sense of spectacular events was quite similar to media events as conceived by Katz and Dayan, except that it implied events occurring in the "real world," not those created or shaped by media or the government.

Viewing the Olympic Games as a media event and a communication process also poses a fundamental difficulty rooted in the fact that the act of human communication involves the problems of transformation of meaning. This transformation takes place as meaning is processed through the encoding and decoding of messages between senders and receivers. The dyad, in fact, becomes a triad—consisting of the sender, the receiver, and the cultural medium through which they communicate. Because of the heterogeneity of the human sign and meaning systems, intercultural communication is always more problematic than intracultural communication. The sender and the receiver often have to negotiate on the invention of a third meaning system, a third culture, in order to communicate. In reality, this has led to a global transcultural communication system that borrows heavily from the dominant world cultures.[57]

The Olympics represent just such a third culture and meaning system, analogous to the United Nations in international diplomacy. As a communication phenomenon, they involve multiple actors, events, media construction, and effects in different nations and cultures around the world. Yet along with the multiple constructions and meanings, there is broad international involvement in negotiating the meaning of the Olympics, from the awarding of the Games to a host city through the years-long preparations, the torch relay, the ceremonies, and the actual competition. There is also a simultaneous global experience, unprecedented in scope, that centers on the opening and closing ceremonies and competition. An important research task is to distinguish those parts of the Olympic communication experience that are "global" from those that are more specific to particular nations, cultures, broadcast structures, or policies.

Table 2.1 identifies the major dimensions of the Olympics as a communication process. The focus was placed on television for the sake of economy, and it implies the central and catalytic role of television in the Olympic Games. Although Table 2.1 includes components of the classic transmission model of the communication process (who says what to whom through which channel with what effect), it should not be construed as a wholesale endorsement of the model. In fact, many aspects of the modern Olympics are better understood by using a ritual view of commu-

TABLE 2.1   Communication dimensions of Olympic television

Aspects of Communication	Levels of Analysis or Comparison
Events, processes, issue areas	Level in international system
Ceremonies (opening, closing, medal)	National: developed vs. developing or
Athletic competition	socialist vs. capitalist
Press conferences	International
News and feature reporting	Transnational
Commercials	
Sources	Cultural
Athletes	Global culture
Media personnel	Particular cultures
Government officials and politicians	East vs. West
IOC, NOC, OCOG officials[a]	
International sports federations	
Corporate sponsors	
Fans	
Messages	Broadcast systems
Nation	Commercial
Culture	Noncommercial
The Olympics and sport	Government
Teams or athletes	Olympic rightsholders vs.
	nonrightsholders
Audiences	Time
Social formations	Los Angeles vs. Seoul vs. Barcelona
Viewing experience	Tokyo vs. Seoul
Size	
Effects	
National image	
Intercultural understanding	
Olympic participants	
Broadcasting and other social institu-	
tions	

[a]IOC = International Olympic Committee
  NOC = National Olympic Committee
  OCOG =Organizing Committee of the Olympic Games.

nication. For example, a ritual perspective may be more helpful for understanding what is occurring when television viewers around the globe gather in villages, living rooms, tearooms, or other viewing locations to watch the Olympic opening ceremony. On the other hand, a transmission perspective may be appropriate for exploring the nature and influence of advertising messages in the Olympic telecast. Both insights are important to an understanding of the contemporary Olympics. The tension between the two perspectives, with all its complexity, must be retained in order to better grasp the Olympics as political communication. Similar contradictory views have emerged from the study of summit meetings as international media events. For example, Daniel Hallin and Paolo Mancini[58] discussed the difficulty in applying a Durkheimian approach to media events, stressing a sense of community and international integration, to the divided and conflictual global "community" of the cold war world.

Table 2.1 also indicates that the Olympics are conceptualized as a media-constructed reality. Rather than showing media coverage of the Seoul Games as accounts of an event to which the press reacted, it depicts the Olympics as a spectacle constructed by the media and other interested groups. This approach draws particular attention to media *messages* and the various influences that shape those messages, a topic explored later in this chapter and in Chapter 3. In general, the producers of messages deserve special attention within a communication system because of the economic, political, and social power that accompanies their role. The Olympic games simply elevate this well-known phenomenon to a more global scale.

The analysis of sources and the interaction between media and sources is a tested and valuable strategy in political communication research. It can be put to good use in research on Olympic media coverage because the question of who speaks is intrinsic to the nature of the reality constructed and the meanings conveyed. For example, how much attention was given to the athletic heroes versus those less well known? Which nations and national or IOC officials were allowed to put their interpretations on events? Which politicians and experts were used to comment on the political situation in Korea and the possible threat to the Olympics from North Korea? What was the amount and nature of attention paid to the media themselves and to corporate sponsors of the Olympics? All of these questions relate directly to the question of control, which is at the heart of Olympic communication from a political point of view. They also point to the centrality of television rights in any analysis of control over Olympic messages. How are the rights negotiated? What do they confer? What are the consequences in terms of the amount and nature of Olympic television coverage around the world?

An analysis of the Seoul Olympics' opening ceremony telecasts in Great Britain, the United States, and Australia showed that the nations most frequently mentioned on all three broadcasts were economically, politically, or athletically strong. Conversely, the ceremony gave viewers a fleeting glimpse, at best, of most smaller island nations, as well as the nations of Africa, Latin America, and South Asia.[59] In some respects, all rightsholding broadcasters had similar privileges and access to Olympic ceremonies and events. In others, their privileges were dramatically different, based on sheer economic power. NBC, whose fee of $302 million represented approximately three-quarters of all television rights fees, set up its main headquarters in a large, separate wing of the International Broadcast Center. Among foreign broadcasters, it also had the largest number of its own (unilateral) cameras to supplement the international television signal provided by the host broadcaster. By contrast, the broadcasting pool representing African nations could not afford the rights fee necessary for access to many Olympic events.

Questions about media *audiences* and media *effects* are no less important to the inquiry, but they must be answered in relation to the various Olympic messages constructed by television and the other major media. As Bennett noted, images are anchored partly in symbolic suggestions and partly in the feelings and assumptions that people have in response to those suggestions.[60] This characteristic of images takes on added importance as people around the world come to live in an information environment that is more and more saturated with the moving, visual, and repetitive images of television.

Image effects among audiences of different nations and cultures have affective components that are of special interest given the rich visual and aural nature of the television message. For example, during one portion of the Seoul Olympics opening ceremony, an international team of sports parachutists formed the Olympic rings in the sky over Seoul and did so again after landing on the field of the main Olympic stadium. But during the extended and visually exciting episode, viewers in many nations of the world may have missed a part of the message that was emphatic for Korean viewers. Throughout the episode, a choir and orchestra rendered specially composed variations on a single tune—the Korean national anthem. It was a powerful evocation of national pride for Koreans and those acquainted with the their language and culture. However, for viewers in other nations, the episode was most likely just another spectacular and precision-timed addition to the ceremony.

The Characteristics of Global Television

The preceding description of the Olympics as a communication event and process touches on the major phenomena that a theory should help to explain. The following passages describing the characteristics of global television as a new medium of communication provide a second dimension of theory that can help to generate a range of questions and hypotheses.

Increased Number of Channels

Worldwide, there has been a steady growth in the number of channels available for broadcast television. Together with the expansion of cable television in many industrialized nations, this is part of the trend toward what many are calling the "intelligent network," with fully integrated delivery of video, voice, and data communications. A larger number of channels theoretically makes a greater diversity of information possible and increases the difficulty for government leaders, international movements like the Olympics, or groups within nations to control the dissemination of information. Witness, for example, the IOC's current concern about the possibility of "ambush marketing,"[61] which might decrease the effectiveness of its sponsorship program. Somewhat paradoxically, the increase in media channels offers new, pervasive, and perhaps more effective means for mounting centralized public information campaigns in support of elections, causes, and policies both domestic and foreign.

Global Reach

Along with an increase in the number of channels available for televised communication comes a dramatic increase in the global reach of some channels, due largely to the rapid development of communication satellites in the 1970s and, more recently, their ease of use technologically and their economic accessibility. The increasingly routine use of space bridges to link television reporters or officials from disparate geographic locations not only affects the activities of the officials and the reporters but may also decisively change the nature of the public sphere and the publics involved. Research findings from the early years of television combine with the more recent study of global media events to suggest that the awareness of a worldwide audience may be one of the most important influences on both the actors and the viewers of television coverage.[62]

Those media events that possess a certain threshold level of reach, measured in terms of audience levels around the world, and international involvement represent a special class and deserve particular scrutiny because they achieve spectacle and also have actual or potential political impact. It is at least an operating assumption of the governments and politicians behind such events that reach translates rather directly into various forms of political impact. Hence, a regional event such as the Pan-American Games or European Basketball Championship is of a different character than the Olympics or World Cup Soccer. Moreover, the central place of nations and nationhood in the Olympic movement expands and accentuates this political communication dimension.

Instant or Timely Broadcasts

Television, like radio before it, is drawn to the live transmission of information about certain kinds of events. Commentator Bryant Gumbel began NBC's telecast of the Seoul Olympic opening ceremony by telling viewers that they would be witnessing the ceremony live and that the time difference between Seoul and the East Coast of the United States was "working to your advantage."

Television's capability for live, global distribution of broadcasts allows viewers all around the world to experience the same event simultaneously. As Eric Rothenbuhler noted, the social formations attendant to the broadcasting of important events like the Olympics are unique types, not adequately dealt with in the existing theoretical lexicon. Not only do the media, principally television, allow widely dispersed individuals to share in an unfolding event, the audience members are also aware of the simultaneity of their experience with the event itself and with the experiences of many others.[63]

Concern with live transmission of major events from the Seoul Olympics, particularly to the large U.S. television market, prompted the Korean government to institute daylight saving time in 1987, for the first time in nearly two decades. In so doing, the government noted that the change would be "beneficial to cultural life during the long summer days."[64] Informally, it was widely understood and acknowledged in Korea that the change would facilitate more live telecasts of Olympic events during peak viewing hours in the United States and Europe. The economic logic behind this move was relatively straightforward: Live telecasts were more likely than delayed broadcasts to attract large audiences, which might increase Seoul's income from U.S. television rights.

Repeatability

The capacity for television images to be rebroadcast and replayed has already emerged as an important characteristic of this medium. Like the instant replay segments in sports, certain especially powerful, dramatic, or symbolic images appear more frequently than others in news coverage of international affairs. Examples abound, such as the assassination of Egyptian President Anwar el-Sadat, the Chinese student facing down a tank on the streets of Beijing, and more recent scenes of the U.S.-led bombing of Bagdhad as reported by three Cable News Network reporters from Iraq's capital city. During the 1988 Seoul Olympics, it is likely that the boxing incident that helped to ignite a wave of anti-NBC and anti-American sentiment among Koreans arose not so much because of the NBC Sports reporting but because scenes of the incident were picked up and shown repeatedly by NBC Television news and other news organizations.[65] However, concern for the repeatability of televised images need not always be directed to the highly dramatic or visually spectacular. Equally important may be the visual backdrop or consistent context provided by, for example, the steps of the U.S. Capitol, the south lawn of the White House, or the desk or fireplace in the U.S. president's Oval Office.

A Visual Medium

Television's visual nature is arguably its most central and widely noted characteristic. Consequently, not only television producers and correspondents (who "wallpaper" their reports with visual segments) but also leaders in a growing number of nations pay inordinate attention to the visual aspects of television news coverage.[66] The visual nature of the television medium gives it an extraordinary capacity to convey emotion, in such disparate contexts as the personal diplomacy and summitry of "great communicators" like former U.S. President Reagan or former Soviet President Gorbachev and telecasts of the Ethiopia famine in the early 1980s or the more recent plight of the Kurds fleeing Iraqi troops in northern Iraq.

In his analysis of the Olympic Games as spectacle, MacAloon argued that "the Games are irreducibly visual. Quite literally, they must be seen, and seen in person, to be believed."[67] He was correct in noting the visual nature of the Games, but his claim that the they must be seen in person to be believed shortchanges the new role of television in creating global spectacles.

Of particular interest is television's well-known capacity to personalize events and convey feelings or emotion and, at a societal level, what Katz called the "sense of occasion."[68] Relatively few people in the world have experienced the emotions evoked by actually attending an Olympic opening ceremony, but literally billions have celebrated or felt a range of emotions in front of a television set that would have been inconceivable in the pretelevision era.

The Seoul Olympic planners recognized this visual power of television and sought to capitalize on it in various ways. The opening ceremony incorporated such elements as the Han River boat parade, a fireworks display outside the Olympic stadium, and the forming of the Olympic rings in the sky above Seoul and again on the stadium field by an international team of parachutists—all elements that greatly enhanced the televised ceremony but had a smaller—or at least a dramatically different—effect on spectators in the Olympic stadium.

Saturation Coverage

The organization of television broadcasts in time rather than space, as in print media, leads to saturation coverage of certain events. Although variously operationalized, saturation coverage occurs when an event assumes sufficient magnitude to occupy all or most of the available airtime, either within a nation or more globally. In the United States, the assassination of President Kennedy, the Iran hostage crisis, and the early hours of the Gulf War are but a few examples. In Korea, one of the most striking recent examples of such coverage involved the televised hearings of the National

Assembly in November 1988 on activities of the Fifth Republic, including the Kwangju uprising and the military response to that movement.[69] With the advent of CNN and the experience of twenty-four-hour-a-day television news, the notion of saturation coverage may need to be operationalized differently, but CNN coverage of the early hours of the Gulf War would seem to indicate that some occurrences can saturate even the longer news day and do so on a global scale.

If the preceding six characteristics of global television are considered in relation to each aspect of the Olympics as a communication process, a number of communication and media theory questions can be explored. For example, the capability for repetition can be examined in terms of (1) the types of events, issues, and processes that lend themselves to repetition, (2) the institutional or personal sources that encourage or discourage repetition of certain messages, (3) repetition in the televised message itself, (4) the impact of such repetition on the audiences for Olympic television, and (5) the broader social, cultural, and economic context in which repeated broadcast of and exposure to televised messages takes place. On a practical level, the question of repeated exposure to television messages suggests concerns that range from the meaning and integrity of the central Olympic visual symbols through the potential of global television for promoting positive Olympic values to the continued profitability of commercial sponsorship as a source of revenue for the Games. Such issues at once suggest theoretical concerns about transcultural meaning flows in a global television era, on the one hand, and an increasingly urgent set of policy questions facing the Olympic movement, on the other.

Levels of Political Communication and Control

A third broad dimension of the theoretical model proposed in this book is political. The need for a politically focused approach stems from the character of the Olympics, their relationship to the international system, and their paradigmatic character as a media event. As Espy stated,

> What is important about the Games is their visibility. The Games are seen by the whole world. For each spectator, whether at the games or watching them on television, it is his country that is competing—and, possibly, winning. One hears about the United Nations and similar forums only indirectly, and there are rarely clear-cut winners or losers. Consequently, what happens in such forums is at best soon forgotten, often completely overlooked.[70]

The contemporary visibility of the Olympics is simply one manifestation, albeit a very important one, of the increased visibility of politics more generally. Indeed, it is the pervasiveness of the media in the global television era that provides a starting point for many students of political communication. The present approach shares with Murray Edelman certain premises about politics. He asked, "What consequences for ideology, action and quiescence flow from preoccupation with political news as spectacle? How does the spectacle generate interpretations? What are its implications for democratic theory?"[71] This book poses a similar set of questions about the modern Olympics as political communication. Its overarching questions are:

- What are the consequences for the modern Olympics, as both political actor and stage, of this broad new role played by global television?
- What does the emergence of global television, internationally and in the Olympics, suggest about a theory to explain contemporary relations between governments, media, and the public more generally?
- What is the nature and political import of the transnational practices in television and commercial sponsorship that have become such a dominant presence in the Olympics and in international sport as a whole?
- What does the central role of global television mean for the host city and nation, in terms of both internal and international politics?

Like Edelman's approach, this study treats the Olympics as a creation of the publics most concerned with the Games. Accordingly, the ordering and analysis of those publics and their actual or potential influence in shaping the global television spectacle is at the heart of the political dimension of this theory and the Seoul case study.

In documents prepared for the first Olympic Broadcast Advisory Committee meeting, RTO '92, the host broadcaster for the Barcelona Olympics, described itself as the "first spectator" for the games.[72] This was an apt description that applies equally well to the role of KBS/SORTO in Seoul and host broadcasters for several prior Olympics. It captures the priority of the many and varied activities that help create the international television signal as required by the Olympic Charter—a signal that becomes the first view of most Olympic events for the majority of world broadcasters. It is the raw material on which they depend in constructing their own national telecasts. In short, the role of first spectator implies nothing less than a central part in the years-long process of planning for global television coverage. This process is tantamount to constructing the central symbolic system that will be seen instantly and in that, future years, will be remembered and replayed as the Seoul or Barcelona Olympics. It is natural that the host broadcaster's work should attract attention, just as the global power of television brings greater concern with the message-making side of the media. Witness the EBU's request following the Gulf War that the European Community Commission help it launch a multilingual alternative to CNN that would present "a European point of view to the global media."[73]

Due in large part to broad international involvement, the Olympics arguably involve more planning and coordination than any other global media event, and planning for the Seoul Olympics was both a long-range and meticulous undertaking. Soon after Seoul was designated in September 1981 as the host city for the Twenty-fourth Olympiad, the Korean Broadcasting System was named host broadcaster, and it formed the Seoul Olympics Radio and Television Operations (SORTO) for the task of coordinating and producing the games. The Korean government treated the 1986 Asian Games that Seoul hosted as a full-scale dress rehearsal for the Olympics. Many of the same venues were used for the sporting events, and the staff of KBS/SORTO, the host broadcasting organization, was responsible for televising the event, just as it would be for the Olympics.

A significant portion of this planning involved the worldwide television broadcasting of the Olympics. The presence of television has increased dramatically in recent Olympiads, in concert with the development of television technologies and their diffusion internationally. The Seoul Olympics were covered by some 10,700 personnel from 130 broadcasting organizations, representing 67 countries.[74] With the addition of print media, the estimated number of international media personnel in Seoul for the Olympics was 14,400, exceeding the number of athletes and officials participating in the Games.[75]

From the very beginning, the Korean government showed a strong commitment to a successful television spectacle, as illustrated by several major capital expenditures. The Korea Telecommunications Authority (KTA) expanded its structure with the construction of a fourth satellite earth station at Poun, which went into service in January 1985 and provided for an increased number of international TV communication channels. The Korean Broadcasting System constructed a new $58-million International Broadcast Center adjacent to its headquarters building to accommodate the many foreign broadcast personnel expected for the Olympics; it was to be used for needed expansion of KBS facilities following the Games. In addition, the government constructed a seven-story Main Press Center building to serve the needs of print media representatives covering the Games.

The international dimension of planning for the Olympic telecasts was also extensive. Much of it revolved around the host broadcast organization, but it also involved the following groups, each of which had a vested interest in the nature of Olympic television coverage:

- the International Olympic Committee
- the host city Olympic organizing committee
- national and regional broadcasting organizations
- corporate Olympic sponsors
- national Olympic committees in each participating country
- international sports federations
- governments
- athletes
- fans
- scholars

The relative influence of each of these publics or spectators in shaping the Olympic media spectacle will be a major concern throughout this book. The broad relevance of this issue of control can be seen through a brief review of some increasingly persistent policy questions in Olympic broadcasting. Each of these will be treated at greater length in ensuing chapters.

One set of questions raised by scholars who have examined Olympic broadcasting has to do generally with the dominance of U.S. commercial networks in the process. For example, it has been suggested that Olympic opening and closing ceremonies be telecast without commercial interruption.[76] NBC's telecast of the Seoul Olympic opening ceremony in the United States lent some weight to the notion of commercial excess. It was interrupted 25 times for nearly 52 minutes of commercials and another 21 times for newsbreaks, interviews, and "Olympic Chronicles" or "Olympics Past" segments averaging 3 minutes, 3 seconds in length.[77]

In the NBC telecast from Seoul, most commercial and other segments cut away from the international television signal during cultural performances and the entry of the athletes. This suggests a second policy issue: whether rightsholders should be required to devote more coverage to the cultural background of the host city.[78] The issue became more complex for Barcelona in 1992 because of the political and cultural status of the host city in relation to both Catalonia and Spain.

Some of NBC's breaks from the international television signal for the Seoul Opening Ceremony showed television in the more positive role of giving viewers a sense of historical and cultural depth that otherwise would be missing from the telecast. Approximately 11 minutes into its live telecast of the ceremony, NBC aired a 4 minute, 13 second background spot tracing the story of Sohn Kee Chung and how he won the Olympic marathon in 1936, competing as a Japanese subject and with a Japanese name while Korea was under colonial rule. The feature used extensive footage from the 1936 race and medal ceremony, with Sohn describing his emotions then, his personal insistence on always using and signing his Korean name, and his continuing campaign to have his name corrected in the Olympic record books.

The feature gave NBC viewers important context on a forthcoming element of the ceremony—the entry of the Olympic torch into the main stadium, carried by Sohn Kee Chung. It no doubt helped them understand the historical significance and the powerful political symbolism of the moment in terms of Korea's relationship with Japan. However, it was also, without question, a very expensive piece to produce and one that was viewed only by a U.S. television audience.[79]

The present arrangement, in which the largest rightsholding broadcasters unilaterally and exclusively telecast such material, poses the question of whether some degree of coproduction and pooling of background segments should be encouraged. Indeed, the degree to which television rights fees dictate access to certain materials was poignantly illustrated by the situation of the Union of African Broadcasters in the Seoul Olympics. Its representatives wanted access to the entire international signal, but that was not possible because they were only able to pay a "symbolic" rights fee. Therefore, the IOC and the Seoul Olympic Organizing Committee approved an arrangement whereby former British and French colonies in Africa could have access to the British and French coverage on the basis of the relatively small rights fee paid.[80]

To place the question of possible coproduction or pooling arrangements in broader context, it may be helpful to view Olympic television in relation to what has happened in commercial television news. Through the 1960s and 1970s, the three major U.S. networks relentlessly pursued journalistic competition and exclusivity (the "scoop") and resisted various suggestions for pooling news. Today, technological change and the realities of the more global competition in television news have forced them, like CNN, to move into more cooperative arrangements.

The Seoul Olympic opening ceremony incorporated television dramatically to convey the breaking of space barriers. Viewers will recall the sports parachutists who formed the Olympic rings in the air above Seoul and once again on the ground within the main Olympic stadium. Television technology will make it possible for future ceremonies to break barriers of time by incorporating televised segments of a historical or cultural nature and to break barriers of space through the use of space bridges via satellite. Should both uses of the technology be freely allowed? This question might be posed with respect to the Olympic Games as a whole, not just the ceremonies. Indeed, President Samaranch's announcement at the ninety-eighth session of the IOC that future Olympic Winter Games might be shared by more than one country, although prompted by the logistical requirements of constructing Olympic venues in difficult climatic and geological conditions, implied a new and more important role for communications technology.[81]

The answers to these and other questions will have a great deal to do with how broadcasters, including the host broadcasting organizations, convey the full range of emotions shown by athletes and spectators in future Olympics. Indeed, the questions are intrinsic to the cultural project of constructing and conveying the global Olympic spectacle. As noted at the outset, they are also essential to the modern Games. It seems certain that they will become increasingly persistent as a more completely global communication infrastructure is put in place. On such questions hinge the nature and degree of mutual understanding and genuine intercultural communication achieved by the Olympics in the future.

Notes

1. John M. Hoberman, *Sport and Political Ideology* (Austin: University of Texas Press, 1984), p. 20.

2. Richard Espy, *The Politics of the Olympic Games* (Berkeley: University of California Press, 1979), p. 9.

3. See, for example, Trevor Taylor, "Sport and International Relations: A Case of Mutual Neglect," in Lincoln Allison, ed., *The Politics of Sport* (Manchester, England: Manchester University Press, 1986), p. 29.

4. Espy, *The Politics of the Olympic Games*, p. 9.

5. D. P. Toohey and K. Warning, "Nationalism: Inevitable and Incurable?" in Jeffrey Segrave and Donald Chu, eds., *Olympism* (Champaign, Ill.: Human Kinetics Publishers, 1981), pp. 118–126.

6. The Korean language is distinguished by several regional dialects. All are mutually intelligible, with the exception of the dialect spoken on the island province of Cheju-Do. Today, nearly all Koreans, including residents of Cheju-Do, can understand and use standard Korean.

7. John J. MacAloon and Shin-Pyo Kang, "Uri Nara: Korean Nationalism, the Seoul Olympics and Contemporary Anthropology," in *Toward One World Beyond All Barriers*, Proceedings of the Seoul Olympiad Anniversary Conference, vol. 1 (Seoul, Korea: Poong Nam Publishing, 1990), pp. 117–159.

8. See, for example, Martin Barry Vinokur, *More Than a Game: Sports and Politics* (New York: Greenwood Press, 1988).

9. Espy, *The Politics of the Olympic Games*, pp. 5, 7.

10. Lincoln Allison, "Sport and Politics," in Lincoln Allison, ed., *The Politics of Sport*, (Manchester, England: Manchester University Press, 1986), pp. 1–26.

11. Vinokur, *More Than a Game*, p. xi.

12. Richard Gruneau, "Sport and the Debate on the State," in Richard Graneou, ed., *Sport, Culture and the Modern State* (Toronto, Canada: University of Toronto Press, 1982), pp. 2–38.

13. Allison, "Sport and Politics," pp. 14, 15.

14. Wallace Irwin, Jr., *The Politics of International Sport: Games of Power* Headline Series 286 (New York: Foreign Policy Association, 1988), p. 10.

15. Espy, *The Politics of the Olympic Games.*

16. International Olympic Committee, *Olympic Charter 1990* (Lausanne, Switzerland: International Olympic Committee, 1990), p. 6.

17. R. Mandell, *The First Modern Olympics* (Berkeley: University of California Press, 1976).

18. Leslie Sklair, *Sociology of the Global System* (Baltimore, Md.: The Johns Hopkins University Press, 1991), pp. 52, 53.

19. Daniel Dayan and Elihu Katz, *Media Events: The Live Broadcasting of History* (Cambridge, Mass.: Harvard University Press, 1992), p. 225.

20. Sklair, *Sociology of the Global System*, p. 74.

21. Dayan and Katz, *Media Events*, p. 226.

22. John M. Hoberman, *The Olympic Crisis: Sports, Politics and the Moral Order* (New Rochelle, N.Y.: Aristide D. Caratzas, 1986).

23. Ibid., p. 14.

24. Ibid., p. 3.

25. Hong Kai, "A Proposal for a New Olympeace Movement," (Paper delivered at the First International Conference on the Olympics and East/West and South/North Cultural Exchange in the World System, Seoul, Korea, August 1987).

26. James W. Carey, *Communication as Culture: Essays on Media and Society* (Boston: Unwin Hyman, 1989), p. 18.

27. Walter Lippmann, *Public Opinion* (New York: Free Press, 1965), p. 18.

28. Herbert C. Kelman, "Social-Psychological Approaches to the Study of International Relations: Definitions of Scope," in Herbert C. Kelman, ed., *International Behavior: A Social-Psychological Analysis* (New York: Holt, Rinehart and Winston, 1965), p. 3.

29. Kenneth E. Boulding, *The Image: Knowledge in Life and Society* (Ann Arbor: University of Michigan Press, 1956).

30. Ibid., p. 16.

31. Ibid., p. 64.

32. Ibid., pp. 64, 65.

33. Karl W. Deutsch and Richard L. Merritt, "Effects of Events on National and International Images," in Herbert C. Kelman, ed., *International Behavior: A Social-Psychological Analysis* (New York: Holt, Rinehart and Winston, 1965), pp. 132–187.

34. Lippmann, *Public Opinion*, p. 11.

35. Bernard C. Cohen, *The Press and Foreign Policy* (Princeton, N.J.: Princeton University Press, 1963).

36. Ibid., p. 13.

37. James N. Rosenau, ed., *Domestic Sources of Foreign Policy* (New York: Free Press, 1967).

38. See, for example, Edward Jay Epstein, *News from Nowhere* (New York: Vintage Books, 1974).

39. Cohen, *The Press and Foreign Policy*, p. 264.

40. Daniel C. Hallin and Paolo Mancini, *Friendly Enemies: The Reagan-Gorbachev Summits on U.S., Italian and Soviet Television* (Perugia: Provincia di Perugia, Italy, 1989), p. 75.

41. Edward S. Herman, "Diversity of News: 'Marginalizing' the Opposition," *Journal of Communication* 35 (Summer 1985): pp. 135–146. Or see Lance W. Bennett, "Toward a Theory of Press-State Relations in the United States," *Journal of Communication* 40 (Spring 1990): pp. 103–125.

42. Bennett, "Toward a Theory of Press-State Relations in the United States."

43. Daniel J. Boorstin, *The Image: A Guide to Pseudo-Events in America* (New York: Atheneum, 1975).

44. For a thoughtful discussion of these issues, see Majid Tehranian, "Events, Pseudo-Events, Media Events: Image Politics and the Future of International Diplomacy," in Andrew Arno and Wimal Dissanayake, eds., *The News Media in National and International Conflict* (Boulder, Colo.: Westview Press, 1984), pp. 43–61.

45. Dayan and Katz, *Media Events*.

46. Cohen, *The Press and Foreign Policy*.

47. W. Lance Bennett, "The Media and the Foreign Policy Process" (Paper prepared for the fifth Thomas P. O'Neill Symposium in American Politics, Boston College, Boston, Mass., April 3–4, 1992).

48. Ibid., pp. 20, 21.

49. Ibid., p. 20.

50. Gaye Tuchman, *Making News: A Study in the Construction of Reality* (New York: Free Press, 1978). Also see David L. Altheide, *Creating Reality: How TV News Distorts Events* (Beverly Hills, Calif.: Sage, 1976); Murray Edelman, *Constructing the Political Spectacle* (Chicago, Ill.: University of Chicago Press, 1988).

51. Karl E. Rosengren, "International News: Intra and Extra Media Data," *Acta Sociologica* 13 (1970): pp. 96–109.

52. Edward S. Herman and Noam Chomsky, *Manufacturing Consent: The Political Economy of the Mass Media* (New York: Pantheon Books, 1988).

53. Dayan and Katz, *Media Events*.

54. Ibid., pp. 4–14.

55. Ibid., pp. 188–217.

56. Deutsch and Merritt, "Effects of Events," p. 135.

57. Majid Tehranian, "Is Comparative Communication Theory Possible/Desirable?" (Paper presented at the Comparative Communication Theory Workshop, Annual Conference of the International Communication Association, San Francisco, Calif., May 25–29, 1989).

58. Daniel C. Hallin and Paolo Mancini, "Summits and the Constitution of an International Public Sphere: The Reagan-Gorbachev Meetings as Televised Media Events," *Communication* 12 (1991): pp. 249–265.

59. James F. Larson and Nancy K. Rivenburgh, "A Comparative Analysis of Australian, U.S. and British Telecasts of the Seoul Olympic Opening Ceremony," *Journal of Broadcasting and Electronic Media* 35 (Winter 1991): p. 82.

60. Lance W. Bennett, *News: The Politics of Illusion* (New York: Longman, 1981), p. 74.

61. "Ambush marketing" occurs when companies that have not purchased official sponsorship rights use promotional techniques that seek to establish an association between their product or company and the Olympics.

62. Kurt Lang and Gladys Engel Lang, "The Unique Perspective of Television and Its Effects: A Pilot Study," in Wilbur Schramm and Donald F. Roberts, eds., *The*

Process and Effects of Mass Communication (Urbana: University of Illinois Press, 1971), pp. 169–188.

63. Eric W. Rothenbuhler, "Live Broadcasting, Media Events, Telecommunication and Social Form," in David R. Maines and C. Couch, eds., *Communication and Social Structure* (Springfield, Ill.: Charles C. Thomas, 1988).

64. Korean Broadcasting System, *SORTO Courier,* 3 (April 1987): p. 18.

65. Horace G. Underwood of Yonsei University called this to our attention during a personal interview in Seoul, Korea, March 1991.

66. For a good treatment of the priority placed on visual coverage by the Reagan White House, see Mark Hertsgaard, *On Bended Knee: The Press and the Reagan Presidency* (New York: Farrar Straus Giroux, 1988).

67. John J. MacAloon, ed., *Rite, Festival, Spectacle, Game* (Chicago, Ill.: University of Chicago Press, 1984), p. 245.

68. Elihu Katz, "Media Events: The Sense of Occasion," *Studies in Visual Anthropology* 6 (1980): pp. 84–89.

69. Personal observation of a nonrandom sort by James Larson during a visit to Seoul in November 1988 indicated that virtually the entire viewing-age citizenry tuned in to these national telecasts, at least during the early and key stages of the hearings. Taxi drivers and others who did not have access to television because of their work tuned to radio.

70. Espy, *The Politics of the Olympic Games,* pp. 197, 198.

71. Edelman, *Constructing the Political Spectacle,* p. 1.

72. RTO '92 First OBAC Meeting, program notes, Barcelona, April 17–18, 1990, p. 8.

73. "Help Sought for 'Euro-CNN'," *International Herald Tribune*, February 28, 1991.

74. Korean Broadcasting System, *KBS Courier* 9 (November 1988): p. 8.

75. KBS/SORTO, production manual, September 1988, p. 51.

76. Bruce Kidd, "The Olympic Movement and the Sports-Media Complex," *Proceedings of the Conference on the Olympic Movement and the Mass Media: Past, Present and Future Issues* (Calgary, Canada: Hurford Enterprises, 1989), pp. 1–8.

77. Larson and Rivenburgh, "A Comparative Analysis," p. 82.

78. See Kidd, "The Olympic Movement and the Sports-Media Complex," and also Jae-Won Lee, "The Symbiosis of Modern Olympics and Mass Media: Policy Concerns for Olympism," (Paper delivered at the Seoul Olympiad Anniversary Conference, September 12–16, 1989, Seoul, Korea).

79. Apparently, German and Japanese broadcasters offered their viewers some background on Sohn Kee Chung, but most other international broadcasters did not. This was discussed in an interview with Cho Sung Min, a member of the IOC TV Commission, in Seoul, Korea, September 8, 1989.

80. Interview with Cho Sung Min, director-general for broadcasting, Seoul Olympic Organizing Committee, in Seoul, Korea, September 8, 1989.

81. Randy Harvey, *Los Angeles Times*, February 5, 1992, p. C1.

3

The Politics of Broadcast Rights, Production, and Media Priorities

The struggle for control over Olympic communication is centered on television, the medium largely responsible for transforming the modern Olympic movement. More precisely, it involves commercial television, which was the driving force in that transformation. Indeed, the contemporary Olympics are a paradigm for the interdependent emergence of global television, on the one hand, and corporate sponsorship of international sport, on the other. As IOC President Samaranch himself has frequently noted, it was the income from television rights that triggered the great expansion of the Olympics after he took office in 1980.[1] But there was concern about too much dependence on television rights revenues, and when the IOC needed a new revenue source to avoid excessive reliance on that one source, it turned to a new, global corporate sponsorship program. These two sources are now the twin pillars of Olympic marketing internationally.

The shaping of Olympic television and other media coverage begins with and, to a large extent, is determined by the negotiation of broadcast rights and rights associated with corporate sponsorship of the Olympics, as discussed in Chapter 4. The sale of rights to broadcast the Games is at once the mechanism through which the Olympic movement raises the single largest portion of its revenues, exerts control over specific characteristics of Olympic telecasts, and sets important priorities among the various broadcasting and print media that cover the Games. The relationship between the Olympics and television encompasses more than the negotiation of rights, it extends to the allocation of rights revenues within the

Olympic movement, the specific forms of control and access that those rights confer on broadcasters, and the more general influence that rightsholding versus non-rightsholding broadcasters exert on the planning and production of the Olympic telecast. Although the rights negotiations take place long before the Olympic telecast and even prior to specific planning by producers and technicians, they anticipate and shape the television event in important ways. Therefore, we will treat them in some detail as an important component in the political economy of the contemporary Games and with emphasis on their role in the construction of the Seoul Olympics as a global television spectacle.

In historical perspective, the whole range of questions posed by new media technologies for the recording, storage, and distribution of audiovisual materials is intrinsic to the negotiation of television rights. As the television industry changes its modes of program production and delivery, audience viewing patterns or ratings tend to change, and, consequently, so do television rights revenues because they depend heavily on both the costs of producing Olympic coverage and the expected audience size for the telecasts. In other words, the very character of television rights is changing over time in response to the introduction of new technologies and their uses by the industry and audiences.

Given such changes in the technologies and economics of television, the various parties involved in the negotiation of Olympic television rights require a common understanding of what such rights are. The detailed description of broadcast and distribution rights in force for the Seoul Games was contained in a version of the *Media Guide*, published by the IOC, as a bylaw to Rule 51 of the 1984 Olympic Charter.[2] The bylaw said, in part, that "the term 'broadcasting' means the placing at the disposal of the public, the official events and ceremonies within the Olympic Games without the circulation of any tangible device. Broadcasting therefore includes notably radio broadcasting and television, and transmission to subscribers by cable or by any other means."[3] The *Media Guide* also covered "distribution" rights, which dealt with such tangible devices as phonographs, records, videodiscs, videocassettes, and the like. It specified that the IOC itself could grant distribution rights and that it would grant television rights jointly with the host organizing committee.

The Increase in Television Rights Revenues

Strictly speaking, television came to the Olympics in 1936, with live coverage of the Games outside the Olympic stadium. A first glimpse of the present global scope of television came in 1964, when the Tokyo Olympics featured the first satellite relay over the Pacific. However, it was in Rome in 1960 that television rights first became an important consideration for the

Olympic movement. The large increases in revenues from television rights took place in the 1970s and 1980s and mirrored the growth of global television more generally. Within this general pattern of an ever-larger role for television in the Olympics, the dominance of the U.S. rightsholding network and the consequences of that dominance for the Olympic movement deserve special attention.

Television Rights as a Proportion of the Olympic Budget

In recent Olympics, television rights fees have become the single largest source of revenues to support the Games. In Seoul, they accounted for 26.1 percent of net revenues taken in by the SLOOC. In Barcelona, they composed an estimated 33.9 percent of net revenues, and for Atlanta, which projects total revenues of $1.162 billion (and expenses of $1 billion), television rights fees are projected to provide $549 million, or nearly 50 percent, of required revenues. Corporate sponsorship is estimated to bring in an additional $324 million, so that—assuming projections are correct—the two related categories will together account for approximately three-quarters of the Atlanta revenues.

Figure 3.1 portrays the increasing proportion of net revenues for Olympic organizing committees that come from television rights and commercial sponsorship. It shows clearly that the 1984 Los Angeles Olympics marked a turning point not only because of a quantum increase in television rights but also because of the introduction of commercial sponsorship on a large scale. These sources accounted for a smaller proportion in Seoul than in Los Angeles, for two major reasons. One was the massive government and private-sector effort entailed in the Seoul Olympics, with 23.4 percent of all revenues coming from donations. The second is the sheer size of the U.S. market and the many corporations in that market that have experience in the use of sports sponsorship in their promotional programs. Those characteristics of the North American market are also illustrated by the projection, shown in Figure 3.1, that 74 percent of all revenues for the 1996 Atlanta Olympics will come from television rights and corporate sponsorship.

In considering the various sources of revenues that support the Olympics, it is important to note that most monies go to the organizing committee charged with preparations for a particular Olympic Games competition and do not support the IOC or the Olympic movement more broadly. The TOP sponsorship program provided another stream of revenue beginning with Seoul. Although that sponsorship income increased for Barcelona and is projected to increase further for Atlanta, it is still far from supplanting television rights as the major source of income for the IOC.[4]

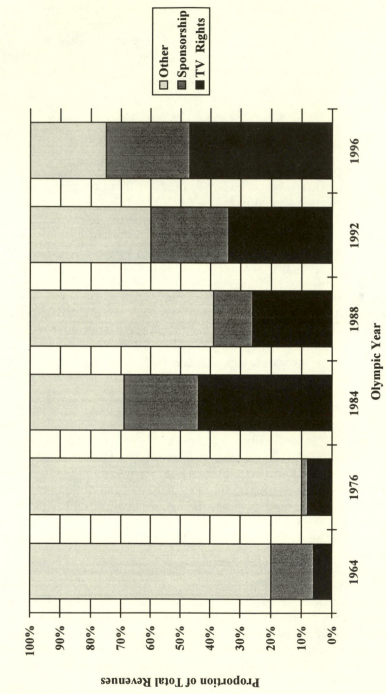

FIGURE 3.1 Olympic Organizing Committee revenues. *Source:* International Olympic Committee.

TABLE 3.1   U.S. network payments for Olympic television rights

Year	Summer Olympics			Winter Olympics		
	Network	Amount Paid ($)	% of Total	Network	Amount Paid ($)	% of Total
1960	CBS	394,000	33.4	CBS	50,000	100.0
1964	NBC	1,578,000	100.0	ABC	60,000	63.8
1968	ABC	4,500,000	46.2	ABC	2,500,000	76.5
1972	ABC	7,500,000	42.2	NBC	6,400,000	75.5
1976	ABC	25,000,000	71.7	ABC	10,000,000	86.0
1980	NBC	72,333,000	82.8	ABC	15,500,000	74.8
1984	ABC	225,000,000	78.6	ABC	91,500,000	89.1
1988	NBC	300,000,000	74.5	ABC	309,000,000	95.1
1992	NBC	401,000,000	66.0	CBS	243,000,000	n/a

Source: International Olympic Committee.

The Dominance of the United States

In recent Summer Olympics, the proportion of worldwide rights fees accounted for by U.S. television networks has remained very high, as shown in Table 3.1. In the case of Barcelona, the proportion accounted for by the United States (NBC) was estimated at something less than 66 percent, due to a proportionally much higher payment by the European Broadcasting Union, with time zone advantages for broadcasts throughout Europe, and increased payments from Japan and other broadcast organizations, as well.[5]

These figures reflect the sheer size and market power of the United States, which have several consequences for the Olympic movement. One of these is that U.S. cities that bid to host the Olympic Games have a built-in advantage over cities in other nations because events can be more easily scheduled to coincide with prime-time hours in the United States. To date, Atlanta represents the best example of this phenomenon, with its location in the U.S. eastern time zone making possible prime-time broadcasts of every big Olympic event. A related factor is that certain large U.S. cities, such as Los Angeles and Atlanta, already possess the telecommunications infrastructure base on which to build in order to meet the demands of a global Olympic telecast. By contrast, Seoul had to construct large parts of that infrastructure almost from scratch.

A second consequence of U.S. market power and dominance in financing the Olympics is that the United States Olympic Committee (USOC) receives special treatment and wields far more power in the movement than any other national Olympic committee. Following the 1984 Los Angeles Games, the USOC negotiated a larger percentage of the IOC's two major revenue streams—from U.S. television rights and TOP. It also gained two seats on the IOC's executive board and an important board position on the Revenue Source Committee.[6]

However, in the view of the USOC and others in the United States, the treatment that country receives is still far from equitable. An analysis published in *The Brookings Review* in the fall of 1989 offered a three-pronged indictment of the current arrangement: "In sum, the funding setup for the Olympics is a travesty. Americans get bilked in three ways. We pay more than our fair share for the games, we have to put up with an excessive number of commercials to see them, and our athletes receive little of the money we do pay."[7]

The first argument was based on the high proportion of worldwide rights fees paid by the U.S. networks and the IOC's encouragement of "bidding wars," in contrast to the "negotiations" undertaken with such organizations as the European Broadcasting Union. Although EBU telecasts to more households than a U.S. network, it has, in the past, paid less than 5 percent of what the U.S. network pays. Antitrust laws currently prevent U.S. networks from banding together to offer a single bid to the IOC. However, in 1980, the three networks undertook negotiations with the U.S. Justice Department in an effort to work out an antitrust exemption, until CBS withdrew from the negotiations.

The argument regarding excessive commercials was based on their sheer number—more than 5,000 during the 179-hour NBC telecast of the Seoul Olympics—together with the fact that interruptions of live events are an irritant. It is now a matter of historical record that the frequent interruptions of NBC's telecast in the United States provoked some negative viewer response and a considerable amount of critical commentary in the press. The topic will be addressed in later chapters.

Finally, an analysis of how the USOC spent its money from 1985 to 1988 provided the basis for the claim that U.S. athletes face greater financial burdens than those in countries where there is state or other support. Given subsequent developments, including the breakup of the Soviet Union and the demise of communism in Eastern Europe, it is worth noting that the argument was bolstered by the high level of state support provided by Communist governments during the cold war era.

The Brookings analysis concluded by recommending three steps to change the current situation. First, it suggested that a U.S. body, either the government or the USOC, hold the auction for U.S. television rights, subject to several conditions: No more than 10 minutes of commercials per hour could be shown, telecasts would be required to be available without fees throughout the United States, and live action could not be interrupted with commercials. Second, the U.S. body would submit an offer for U.S. broadcast rights to the IOC, indexed to what other nations pay for such rights. Eventually, this would result in payments proportionate to the per capita incomes of nations, adjusted to reflect the attractiveness of the location of the Games for viewing in certain time zones. Finally, the U.S. body would spend the difference between the revenue raised at its auction and the amount paid to the IOC on direct support of athletes training for the Games.[8]

After the Seoul Olympics, the disagreement between the USOC and the IOC over allocation of U.S. television rights surfaced publicly, with the USOC arguing that it deserved more than the 10 percent it had agreed to before Seoul. From one perspective, the fundamental issue in the dispute was the question of whether the advertising revenue generated by telecasting the Olympics in the United States is "American money" or money that belongs to the Olympic movement. This issue raised some fears in Olympic circles that if the USOC pushed hard enough, the U.S. Congress might seek to impose a tariff restricting the "export" of the rights fee.[9] Indeed, during the fall of 1990, a bill was introduced into Congress that would have required the U.S. networks to negotiate with the USOC instead of the IOC. This move raised fears of governmental bureaucratic oversight and was credited with moving the USOC and the IOC toward eventual agreement in their negotiations.

In addition to the question of U.S. versus Olympic movement ownership of revenues from the U.S. telecast, there was another major element in the dispute. From the viewpoint of the USOC and its president at the time, Robert Helmick, the central issue was one of replacing income lost by the USOC as a direct result of the activities of the rights-holding U.S. television network. They noted that a network's sale of the Olympic rings to sponsors for use in commercials damaged the USOC's ability to attract sponsors because it could not offer them exclusive use of the symbol. This question of conflict between television and Olympic sponsorship is also a major unresolved issue for the IOC and ISL Marketing, which manages its global sponsorship programs.

For most of the period from 1972 to 1989, the USOC did not have representation on the IOC Executive Board and, in fact, had generated some resentment among IOC members due to its dominant presence in both sport and the media. On the issue of how much of the U.S. network rights revenues should go to the USOC, Helmick made a revealing comment: "There is a lot of divisiveness because the IOC is not getting the right information. It is not having these things explained. My objective is to bring the IOC and the USOC together. I have told Samaranch that we (the IOC and the USOC) could work together instead of fighting all the time."[10]

By 1991, an agreement had been reached on some of these issues. IOC Vice President Richard Pound, who handled financial negotiations with the USOC, said that discussions between the IOC and the USOC would give the USOC a large portion of revenues. "The USOC will receive 10 percent of U.S. television rights fees under a 1989 agreement and, starting in

1996, will receive half of any increase in the rights fees. It will also continue to receive 20 percent of the IOC's TOP revenues."[11]

Finally, a caveat is in order concerning U.S. dominance. Although the United States and its commercial television networks presently exert strong leverage on Olympic television, the logical outcome of current developments will be to decrease that relative influence. With changes in television technologies and markets around the world, there will likely be significant alterations in the financing, negotiation, and production of Olympic television, assuming continued growth and expansion of global television generally in tandem with an Olympic movement of worldwide scope. Take, for example, the vast Asian region. Given the economic dynamism of many of its nations, together with potential regional television audiences in the billions of viewers, it seems poised, if not destined, to play a new and more powerful role in Olympic television.

Negotiation and Distribution of Rights Revenues

Rule 21 of the Olympic Charter 1984 provides, in part, that "all sums arising out of the celebrations of the Olympic Games belong to the IOC and that the IOC reserves the right to give a portion of those monies to the host city organizing committee, to the international sports federations, and to the national Olympic committees.[12] Rule 10 of the charter is even more explicit: "The Olympic Games are the exclusive property of the IOC which owns all rights over their organization and exploitation and over their transmission and reproduction by any means whatsoever. The IOC may grant concessions or licenses in respect of these rights."[13] Accordingly, the television rights for the Olympic Games for Seoul and Barcelona were negotiated by the IOC, together with the host organizing committee. However, both the manner of negotiation and the distribution of rights has changed dramatically since the 1960 Olympics in Rome, as the following chronology indicates.[14]

- Rights paid for the 1960 Rome and 1964 Tokyo Olympics belonged completely to the organizing committees. The IOC had foregone them, instead receiving a single contribution from the Olympic cities at the time of their election.
- Beginning with the Mexico City Olympics in 1968, the IOC asked for a lump-sum payment for television rights (which were becoming large) and renounced the previous contribution that the elected cities had been asked to pay.
- For the Munich Olympics in 1972, the IOC adopted a distribution scale: The first million dollars in their entirety, two-thirds of the second, and one-third of the next million belonged to the IOC, with the

remainder going to the host organizing committee. "However, in 1969, the IOC discovered that the Munich Organising Committee had entered into a contract for the sale of rights for the United States of America in two parts. The first, amounting to US$ 7.5 million, covered the rights themselves. The second, worth US$ 6 million, related to 'technical costs'. Thanks to this restrictive interpretation of the notion of rights, US$ 6 million belonged exclusively to the OCOG, in addition to its share of the US$ 7.5 million."[15]

- The IOC responded as part of its ongoing efforts to gain control over rights and their negotiation. Beginning in 1976, the distribution of the amounts paid by the broadcasters was divided into broadcasting rights and costs for setting up the production center and broadcasting of the basic signal. These "technical costs" amounted to US$ 17 million in 1976, US$ 51 million in 1980, and nearly US$ 130 million in 1984.

- From 1972 on, the IOC's share of rights revenues has been divided into three parts: one for the national olympic committees through a solidarity fund, one for the International Sports Federations, and one for the IOC itself.

The original plan for distribution of television rights revenues from the Seoul Olympics called for 20 percent to be paid to the Seoul Olympic Organizing Committee, to ensure an optimal meeting of technical requirements; two-thirds of the remaining amount would go to the SLOOC and one-third to the IOC. The IOC portion would then be divided into the three parts described earlier, after deducting—as begun in 1984—10 percent for expenses of all referees and judges at the Games and another 10 percent that was used to pay the travel and sojourn expenses of a certain number of athletes.[16] As it happened, the IOC increased its technical assistance contribution to the Seoul Olympic Organizing Committee to US$ 125 million, or about 30.6 percent of worldwide rights revenues, after IOC President Samaranch responded affirmatively to a formal request from South Korean President Roh Tae Woo.[17] With this modification, the preceding formula for allocation of rights revenues was followed.

Beginning in 1996, a new arrangement will send 60 percent of television rights revenues to the local organizing committee; the USOC, the IOC, and the international sports federations will each receive 10 percent, and the remainder will go into a pool for the other nations. At the same time, the IOC itself will take control of television rights negotiations in a move that acknowledges their increasing complexity as well as the need to balance the competing goals and interests of various parties. President Samaranch described the change as follows: "We feel it's a much better arrangement. The negotiations will also be held by the IOC, not the local organizing committee. In the future, we are going to not only be interested in getting the greatest amount of money, but also the greatest amount of coverage."[18] Other members of the IOC and its staff are also keenly aware of the trade-off between maximizing rights fees and achieving the most extensive coverage. They understand the essential role of television and other media in disseminating messages about Olympism, including its central symbols. From such a perspective, television rightsholders are more central and beneficial to the Olympic movement than commercial sponsors. Once television purchases the rights, its ensuing activities generally help the IOC and the movement as a whole. Sponsors, on the other hand, characteristically want their own corporate names in the forefront, linked closely with Olympic symbols.[19]

Such IOC concerns reflect a broad issue facing the contemporary Olympic movement. As the following chapter will explore, the effort to create an association between a corporate name or image and the sports event is intrinsic to contemporary commercial sponsorship of sport. In contrast to this promotional role, rightsholding broadcasters play a journalistic or reporting part in the Olympics. Given the present dominance of commercial broadcasters, these two roles are inevitably and closely related, yet the question of how they should be balanced persists and is likely to grow in importance.

Negotiating the Rights for Seoul

The forthcoming change to give the IOC control over television rights negotiations represents a major shift in the pattern followed through the Seoul Olympics. It stems both from difficulties encountered in the Seoul negotiations and from evolutionary changes in the television industry and its relationship to the Olympic movement, as well. The SLOOC negotiated television rights for Seoul, working with the advice and approval of the IOC. In September 1983, it signed an agreement with the IOC regarding distribution of proceeds from the sale of television rights, and in February 1984, a joint IOC-SLOOC committee was formed to negotiate with world broadcasting organizations. The IOC and SLOOC agreed that they would first sell rights for the U.S. territory and then pursue sales to other nations. In some cases, the SLOOC led negotiations with broadcast unions or independent broadcast organizations; in other cases, the IOC did. But in all cases, the final outcome was approved by the IOC.[20]

The story of how the television rights for the Seoul Games were negotiated is instructive not only for the Olympic movement globally (and as an increasingly important transnational actor), but also for the future place of Asia in that movement. On the Korean side, one individual, Kim Un-Yong, was particularly influential in those negotiations. He served as vice president of the Seoul Olympic Organizing Committee and was in charge of the television rights negotiations. He had also been a member of the International Olympic Committee since 1986, joining its executive board in 1988 and becoming chairman of the IOC Radio & TV Commission in 1989. It is worth noting that Kim's long career in the world of sport, rather than the Seoul Olympics per se, was responsible for his assumption of key responsibilities for the SLOOC and the IOC. He had served as president of the World Taekwondo Federation since 1973, and in 1986, he became president of the General Association of International Sports Federations (GAISF).[21]

At the outset, the negotiations for television rights to the Seoul Olympics were strongly conditioned by several factors. One was the pattern of sharply rising television rights fees, which fostered an expectation on the part of the organizing committee that the trend would continue. Another was Korea's lack of experience with U.S. commercial television and the various considerations in estimating a rights fee. Finally, there was the cultural gap between Korea and Western countries, which would result in dramatically different approaches to the negotiation process. These cultural factors can hardly be overemphasized. Despite long military and geopolitical proximity, incidents involving cultural differences or misunderstandings are a persistent leitmotiv in relations between Korea and the United States.

The Seoul Olympic Organizing Committee entered the negotiations expecting to receive $500 to $600 million in television rights fees, based on the past rate of increase in such revenues.[22] In the United States, however, the market situation was far from optimal, due to three major factors. One was the 14-hour time difference between Korea and the East Coast of the United States. A second was the uneasiness in the minds of television network executives about a possible boycott by Socialist nations. Third and not least important was the concern in the United States and other Western nations about both internal and external terrorist threats.

The Games schedule, especially as it relates to time differences in major world television markets, is always a prominent consideration in the negotiation of Olympic television rights. This is because the value of these rights depends directly on audience size, which is, in turn, dependent on the scheduling of live telecasts of the most popular sports and the finals in those competitions.

Among the guidelines provided to host broadcasters by the IOC is a "minimum requirements" document, which is compulsory and binding upon host cities and is governed by the Olympic Charter and its accompanying *Media Guide*. Section IV of the minimum requirements document contains the following language concerning the Games schedule:

> The final programme of the Olympic Games will be decided by the IOC on the recommendation of the Organising Committee and with the advice of the International Federations. However, before slotting the various events

into the final schedule, please discuss the suggestions from the press organizations and the broadcasters in order to achieve the best possible programming and, in particular, to reduce timetable clashes between the most
important events.[23]

Seoul provided a powerful illustration of the influence of events schedules in television rights negotiations. David Klatell and Norman Marcus
described the strategy of the U.S. networks:

> Time zones and the location of the Games have traditionally represented
> the greatest challenge to the networks and have come to represent the most
> important consideration in bidding for Olympic rights. ... The network's
> interest is in getting the organizing committee to schedule as many events
> as possible—particularly those involving the U.S. teams—so they will oc-
> cur when it is prime time in the U.S., regardless of the time of day at the
> Games. Thus in Korea, a number of events were scheduled at 8 A.M to ac-
> commodate this desire, even though the other nations' teams were un-
> happy about it.[24]

The time difference between Seoul and New York is 13 hours, which
meant that for live telecasts to coincide with prime-time television viewing in the United States—8:00 to 11:00 P.M.—events would have to be
scheduled in the morning, Seoul time. The schedule initially proposed by
the organizing committee called for such morning finals in several of the
Olympic events most popular with television viewers in the United States
and, for that matter, many other parts of the world.

In addition to the general concern with live, prime-time broadcast of
the Olympics, the U.S. television networks generally seek to achieve several things in their rights negotiations: to include as many weekend days
as possible in the competition, thereby maximizing both commercial in-
ventory and peak sports viewing periods; to spread out of those events
considered most prestigious in the United States so they will not overlap
or conflict; and to protect network affiliates' evening newscast periods,
which are major revenue sources for the local stations.

Early in the bidding for rights to the Seoul Olympics, ABC reportedly
proposed that the entire nation of South Korea move its clocks ahead by 1
hour for the duration of the games, to ameliorate the 13-hour time difference between Seoul and New York. According to one account, "The aston-
ished South Korean government declined to participate, citing the havoc it
would wreak in military, industrial and financial arrangements worldwide."[25] Yet what this account failed to note is that the South Korean government decided to establish daylight saving time from the second Sunday in May through the second Sunday in October, beginning in 1987:
"The government noted that 'Daylight-Saving Time' will be beneficial to

cultural life during the long summer days."[26] However, the move was widely and informally recognized as a response to the needs of television during the Seoul Games. In its official newsletter, host broadcaster KBS/SORTO published a world time chart showing the new time differences between Seoul and other major cities due to daylight saving time, noting that "nonetheless, the competition schedules for the 1988 Seoul Olympic Games will show no changes."[27]

When the Seoul Olympic Organizing Committee first publicly announced the schedule containing morning competition, a number of international sports federations objected. Concern centered on three sports—athletics, swimming, and gymnastics. One leading gymnastics coach commented that "if the finals are held at 10:00 A.M., the warm-ups should start at 7:30 A.M.—and the athletes have to get up two hours before that! That's impossible for young gymnasts."[28]

The morning final schedules became a major topic of conversation at the November 1984 International Symposium on Sport, Media and Olympism. IOC President Samaranch himself took note of the controversy and indicated that the IOC, after receiving the proposed schedule from the SLOOC, had contacted the three respective international federations. As he mentioned,

> We consulted the International Federations, because, I repeat, I believe they are better informed than other organisations of athletes' requirements. The International Federations, I am now referring to these three Federations quoted previously, athletics, swimming and gymnastics, wish, in the athletes' interests, to remain within the traditional timetable, and the IOC's position will, of course, be to respect the request from the International Federations. In these three cases, I believe we will have the definitive time-tables for the Olympic Games in Seoul in several weeks' time. Afterwards, when we have approved these time-tables, we can begin contracts with the television networks.[29]

The Seoul experience led one senior official of the host organizing committee to argue, based on his experience, that the Games schedule should be considered a product, with business value. That value related directly to the growing popularity of certain Olympic sports around the world and, by implication, the role of television in popularizing those sports. Consequently, he argued that "the facade up to now that the competition schedule which has business value, does not, should be discarded."[30]

In addition to the Games schedule, two other general elements enter into the negotiation of rights. One is the balancing of interests between the IOC, the international sports federations, the television networks, and the host organizing committee. The concerns of television organizations might involve not only advertising revenue, as in the case of commercial networks, but also the popularity of certain Olympic sports and, hence, the audience reach in those nations. The sports federations are generally concerned about how the schedule will affect competing athletes.

The second general element is the marketing strategy and tactics pursued by the major U.S. networks. In deciding how much to bid, all these networks must make an estimate of the size of profits they expect to earn. Making such an estimate three or four years in advance is a complex exercise that involves a projection of audience size, cost of producing the telecast, future international currency exchange rates, the risk of boycotts, and so forth. Although such considerations are common to all commercial networks, there are also idiosyncratic factors that explain why one network may value television rights differently than another and even why, on occasion, a network may bid more for the rights than they alone are worth. For example, because an Olympic telecast may generate additional viewers for the network's other programs, the rights may mean more to a network with low overall ratings than to one whose ratings are already high. Also, if one network is more skilled or experienced in sports telecasts than another, it presumably would attract a larger audience for its Olympic telecasts.[31]

To better understand the strategies of U.S. television networks, the SLOOC hired the same media consultant that dealt with the Calgary organizing committee, Trans World International (TWI) of the United States. Trans World is the television branch of the Mark McCormack sporting empire. McCormack is a sports business manager whose activities range from managing sports events to handling the financial dealings of athletic superstars.[32] Nevertheless, according to a senior SLOOC official, "the organizing committee ... did not have enough knowledge about the strategies of TV networks and the timing of the sales of the rights was not so great. As a result, Seoul's revenues from selling the rights were not as successful as those of other games."[33]

SLOOC officials responsible for television rights negotiations held discussions with the IOC and gave a briefing to the U.S. networks early in 1984. Proposals were sent to the three networks in August of that year.[34] However, the official television rights negotiations with the U.S. networks took place during the following series of meetings.

Date	Place
September 12–13, 1985	Lausanne
September 27–28 (approx.)	New York
November 11–26, 1985	New York
January 13–20, 1986	New York
March 13–24, 1986	New York
March 26, 1986, contract signing	Lausanne

The first of these meetings involved representatives of all three U.S. networks, the IOC (led by its vice president, Richard Pound), and the Seoul Olympic Organizing Committee. The initial bids, which were in the $300-million range with various incentives, surprised the SLOOC delegates, who had been expecting more than $500 million as an initial offer. One who apparently was not surprised was Kim Un-Yong, leader of the delegation. He later wrote that "I was caught between Korea's national pride and the cold reality of a maximum market price."[35] At the second negotiating session, held in New York, NBC agreed to a $300-million guarantee plus $200 million on a risk-sharing basis. However, a series of difficult negotiations followed before the contract was finally signed in March of the following year. The revenue-sharing agreement with NBC shifted some of the risk of low advertising fees from the network to the Olympic organizers in Seoul. At the same time, it may have lowered the total amount of revenue to be shared by reducing NBC's incentives to sell advertising time. With an ordinary fixed-price contract, NBC would keep all extra revenue generated by an extraordinary sales effort, but with the revenue-sharing agreement, it would be entitled to only a portion of that.[36]

From the SLOOC point of view, "Negotiations were not moving as quickly as expected because of the complicated nature of the talks and demands by NBC, which wanted to protect its rights from all possible angles."[37] Because NBC had suffered financial losses in its coverage of the 1980 Moscow Olympics, repayment conditions, which would take effect if the Games were canceled, postponed, or not held in Seoul, became a key issue in the negotiations. "The biggest hurdle was the letter of credit to be issued by the Korea Exchange Bank in the amount of $330 million to cover total repayment, which could be automatically triggered by NBC."[38]

As Kim Un-Yong put it, "The request for a letter of credit was received as an insult to Korea."[39] Its eventual approval required discussions and approval by President Chun Doo Hwan in the Blue House, the official residence of South Korea's head of state.

During the final set of negotiations in March 1986, the key issues on which agreement was reached were described in this way:

> Agreement was reached on a wide range of items, including production of an international signal, free space in the IBC, parking space, free and purchasable tickets, auditing of advertisement sales, repayment conditions, how to inform cause of repayment, terms of reduction, scope of reduction, damage of equipment except by NBC's fault, no broadcasting if U.S. team did not participate, time of repayment and reduction, tax, arbitration and court proceedings. NBC was afraid of a congressional inquiry on the contract provision stipulating an introduction of Korean heritage and development, but Watson [President, NBC Sports Division], in a letter, accepted my proposal to do so.[40]

As part of the final accord, NBC agreed to allow Korean-language television stations in the United States to broadcast some of KBS's coverage of the Seoul Olympics. "Initially, NBC opposed this idea because it worried about a similar request from Barcelona for the numerous Spanish stations in the U.S. if it got T.V. rights for Barcelona. NBC finally agreed to broadcast four hours a day in Los Angeles and five other KBS stations in the U.S."[41]

In retrospect, the difficulties in negotiating broadcast rights with NBC prefigured the major controversy that would erupt during the Seoul Olympics over NBC and the nature of its coverage. NBC approached the Seoul Games much as it would any other major international sports telecast, with a focus on the logistics and details of television production and transmission. One telling aspect of that approach was the network's failure to place its own bilingual staff in Seoul until after June 1987, following resolution of the political crisis in South Korea. This occurred despite the size of its investment in the Olympic telecast and the importance of the earlier 1986 Asian Games as a rehearsal for Seoul. Given the cultural gap between East and West and the legendary difficulty Westerners have with the Korean language, such contrasting views of the Olympics project were not a good omen. The controversy over NBC and the accompanying wave of anti-American sentiment in Korea are dealt with at length in Chapters 7 and 8.

The second set of television rights negotiations involved discussions with the pool of Japanese broadcasters, representing NTV, Fuji, Asahi, TBS, and TV Tokyo. The SLOOC had engaged a well-known U.S. consulting firm to assist its negotiations with the U.S. networks, but in the dealings with Japan, it drew on its own considerable expertise. When questioned in a 1991 interview about the role of McCormack's TWI corporation, Kim Un-Yong replied, "Do you think McCormack would know how to negotiate with the Japanese?"[42] This comment underscored a consideration that had doubtless been taken into account by the IOC and SLOOC in choosing him to handle the negotiations. It also offered a hint of the future role that he and colleagues from Korea might play in Asian television rights negotiations should Beijing succeed in its bid for the Olympic Games in the year 2000.

Because the NBC negotiations had caused so much adverse reaction in government and civilian circles in Korea, the Japan TV rights negotiations attracted a great deal of attention. A major goal of the SLOOC was to secure a high enough rights fee so that total worldwide television rights revenues would exceed those paid for the Calgary Winter Games.[43]

Negotiations with other television networks or broadcast unions ensued. Among these, the agreement with OIRT is noteworthy. Because Korea had no diplomatic relations with the Soviet Union and Eastern European countries at the time of the negotiations, it did not consider the amount of the rights fees for those areas to be very important. Instead, negotiations with OIRT were viewed as a means to help guarantee the security of the Games by ensuring full participation. Because the OIRT member networks were all government-supported broadcasting organizations, the negotiations served as a very important indicator that all these nations would actually participate in the Seoul Olympics.[44] In this manner, television rights negotiations, like all other aspects of planning for the Games, were enlisted in the service of South Korea's Northern policy.

New Technologies and Future Rights Fees

As mentioned earlier in the chapter, new or emerging communication technologies will be a factor in future bidding for television rights because they directly affect both the size and nature of the audience for Olympic television, as well as the cost of producing and distributing it. Consider the manner in which cable television and associated technologies for distributing Olympic coverage have already become important considerations in decisions about television rights. In the first formal negotiations between the SLOOC, IOC, and U.S. network representatives in New York, ABC's Roone Arledge offered $225 million plus an additional guarantee by ESPN, the sports television cable network, for a maximum of $135 million as an initial bid.[45] ABC was not successful, but NBC incorporated a large, pay-per-view cable subcontract as part of its successful bid for rights to the 1992 Barcelona Olympics. Indeed, NBC's high bid was made possible only through a somewhat optimistic assessment of the likely revenues from pay-per-view cable.

The emerging technology of high-definition television (HDTV) provides another illustration of how new media technologies might change the character of television rights. HDTV promises to influence both the costs of producing Olympic television and the audience viewing preferences. For the Seoul Olympics, Japan was the only country to cover the competition in HDTV. Its costs to produce such telecasts were much higher than those incurred by other world broadcasters using conventional television. As with other new or "cutting-edge" technologies, the cost of HDTV will decline over time. However, during the Seoul Olympics, it was still high on its cost curve. Although the technology had advanced considerably by 1992, HDTV production of Olympic coverage was done on a limited, although significant, basis even in Barcelona. If the host broadcaster were required to use such new technologies for production of the international television signal for the entire Olympic telecast, the overall cost would increase greatly. Nevertheless, the pressures to employ technological advances in Olympic television are great, given the status of the Games as a showcase for the international television industry. Viewing audiences will also have a say on when and how HDTV will be introduced around the world insofar as they influence the size and character of market demand.

What Rights Confer: Control and Access

When representatives of television and the press descended upon Seoul in September 1988, they formed a global village of their own, outnumbering all the athletes and officials participating in the Olympics. The total number of accredited broadcast personnel alone was more than 10,000. In effect, the residents of this "global media village" were all employed in the production and dissemination of the televised or otherwise reported Olympics. To go about their daily life in the village, they required places to eat, sleep, and work, as well as considerable assistance with communication and transportation. Providing the infrastructure to house, feed, and assist the broadcasting and press personnel was a major task for the Seoul Olympic Organizing Committee. However, not all residents of this large village were given free rein to wander throughout. Limitations of size and space in the International Broadcast Center, the Main Press Center, sports venues, and other facilities dictated that a set of priorities be established for access to key locations within the Olympic host city and in outlying venues, as well.

The agreement on television rights sets up an important hierarchy among broadcasters and among the media more generally, in which television is preeminent and the rightsholding U.S. network plays a dominant role. The remainder of this chapter examines the nature of access and control made possible through that hierarchical system.

Rightsholding Versus Non-Rightsholding Broadcasters

The mechanism through which the Olympic movement controls access to coverage of the Games is accreditation. As noted in the IOC *Media Guide*, "Accreditation basically guarantees access to Olympic events. If necessary restrictions exist, the IOC will make every effort to meet the requirements of accredited media."[46]

As a rule, larger rights payments translate into a greater number and higher levels of accreditation cards for a broadcasting network or union. Figure 3.2 provides a quantitative representation of this relationship by

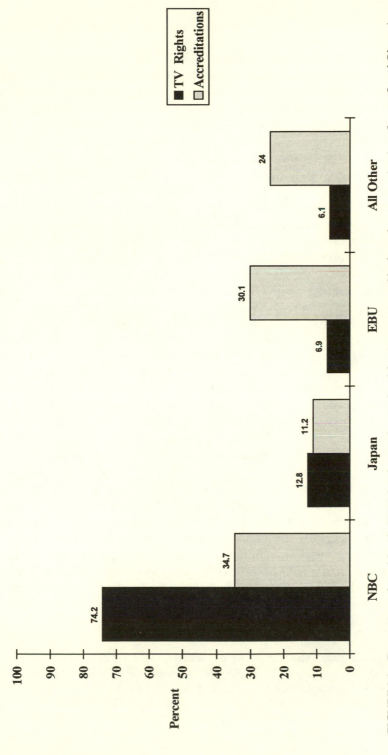

FIGURE 3.2   Proportion of worldwide TV rights fees and accredited foreign personnel by broadcast organization. *Source:* Seoul Olympic Organizing Committee, "Report on Television Broadcasting Operations for the Games of the XXIVTH Olympiad," April 1989, p. 5.

comparing the proportion of worldwide television rights fees paid by major broadcasting organizations with their proportion of total broadcasting accreditations. Those organizations with more accredited personnel have more extensive access for larger numbers of people to the locations at which Olympic ceremonies and events take place. As anyone who has attended a recent Olympics will attest, the official accreditation card issued to all broadcasters, press, athletes, officials, and other members of the Olympic family quickly becomes object of interest and a status symbol in the host city. The cards are plastic-laminated and contain a photograph of the accredited individual, along with letters in large print identifying the level of his or her accreditation. They come with a small chain so they can be worn as necklaces, and they are required for admission to virtually all Olympic locations and activities. During September 1988, more than 26,000 people wore these accreditation cards more or less continuously in navigating their way around the city of Seoul. Among these many individuals, it was the largest rightsholding broadcasters—starting with NBC television—who had the most free and extensive access to Olympic venues and other locations of interest around the city, exceeded only by members of the host broadcasting organization itself.

The significance of the extent and quality of access afforded to NBC and other large rightsholders does not lie in the accreditation and ability to move about freely per se. Rather, it is because access for the broadcast journalists who produce the global telecast translates into vantage point and perspective. The television pictures seen by audiences around the world, tantamount to the Olympic experience as conceptualized in this book, are, in important ways, determined by the number and location of camera operators, producers, and commentators. The accreditation procedure for broadcasting personnel regulates their vantage point in much the same way as tickets to an athletic competition in a large venue do for the fans who attend. Generally, the higher the ticket price, the better the view. This is roughly the principle that links Olympic broadcast rights and accreditation. It explains why RTO '92, the host broadcaster for the Barcelona Olympics, referred to television as "the first spectator" in the Olympic Games.

For those broadcasters who are not rightsholders, the IOC *Media Guide* places the following limitation on their coverage of the Olympics:

> Without prejudice to the granting of exclusive rights as defined hereafter, the showing, free of charge, of newsreels covering the Olympic Games is authorised in regular news programmes in which the actual news element constitutes the main feature, whether in cinemas, over the whole of a television network or on a single station, but shall be limited to three reports of two minutes each per day, separated by an interval of at least three hours.[47]

The Issue of News Access

This restriction on news coverage of the Olympic Games by organizations that do not hold television rights has caused a growing problem in an era in which changing technologies, economics, and overall patterns of visual newsgathering have brought an increasing number of national, regional, and local television organizations into international television coverage. The issue has been particularly acute in Europe, where leaders have sought to introduce transborder television along with overall economic unification of the continent. Article 9 of the European Convention on Transfrontier Television, adopted on March 15, 1989, by the Committee of Ministers of the Council of Europe, states that

> each Party shall examine the legal measures to avoid the right of the public to information being undermined due to the exercise by a broadcaster of exclusive rights for the transmission or retransmission ... of an event of high public interest and which has the effect of depriving a large part of the public in one or more other Parties of the opportunity to follow that event on television.[48]

The need to establish some balance between the rights of the public for access to information about the Olympics and the contractual right to property and exclusivity surfaced at the Seoul Games and promised to be an even greater question in Barcelona in 1992. A communications trade publication carried the following account of the situation in Seoul:

> Left out in the cold are hundreds of TV stations that have representatives in Seoul without any TV rights. They aren't allowed in IBC, can't take their cameras into venues and are severely restricted on what they can air. Most, from the U.S. and elsewhere, are following hometown heroes. "The rules are just plain stupid as to what we can and cannot air," a reporter from a midwestern TV station told us. Restrictions, of course, don't apply to non-event coverage that stations pick up on their own outside venues. Their cameras can't be taken onto sites until an hour after the end of competition. An ABC Sports official said the network "will be doing very little" coverage of Olympics events. "The highlights will be very old by the time NBC allows us to use them." CBS is taking different tack, and said it is planning to use its ingenuity to "do a lot of different things to provide news coverage."[49]

European discussions of the conflict between television as an issue of property rights and the public's right of access to information have suggested the general principle that exclusive rightsholders should accept— where appropriate and with the event organizer's consent—a limitation on their property rights. If agreement could be reached on such a general principle, then two other subsidiary principles could be established. The first would govern the conditions under which the holder of exclusive rights would give secondary broadcasters short reports relating to the event (in this case, the Olympics). To protect legitimate interests, the primary broadcaster might control the content of the short reports and the time lapse required before their broadcast. Secondary broadcasters would agree not to exploit short reports or sell them to third parties. The second principle would establish similar provisions governing longer summaries.[50]

The preceding discussion of news access and even the language of the Olympic Charter itself tend to presume a clear distinction between news and sports coverage. However, there are frequent instances during the Olympics in which sports events come to have news value. This was clearly demonstrated during the Seoul Games by the boxing incident, in which a disputed decision, a melee in the ring, and a 67-minute sit-in by a Korean boxer became a news event and contributed to a larger news controversy about NBC's coverage itself. The manner in which sports can generate news was even more emphatically demonstrated in Seoul when Canadian sprinter Ben Johnson was stripped of his gold medal in the 100-meter race after failing a drug test. That incident became by far the major international news event associated with the Seoul Olympics. However, those Games were not unique in this respect. The Olympics involve sport and the nature of news that will emerge during any particular Games is uncertain, but it is highly predictable that the modern Olympics will generate news of national and international interest if for no other reason than the news value inherent in sport itself.

Third World Access

As in the structure of international media generally, the issue of access to Olympic television and other communication is most acute in the poor nations of the Third World. These nations have less in the way of communications infrastructure and broadcasting systems and a concomitant lack of resources to pay television rights fees. As noted in Chapter 2, the Union of African Broadcasters initially sought access to the entire international signal from the Seoul Olympics but was only able to pay a small and "symbolic" rights fee. Therefore, the IOC and the Seoul Olympic Organizing Committee approved the use of England and France's coverage by former African colonies of those two nations.[51] Following the Seoul Olympics, the IOC Television Commission began studying a proposal under which the IOC would designate Third World countries that would be able to use much more than two minutes of Olympics coverage three times a day for free, along with the Olympic summary.[52]

Print Versus Broadcast Media

Communication researchers have long known that the introduction of a new medium, such as radio in the earlier years of this century or television more recently, may dramatically change the functions of existing media. However, this knowledge does not necessarily ease the transition, especially for practitioners working in one or the other media. Within the Olympic movement and in the communication media more generally, there is an ongoing debate and tug-of-war between the print and broadcast media. This was illustrated by the following exchange between a senior official of the Seoul Olympic Organizing Committee and a representative of the IOC Television Commission during the April 1988 meeting of the Olympic Broadcast Advisory Committee in Seoul.

> [SLOOC Official:] May I ask a favor of you before going to the IOC meeting? I realized there's considerable problems within SLOOC while working for broadcasting operations. To be specific, the press has power over the broadcasters. In the IOC meeting I hope that you make a strong point on behalf of the broadcasters that broadcasting is much more important than the press and let the SLOOC be notified of that fact.

> [IOC TV Commission Member:] I'll never accept the fact that the press is more important than the broadcasting, the people who take the news to the world today, TV and radio. The press follows up. But no longer are the news media taking the news or anything including Olympic Games to the world. The other thing which makes broadcasting more important is the fact that a very large amount of money available to run the games comes from the TV rights paid by broadcasters for the privilege of broadcasting the games while the press pays nothing. But I think whenever you get demands from the press in SLOOC which clash with requirements of broadcasting, then this should be pointed out to those people who are involved, broadcasting is in fact the organization to take the news to the world and also is the organization that's paying a very large part of the games budget for the staging of the games.[53]

The Negotiation of the Olympic Telecast

The actual planning of the global telecast from Seoul was an international and transnational project that involved representatives of the IOC (especially its television commission), international broadcasters, host broadcaster KBS/SORTO, and the Seoul Olympic Organizing Committee. Because the Games were held outside the large U.S. media market, the proportion of international media personnel relative to domestic personnel was far higher in Seoul than it had been in Los Angeles in 1984.

KBS/SORTO received international input into planning of the televised spectacle both formally and informally through several means.

The first and broadest level was represented by the World Broadcasters' Meetings convened in November 1986 and again in May 1988. The initial meeting was attended by 133 individuals representing 34 broadcasting organizations of 27 countries,[54] and the second meeting involved more than 270 delegates representing 65 broadcasting organizations and unions from a much larger number of countries.[55] The purpose of these meetings was to brief world broadcasters on Korea's preparations for the Olympic Games and to solicit input from them about production plans.

The second level of international planning took place through meetings of the smaller Olympic Broadcast Advisory Committee, which included representatives from the International Olympic Committee Television Commission, broadcasting unions such as ABU, EBU, OTI, and OIRT, and broadcasters from Japan, Hong Kong, the United States, Australia, New Zealand, Canada, and England. OBAC meetings also included delegates from the Seoul Olympic Organizing Committee, the Korea Telecommunications Authority, and KBS/SORTO. In short, the OBAC was a working group. It met once during the Asian Games in 1986, twice in 1987, and twice in 1988. During the Olympic Games themselves, there were daily OBAC briefings at the International Broadcast Center.

The third level of planning was less formal but perhaps no less important. KBS/SORTO held numerous group or individual meetings in Seoul and elsewhere around the world with members of the IOC TV Commission Technical Group and with other producers and technicians whose expertise was valued. The 1986 Asian Games were the occasion for some of the most important such meetings.

Several themes emerged with clarity in the discussions of the Olympic Broadcast Advisory Committee as it met to prepare for the Seoul Olympics. First, there was the rivalry for resources and priority between representatives of the broadcast and print media, as noted earlier in this chapter. The broadcasters asserted their priority over the print media and stressed their need for certain facilities and types of information on a more instantaneous or timely basis.

A second, related concern was the priority that should be accorded to rightsholding broadcasters, over and against those broadcasters who did not hold rights, and representatives of rightsholding broadcast unions versus individual members of those unions. For example, during the June 1987 OBAC meeting that followed a larger World Broadcasters' Meeting (WBM), a representative of the EBU expressed this view: "I think here are the people who can talk in a responsible way for the broadcasters who have the rights. If you have heard different opinions in the WBM, that is no surprise because there actually were. I can talk for EBU. There were more than 50 people from EBU and everybody had their own opinion. But there is in the end, one EBU opinion."[56]

A third general issue had to do with how well suited the venues were for television coverage. Concerns ranged from criticism of the color of the floor mats in the Asian Games gymnastics venue to more extended discussions of the location of camera and commentator positions.[57] Although the OBAC discussions themselves were frequently highly technical and detailed, they cumulatively carried important implications for the television pictures through which most of the world would experience the Olympics.

A fourth theme that pervaded the OBAC discussions was the importance of live, rather than delayed, coverage of as many events as possible. The international broadcast community generally approaches international sports competitions with the notion that viewers prefer to see the competition instantaneously. As discussed elsewhere in this chapter and in other parts of this book, this preference for live coverage relates not only to production planning and practice but also to questions of exclusivity and broadcast rights. The longer the delay of a telecast, the greater the chance that a viewer might learn of results or see part of a competition through another channel. The more live coverage of popular events that can be provided at attractive times, the larger the viewing audience and the higher the rights fee.

During the June 1987 meeting of the OBAC, there was extensive debate on the number and nature of television feeds to be provided by the host broadcaster from the gymnastics venue. To satisfy the majority of broadcasters, it became necessary to consider an integrated feed, composed of coverage from several of the different events taking place in the venue. NBC alone opposed that plan, on the grounds that it would force the network to rely on tape-delay coverage of some of the gymnastics competition. The issue became one of the major disagreements in the meeting, with NBC holding to its position until the final hours of the three-day meeting.[58]

The 1986 Asian Games were planned and widely acknowledged in Seoul as a dress rehearsal for the 1988 Olympics. From a television standpoint, they provided a timely opportunity to test not only the various electronic technologies involved but also and most importantly the production skills that would be required of personnel working for the host broadcaster. The NBC delegation sent to observe the Asian Games was "pleasantly surprised" at the quality of the feed produced by KBS/SORTO. NBC executive producer Mike Weisman assessed it as "very simple, very safe, very by-the-book coverage."[59] However, the visit also pre-

saged some key problems that were to balloon into major issues in the
Seoul Olympics. They were described by a columnist for *Sports Illustrated:*

> For one thing, there was little sense of drama or color in the Korean tele-
> casts. When the Japanese winner of the steeplechase collapsed at the finish
> line and writhed in pain, the cameras followed the other runners as they
> crossed the line. Too often the coverage seemed regimented. In water polo,
> the director called up crowd shots after every goal, even when the crowd
> was sitting on its hands.
>
> The Korean replays tended to be inconclusive and end too soon. In basket-
> ball, for instance, it was impossible to analyze a contested charge because
> the replay cut out before the defending player fell backward. And in box-
> ing, the knockout punch was shown, but jabs that set up the punch were ig-
> nored. Another problem: Korean microphones consistently picked up the
> crowd noise but rarely were in position to catch the grunts and groans of
> the contestants.
>
> NBC staffers were pointing out these and other problems to the Koreans
> last week, but always in the gentlest fashion. "Like all creative people they
> have fragile egos and a lot of pride," said Weisman. "Any criticism is awk-
> ward to give. You try to be diplomatic."[60]

In retrospect, this description offered hints that NBC and the Korean
hosts had vastly different views of Olympic television. The U.S. network
saw it as another sports event, but for KBS—the host broadcaster—it was
that and much more. One piece of evidence on the early NBC perspective
is that, though the network sent a large delegation to the Asian Games, by
that point it had not yet established even a preliminary or skeleton staff of
its own in Seoul.

However, the most suggestive and telling evidence in the *Sports Illustrated* article was contained in the following paragraph:

> If anything threatens to disrupt the harmonious relationship between the
> television crews it is the supercharged Korean political scene. During the
> Asian Games, the Koreans objected to an NBC News story reporting the
> bombing at Seoul's Kimpo International Airport and the demonstrations at
> the opening ceremonies. Korean officials argued that NBC has a vested in-
> terest in the success of the Olympics. This discussion will surely continue as
> the Games approach.[61]

With the advantage of hindsight, these comments appear prescient.
They clearly called attention to the difference in cultural norms about ac-
ceptable behavior for broadcasters, with NBC proceeding on the basis of
one set of standards and the Korean hosts operating with another. The situation was broadly analogous to what happens with increasing frequency

in international news coverage when Western reporters fly into an unfamiliar setting to cover a major event. The latter practice is well known in the scholarly literature as "parachute journalism" or the "firehouse" model of reporting.

However, the author of the *Sports Illustrated* column could not have foreseen the magnitude of the clash that would emerge between NBC and its Korean hosts during the 1988 Olympics or the international dimensions the incident would assume. By focusing on disagreements over reporting, the column illuminated only the tip of the iceberg. Beneath the surface was the important political reality that Korean-U.S. relations started on a rocky road years earlier and that the breadth and nature of anti-American sentiment had changed in important respects during the 1980s. In historical perspective, the eruption of anti-Americanism on the occasion of the Olympics was hardly surprising. How and why it occurred will be a major subject later in this book.

In summary, the analysis in this chapter shows that broadcast rights, in addition to providing the major stream of revenue for the modern Olympic movement, are part of a political process through which actors in that movement negotiate its most important product—the global telecast of the Summer Olympic Games. The payment of rights fees establishes an orderly hierarchy among world broadcasters, not unlike the ordering of ticketholding spectators at any athletic event—ranging from those in the box seats or front row to others seated on distant bleachers. The U.S. commercial networks have long dominated Olympic television, and the situation in Seoul was no exception. NBC's large payment for television rights made it a major influence in the scheduling of key athletic events in the host city and also provided the network with more and higher levels of accreditation than other television organizations—a "front row seat," if you will, equaled only by the presence of personnel from KBS/SORTO itself.

The central role of broadcast rights fees as a mechanism for regulating access to the Olympics in order to construct a global television spectacle clarifies a persistent dilemma facing the Olympic movement. On the one hand, it requires commercial broadcasting, both as a revenue source and because that is the principle medium of the modern Olympic experience. On the other hand, the priorities of commercial television, with its impetus toward exclusivity in coverage, may not serve the expressed universalist goals of the IOC, both for worldwide audience exposure and for a telecast that will consistently convey certain central Olympic symbols and values. Consideration of the dilemma requires attention to the growing role of commercial sponsorship, which is closely interdependent with global television. Indeed, one of the "rights" purchased by NBC Television was the right to promote itself in the United States as the official network of the

Olympic Games in Seoul. The following chapter takes up the whole topic of sponsorship.

Notes

1. Morley Myers, "IOC Chief Warns of Olympic Growth," United Press International (San Juan, Puerto Rico), August 29, 1989.

2. Note that Rule 51 of the 1984 version of the Olympic Charter became Rule 49 in the 1990 version and Rule 59 in the totally revised 1991 version.

3. International Olympic Committee, *Media Guide* (Lausanne, Switzerland: International Olympic Committee, 1985).

4. Personal interview with Kim Un-Yong, IOC member and chairman of the IOC Radio and Television Commission, Olympic Center, Seoul, Korea, April 14, 1992.

5. Based on negotiations concluded as of January 1991, the Organizing Committee for the Barcelona Olympic Games (COOB) reported total television rights revenues of $632.65 million, including $416 million from NBC ($415 in cash and $15 million in advertising). See COOB '92, S.A., Image and Communication Division-Press, *Press Dossier*, Barcelona, Spain, January 1991, p. 21.

6. Holt Hackney, "Getting Some Gold," *Financial World*, March 5, 1991, p. 48.

7. Robert Z. Lawrence, with Jeffrey D. Pellegrom, "Fool's Gold: How America Pays to Lose in the Olympics," *The Brookings Review* (Fall 1989): p. 5.

8. Ibid., pp. 5–10.

9. "Feathers Fly over the Games' Golden Goose," *London Times*, April 5, 1990.

10. Randy Harvey, "Controversial USOC Chief Elected to Olympic Board," *Los Angeles Times*, August 31, 1989, sports sec., pt. 3, p. 1.

11. Hackney, "Getting Some Gold."

12. International Olympic Committee, *Olympic Charter 1984*, (Lausanne, Switzerland: International Olympic Committee, 1984), p. 14.

13. Ibid., p. 8.

14. Monique Berlioux, "Income: Television Rights" (Paper delivered at the Symposium International Sport Medias Olympisme, Lausanne, Switzerland, November 23–26, 1984), pp. 89–93.

15. Ibid., p. 90.

16. Ibid.

17. Kim Un-Yong, *The Greatest Olympics: From Baden-Baden to Seoul* (Seoul, Korea: Si-sa-yong-o-sa, 1990), p. 287.

18. William D. Murray, United Press International (Portland, Ore., February 20, 1989).

19. Personal interview with Kim Un-Yong.

20. Seoul Olympic Organizing Committee, "Report on Television Broadcasting Operations for the Games of the XXIVTH Olympiad," April 1989, p. 5.

21. Kim, *The Greatest Olympics,* pp. 295–303.

22. Ibid., p. 87.

23. International Olympic Committee, *Minimum Requirements for the Electronic, Written and Photographic Coverage and Broadcasting by Radio and Television of the*

Games of the Olympiad and the Olympic Winter Games (Lausanne, Switzerland: International Olympic Committee, n.d.), p. 3.

24. David A. Klatell and Norman Marcus, *Sports for Sale: Television, Money and the Fans* (New York: Oxford University Press, 1988), p. 184.

25. Ibid., p. 173.

26. Korean Broadcasting System, *SORTO Courier,* 3 (April 1987): p. 18.

27. Ibid.

28. Vincent J. Ricquart, *The Games Within the Games* (Seoul, Korea: Hantong Books, 1988), p. 169.

29. Juan Antonio Samaranch (Comments in the official report of SISMO '84, Symposium International Sport Medias Olympisme, Lausanne, Switzerland, November 23–26, 1984), p. 231.

30. Lee Dong Wook, *How to Prepare for the Olympics and Its Task* (Seoul, Korea: Lee Dong Wook, 1988), p. 99.

31. John McMillan, "Bidding for Olympic Broadcast Rights: The Competition *Before* the Competition," *Negotiation Journal* (July 1991): pp. 255–263.

32. Ricquart, p. 167.

33. Lee, *How to Prepare for the Olympics and Its Task,* pp. 237–238.

34. Ibid., p. 235.

35. Kim, *The Greatest Olympics,* p. 89.

36. McMillan, "Bidding for Olympic Broadcast Rights," p. 261.

37. Kim, *The Greatest Olympics,* pp. 91, 92.

38. Ibid., p. 92.

39. Ibid., p. 93.

40. Ibid., p. 94.

41. Ibid., p. 96.

42. Kim Un-Yong, personal interview, at Kuk Ki Won (headquarters of the World Taekwondo Association), Seoul, Korea, September 12, 1991.

43. Kim, *The Greatest Olympics,* p. 99.

44. Ibid., p. 104.

45. Ibid., pp. 88–89.

46. Seoul Olympic Organizing Committee, *Media Guide,* (Seoul, Korea: Seoul Olympic Organizing Committee, 1985), p. 34.

47. ibid., p. 44.

48. Alfonso de Salas, "Exclusive Rights and News Access," Proceedings of "Sport and the Media," 23rd Congress of the General Association of International Sports Federations, Budapest, Hungary, October 18–21, 1989, pp. 41, 42.

49. "Doing 'Hell of a Job': Halfway Through Seoul Olympics, NBC Is Playing Catch-Up," *Communications Daily* 8 (September 27, 1988): p. 7.

50. de Salas, "Exclusive Rights and News Access," pp. 43, 44.

51. Personal iInterview with Cho Sung Min, director-general for broadcasting, Seoul Olympic Organizing Committee, Seoul, Korea, September 8, 1989.

52. Alex Gilady, "The New Ways of Television," Proceedings of "Sport and the Media," 23rd Congress of the General Association of International Sports Federations, Budapest, Hungary, October 18–21, 1989, pp. 17–22.

53. Korean Broadcasting System SORTO, "OBAC Meeting Transcript," April 6–8, 1988, p. 139.

54. Korean Broadcasting System, *SORTO Courier* 2 (December 1986): p. 4.

55. Korean Broadcasting System, *KBS Courier* 8 (June 1988): p. 4.

56. Korean Broadcasting System/SORTO, "2nd OBAC Meeting Transcript," June 10–12, 1987, p. 19.

57. Alex Gilady, a U.S. member of the IOC TV Commission, stated that during the Asian Games, the floor mats were "a very boring green." Note that in the Calgary Winter Games, the host organizing committee tore up the ice in a skating venue and put in ice with a different color background after criticism from ABC television.

58. Korean Broadcasting System/SORTO, "2nd OBAC Meeting Transcript," pp. 19, 83.

59. William Taafe, "Television Diplomacy," *Sports Illustrated* (October 13, 1986): p. 20.

60. Ibid.

61. Ibid.

4

The Introduction of
Commercial Sponsorship
on a Global Scale

The Seoul Olympics, together with the Calgary Winter Games earlier in 1988, ushered in a new era of commercial involvement with the Olympics. For the first time in Olympic history, corporate sponsorship activities were planned and carried out on a truly global scale. In the words of an industry publication, "The Games of the XXIV Olympiad marked the culmination of an unprecedented cooperative initiative on the part of the hundred-plus organizations which comprise the Modern Olympic Movement."[1] The initiative was called The Olympic Program (TOP), and it was negotiated over a period of years by the International Olympic Committee, the organizing committees for the Seoul and Calgary Games, and more than 150 separate national Olympic committees.

Continuing the line of analysis begun earlier, this chapter suggests that TOP also marked an important stage in the interdependent development of both global television and the marketing practices of transnational corporations. With it, the Olympic movement entered an era in which decisions about television, advertising, and sponsorship affect not only its major sources of revenues but also the shape of international television broadcasts and, consequently, many of the meanings that come to be associated with the Olympics around the world.

In this chapter, we look briefly at the history of sponsorship, then at its more recent role in sports and its incorporation into the Olympic movement. We draw heavily on the experience of Seoul to illustrate the new TOP program and to examine the other levels of commercial activity associated with the modern Olympics.

Origins and Understandings of Commercial Sponsorship

Patronage of sport, the arts, and entertainment has a long history. Just how long *commercial sponsorship* of sport has existed depends upon how restrictive or expansive a definition of sponsorship is used. Merchants in ancient Greece supported local athletes in training for the Games and enjoyed goodwill and increased business from the community as a result.[2] However, commercially motivated support is generally thought to be a more recent development. In the mid-nineteenth century, a British corporation sponsored an English cricket team on a tour of Australia, and in 1887, a French magazine sponsored an auto race.[3] During the early twentieth century, sponsorship became well established in the United States before the surge in sponsorship expenditures in Europe during the 1960s and in Japan during the 1970s.

As noted in Chapter 1, the decade preceding the Seoul Olympics saw a massive growth in the world sports calendar, with the number of international events more than doubling. In Britain, as an example, annual sponsorship expenditures in 1987 were $235 million, with 2,000 companies involved. Only fourteen years earlier, the market was worth just $3.5 million.[4] A 1987 estimate by ISL Marketing, Ltd., put worldwide sponsorship expenditures at $4.1 billion, a figure that represented between 2.5 and 3.5 percent of all advertising spending worldwide. The United States and Western Europe accounted for 45 percent and 32 percent of total sponsorship expenditure, respectively. The ISL report placed particular emphasis on the recent growth of sponsorship in the Pacific Basin, with Japan alone accounting for 10 percent of worldwide expenditure.[5] Another estimate put global sponsorship expenditures at $5 billion in 1989.[6] One recent analysis projects a slowed rate of growth in sports sponsorship in the United States and Europe, while the less-developed markets of Asia, Australia, and South America will experience considerable future growth.[7]

In South Korea as well, the sports calendar burgeoned as the nation embarked on an intense effort to build a world-class sports program, especially beginning in 1981 when the Olympics were awarded to Seoul. The following year, South Korea established a Ministry of Sports, and a nationwide drive was undertaken to scout for athletic talent, with 6.2 million young people put through athletic aptitude tests. From those tests, 4,300 youths were identified as highly promising.[8] However, the effort to build a sports program extended far beyond the recruitment of potential Olympic athletes. New professional sports were introduced into Korea and immediately showed up on television. Boxing had been the first Western sport to become commercialized in Korea, during the Japanese colonial rule earlier in the century. Golfing came next, with a Korean golfer winning a tournament in Japan in the 1940s. Soccer and baseball followed some years later. For example, professional baseball began in 1982 with six teams: the MBC Chongryong, Sammi Super Stars, OB Bears, Haitai Tigers, Samsung Lions, and Lotte Giants. The club owners were leaders of top business groups in Korea.[9]

Along with these developments, the three Korean television networks increased their coverage of sports accordingly. A study by Suh Chung Woo showed that in 1981, KBS-1, KBS-2, and MBC devoted 18 percent, 19.7 percent, and 18.9 percent of their airtime to sports, respectively, for an average of 19.0 percent. By 1984, the figures had increased to 33.3 percent, 21.2 percent, and 25.3 percent. This was already significantly higher than the BBC (14 percent), ZDF of West Germany (9.8 percent), and NBC (5 percent).[10] By the mid-1980s, the Fifth Republic under President Chun Doo Hwan was widely viewed in South Korea as the "Sports Republic," and Koreans were known to grumble about the number of sporting events on television. In the context of widespread public discontent with the military dictatorship, including specific irritation at its strict control of the media, such a response to governmental efforts to increase the overall amount and range of televised sports was understandable.

Most industry analyses of sponsorship acknowledge that the key factor behind its worldwide growth is its particular suitability as a global communications medium. More specific factors include (1) government policies on the advertising of tobacco and alcohol, (2) escalating costs of media advertising (3) new opportunities because of increased leisure activity, (4) the proven ability of sponsorship to increase consumer recognition, (5) greater media coverage of sponsored events, and (6) inefficiencies in traditional media, such as clutter and zapping.[11]

As one marketing scholar succinctly put it, "In an environment of media clutter and audience fragmentation, sponsorship can overcome the now severe difficulties encountered by advertisers in gaining attention and interest from a wide range of publics who may have limited interest in the sponsor's advertising."[12]

Defining Commercial Sponsorship

After reviewing various industry efforts to define sponsorship, the Global Media Commission of the International Advertising Association proposed the following definition in 1988: "Commercial sponsorship is an investment, in cash or in kind, in an activity, in return for access to the exploitable commercial potential associated with that activity."[13]

Several components of this definition capture the breadth and highly negotiated nature of sponsorship. The term *activity* embraces events, individuals, teams, series books, and broadcast programs. The term *access* has the flexibility to describe the purchase of third-party rights, at one end, and the creation of rights in the name of the sponsor, at the other. Finally, *investment* by the sponsor constitutes the purchase price of this association—emphasizing that it is a commercial investment.

The key factor distinguishing sponsorship from such terms as *philan-thropy, patronage,* and, to a lesser extent, *charitable donations* is motivation for involvement. When commercial organizations decide as a matter of policy to donate to charitable causes or philanthropy, the motivations be-hind such donations are essentially charitable, rather than commercial. On the other hand, sponsorship encourages investment *for corporate gain*.[14]

Sponsorship in the Olympic Movement

The historical evolution of sponsorship within the Olympic movement must be seen in relationship to the IOC's perennial problem of amateurism versus professionalism and the inexorable commercialization of sport throughout the world. Commercialization was a favorite topic of IOC President Brundage, beginning during the Fifteenth Olympiad following the 1952 Olympic Games in Helsinki. After the 1956 Olympics, there was a controversy over revenue-sharing—the problem of how to distribute reve-nues from the Olympics among the various amateur organizations. This controversy generally reflected growing participation in international sport and the increasingly commercial nature of such sport.[15] In that con-troversy, Brundage argued, to no avail, that the size of the Olympic Games should be decreased because they were becoming unmanageable.

Of course, the increases in television rights fees were an important part of the commercial pressures brought to bear on the Olympics. For the 1960 Rome Games, when total television revenues were approximately $1.2 million, 46 corporations donated goods or made services available to the Games.[16] This level of commercial involvement was only the beginning of a long and controversial evolution of corporate involvement in the Olym-pics. The 1968 Winter Games produced a conflict over manufacturers' names appearing on skis, and during the Summer Games that year, it was revealed that Adidas and Puma, the two leading track shoe manufacturers in the world, were paying athletes to wear their gear.[17]

The trend toward higher television rights revenues and generally in-creased commercial involvement continued through the 1976 Montreal Olympics, which were an important turning point because of the amount of money they lost—reportedly, $1.5 billion. There were 168 "official prod-ucts" in Montreal. In the the 1980 Moscow Olympics, there were 200 Olympic products, and the 1980 Winter Games at Lake Placid attracted 381 corporate sponsors.[18] Despite the increasing number of sponsors, there were two growing problems. The first was low average sponsorship prices (reportedly as low as $10,000), and the second was the related difficulty of sponsorship clutter.[19] Cumulatively, these developments set the stage for what would be dubbed the "Hamburger Games" in Los Angeles, a reference to the prominent commercial involvement of the McDonald's Corporation.[20]

Having seen the city of Montreal saddled with debt, the citizens of Los Angeles were understandably reluctant to support the Olympics if that cost them any money: Thirty-four percent of them said so in a citywide referendum. Consequently, the IOC reluctantly allowed the United States Olympic Committee and a private, nonprofit corporation to be jointly responsible for financing the Olympic Games. This corporation formed the Los Angeles Olympic Organizing Committee and hired Peter Ueberroth as its president.[21]

Ueberroth's solution to the growing problems with sponsorship was founded on a "less-is-more" philosophy. He sought fewer sponsors, each paying much more money. In exchange, they received more rights, more attention on their corporate name or products, and the right to be exclusive sponsors within their respective product categories.[22] Whereas the 1980 Lake Placid Olympics had 381 corporate sponsors and raised approximately $10 million, Los Angeles had just 35 sponsors but raised approximately $100 million.[23]

> Atlantic Richfield Co. helped to refurbish the Los Angeles Coliseum; Southland Corporation (7-Eleven Convenience Stores) agreed to build the velodrome; IBM committed itself to supply computer equipment; AT&T agreed to set up the communications; General Motors to provide the cars; Levi Strauss to provide "official" clothing. McDonald's ...put its money into the construction of the Olympic pool.[24]

The financial success of the Los Angeles Olympics enraged some members of the International Olympic Committee, who did not think that the LAOOC returned an appropriate portion of the proceeds to the Olympic movement. However, the Games also helped to convince IOC President Samaranch that a marketing approach involving the IOC and all of the NOCs worldwide could be beneficial to the movement. The notion had been under serious consideration at least since 1983, when ISL Marketing made a presentation to the New Delhi meeting of the IOC.

Samaranch had two main concerns that motivated the move toward TOP. First, as noted earlier, he felt the IOC was becoming too dependent on television rights as a source of revenue. Second, he thought that Olympic competition had come to be dominated by teams with superior financial resources. TOP could help with both of these problems by raising more revenue and sharing it more equitably among the nations of the world.

In particular, the IOC president defended the "much needed commer-cialization" of the Olympics, saying it was the IOC's duty to raise money from television rights, sponsorship fees, and other sources.[25] "The only problem I see with commercialism, is that the money generated by sports must go back to the sport. The more money there is around the world for sports, the better it will be for the athletes."[26] The International Olympic Committee announced in September 1990 that it expected to bring in $1.84 billion in revenue for the period from 1989 to 1992, largely from television rights and its TOP program for the worldwide marketing of Olympic sym-bols.[27]

TOP was also very attractive for the largest of corporate sponsors. Be-fore TOP, the implementation of a global marketing strategy required "a long series of time and labor-intensive negotiations with dozens of NOCs worldwide, as Coca-Cola had discovered when it tried to leverage its sponsorship of the Los Angeles Games outside the United States."[28] By contrast, TOP offered a select group of corporations exclusive worldwide sponsorship rights, entailing the use of the Olympic rings and other sym-bols of the Games in Seoul and Calgary, as well as the symbols of 154 na-tional Olympic teams.[29]

Commercial Involvement in the Seoul Olympics

By the summer of 1987, a visitor to Seoul could see highly visible evidence of the forthcoming Olympic Games. All the larger taxis, formerly referred to as "call taxis," were now "88 taxis," with the numbers displayed promi-nently on their roofs. Throughout the city and, indeed, throughout the country, electronic and manually changed signboards continued the countdown of days until the Olympic opening ceremony. The Olympic slogan, "The World to Seoul, Seoul to the World," was ubiquitously dis-played. A brand of "88" cigarettes was already very popular in a nation with many smokers, especially among men. This occurred despite the fact that the IOC prohibits Olympic endorsements of tobacco items and liquor. However, among the most interesting messages about the forthcoming Olympics were found in names like the 88 Insam Chip (88 Ginseng Tea House) in Naija Dong, near the heart of the city; the 88 Paint Store, south of Shinchon Rotary; and countless other examples where ordinary citizens and small businesses owners; saw the opportunity for a profitable associa-tion with the 1988 Olympics and simply renamed their places of business to form that association. They were doing (albeit on a more modest level) the same thing that Visa, Panasonic, and Coca-Cola sought to do on a global scale—to exploit an association between the Olympics and their own product or business. Regarding businesses adopting the Olympic "88," without official endorsement, a SLOOC official said, "It's not something we're happy about but we can't control the simple use of the figures '88. If they use 'Seoul 88' or '88 Olympic Games,' or '88 Olympiad,' then we can exercise our control."[30]

As these activities illustrate, the public visibility of the Seoul Olympics, especially in Korea but also in the rest of the world, stemmed in important measure from the various revenue-generating commercial activities associated with the Games. In addition to television rights, corporate suppliers' sponsorship, and licensing, revenues for the Seoul Olympics came from the sale of coins, stamps, and medals, as well as the Olympic lottery.

Types of Sponsorship

Sponsorships for the Seoul Olympics took the following forms.[31]

- The Olympic Program: This worldwide program brought together rights from the International Olympic Committee, the national Olympic committees, and the Olympic organizing committees.
- National Olympic Program: Under this program, a company could sponsor from 2 to 150 national Olympic committees and use their local marks and emblems in their countries.
- NOC sponsorship: A corporation could sponsor a national Olympic committee. These rights were negotiated on an individual basis, and some NOCs had multiple sponsors.
- Official team sponsor: A specific team could be sponsored by a corporation, and teams might have multiple sponsors.
- Official supplier: Under this arrangement, a company became the official supplier of a specific product for an NOC or for the organizing committee (in the case of Seoul, the SLOOC).
- Official licensee: A company could become the licensee for the Seoul Olympics, for a specific NOC, or for specific teams in a particular country.
- Olympic barter program: In this arrangement, valid only with the United States Olympic Committee, sponsors provided a combination of money and services (of in-kind value) to the USOC and its athletes.
- Sponsors of television coverage: Although not a Games sponsor, NBC secured the television rights and, in turn, was allowed to use the Olympic rings with its peacock logo as agreed in the rights negotiations.

The Olympic Program included 44 product categories with global markets; such products as beer and automobiles are considered regional, rather than global, so they were not included. The Seoul Olympic Organizing Committee decided to participate—"but alertly"—in TOP, according to Kim Bum Il, its marketing director.[32] For example, home appliances fell into the 44 TOP product categories, but the SLOOC objected because local firms like Goldstar and Daewoo were in the market and would be hurt if exclusivity were given to non-Korean companies.

Nine multinational corporations—Coca-Cola, Kodak, Philips, Brother Industries, Matsushita, Federal Express, Visa, 3M, and Time Magazine— paid a minimum of $5 million and up to around $15 million to have their names exclusively associated with the Olympics within their product category in 150 countries. The sponsorship package gave ten rights to the original nine sponsors:

1. Product exclusivity. Each participant was the only sponsor in its product category. The NOCs and the Seoul and Calgary organizing committees were free to take on additional sponsors, as noted earlier, but only in product categories not previously claimed by TOP or designated as a global industry.

2. Use of marks and designations. In the most tangible aspect of the program, each sponsor had the right to display the logos and specific designations (i.e., "official sponsor," "official product," and so forth) of the Olympics, the events in Seoul and Calgary, and each of the national teams.

3. Public relations and promotional opportunities. There were tie-ins with officially sanctioned events, as when Federal Express created a press kit and promotional video, "A Call to the Games" in coordinating overnight delivery of the IOC's official Olympic invitations to more than 160 nations.

4. Access to Olympic archives. The IOC loaned Olympic art and artifacts from its archives in Lausanne, Switzerland, for sponsor use at trade shows or sales meetings.

5. Olympic merchandise and premiums. Sponsors had the exclusive right to use these for sales and promotional incentives.

6. Tickets and hospitality. Sponsors were given preference in purchasing tickets to some of the most popular Olympic events and received hospitality services in Seoul to entertain their guests.

7. Advertising options. Depending on the nation and IOC's contract with its broadcast entity, sponsors received priority access to purchase advertising during the telecast of the Games.

8. On-site participation. Each sponsor could showcase and sell products during the Games through franchises with the organizers and venue concessions.

9. Research. Studies were done for each sponsor on public perceptions of them as a sponsor.

10. First right to direct negotiation on sponsorship for the next quadrennial. Sponsors were given this right to ensure that a competitor could not preempt their continued worldwide sponsorship during the forthcoming Olympiad.

The Implementation of Sponsorship in the Seoul Olympics

The Olympic Program in Seoul was less successful than originally hoped. ISL Marketing had set a goal of attracting 20 corporate participants but only managed to sign 9. Furthermore, 11 of 161 NOCs, including those of Cuba, Libya, Venezuela, and Greece, refused to join TOP, some of them disagreeing with the commercialization of the Olympic Games.[33]

In light of the separate contractual procedures for sponsorship and for radio and television advertising, being a TOP sponsor or any other kind of Olympic sponsor did not guarantee a company the right to advertise on television. Television and radio contracts were negotiated separately, and the network then sold Olympic ads to the highest bidder, which was not necessarily the official Olympic sponsor. The SLOOC tried to overcome this problem by advising the networks that had bought the Olympic television rights to give preferential treatment to official Games sponsors.

Companies advertising on South Korean television were bound by strict rules. One regulation stipulated that foreigners could not appear in television advertising. Therefore, companies like Coca-Cola and Kodak redesigned and reshot their commercials for use in Korea. American Express, which was not an official Olympic sponsor, hosted a radio show on South Korea's MBC station to teach English to Korean taxi drivers. Although there was no major problem with Visa in this matter, the move may have foreshadowed the famous controversy that erupted during the 1992 Olympic Winter Games when American Express aired television advertising that evoked images of the Olympic area around Albertville, France, in an effort to counter Visa's claims that only its credit card would be accepted at the Olympic Games.

There were a total of 23 Olympic sponsors (including the 9 TOP sponsors), 65 exclusive suppliers of equipment for the Games, and 61 licensees that manufactured souvenirs and other goods specially designed for the event. Firms could sponsor a country's Olympic team, individual athletes, or even a national Olympic committee. The Korean team was not sponsored by any business concern, but it was supplied with training shoes by ProSpecs and with sports equipment by Kolon.

In 1987, the Korean firms Goldstar and Samsung, along with Philips from the Netherlands and Japan's Matsushita, were named official suppliers of electronics products for the Seoul Olympics.[34] Hyundai launched its new car, the Stellar 88, at the Games, and it became the official car of the Seoul Olympics. IBM Korea supplied data processing equipment; Adidas supplied soccer and handball gear. The majority of Olympic suppliers were Korean companies.

The largest Korean corporations, such as Lucky-Goldstar, Samsung, Hyundai, and Daewoo, undertook a range of activities relating to sponsorship. The Goldstar Company, part of the Lucky-Goldstar group, provides a representative illustration. In conjunction with the Olympics, Goldstar constructed a 1,500-square meter exhibition hall at its Pyung-taek manufacturing plant south of Seoul and invited approximately 3,000 international visitors, including athletes, reporters, and buyers, to the hall during the Han River festivals. The hall, built at a cost of about $400,000, contained five sections with displays on Goldstar's history, its prospects for the future, and special goods for the Olympics, home, factory, and office automation. Goldstar's special Olympics products included various consumer electronics and other appliances emblazoned with the Seoul Olympic emblem. To sell these products in Korea, the company could make use of its extensive distribution network, easily the most visible and ubiquitous in the country, with all its store exteriors painted in the distinctive yellow and black corporate colors. During the buildup to the Olympics, Goldstar designated a large number of these as official distributors of "Olympics products."

In a distinctive effort by a supplier, Samsung Electronics gave each of the 100,000 persons attending the opening ceremony a small (4.5 cm × 2 cm × 1 cm), clip-on FM receiver weighing just a few ounces and earphones through which the spectators could tune to a narrative description of the ceremony in English, German, French, Korean, Russian, Spanish, Arabic, or Japanese. This program had several advantages: It was the first time in Olympic history that such technology was used, it targeted a highly influential group of spectators, and it generated a great deal of additional television and press coverage.

Seoul Olympic sponsorship brought in $140 to $150 million, 30 percent of which was received in products and services used during the Games (known as in-kind support). This was slightly more than the $122.5 million raised at the Los Angeles Games in 1984. Overall, a total of $900 million was raised through commercial ventures, most coming from the sale of television rights, which brought in $407,133,000.[35]

Sponsorship and the Visibility of Olympic Symbols

During the weeks immediately surrounding the Seoul Olympics, South Korea's capital city was decorated like never before. It was festooned with banners—some floating in the air above buildings and supported by large balloons in the Olympic colors, others on the sides of large and small buildings, and yet others hanging from streetlights. Every major rotary and intersection in the city was decorated and lined with live flowers, and many contained large, pyramid-shaped "flower towers" emblazoned with the Seoul Olympic emblem or mascot. At City Hall Plaza, a large electronic display counted down the days remaining until the opening ceremony, and the Seoul Olympic emblem was formed in flowers on a large pyramid. The perimeter of its traffic island had flagpoles flying the flag of every participating country in the Twenty-fourth Olympiad.

In short, for the period immediately preceding and during the Olympic Games, Seoul was completely refurbished and redecorated. Indeed, the Seoul Olympic Organizing Committee had hired an environmental design firm to coordinate the colors and overall appearance of the hundreds of thousands of banners and visual displays used during the Games. Amid this massive visual display of decorations and symbols, the most prominent were the Olympic rings, the Seoul Olympic emblem, the Olympic mascot, Hodori, and the slogan "The World to Seoul, Seoul to the World."

Of course, the Olympic rings were the most ubiquitous symbol of all. In addition, thousands upon thousands of Olympic flags and banners bearing the Seoul Olympic emblem were displayed throughout the capital and all major cities of South Korea. And the official display of the Olympic rings was multiplied many times over because those rings were incorporated into all Olympic symbols at all levels of commercial sponsorship.

There were also some interesting appropriations of Olympic messages by corporations. For example, one very large billboard outside the main Seoul railroad station, done in the well-known yellow and black colors of the Lucky-Goldstar group, declared "The World to Seoul, Goldstar to the World." More generally, the Seoul Olympics appeared to add impetus to the development of Korea's advertising and media markets. For one thing, sports sponsorship, as with certain other types of marketing practiced elsewhere in the world, was not well known or widely used in Korea before the Asian Games and Olympics buildup.

However, as noted by an English-language business journal in Seoul during September 1988, "Olympic sponsorship has had a big impact on advertising in Seoul. Only a few years ago, neon signs and billboards were forbidden, and advertising on buses and taxis unknown. But as companies came to see the commercial potential of the Games, restrictions were lifted and Seoul's skyline now rivals that of Hong Kong or Tokyo."[36]

Royalties received for use of the Olympic emblem and mascot are important as a revenue source for the modern Games and also because they become the most highly visible symbols linking the host country and its culture to the Olympics. During the Los Angeles Olympics, royalty payments for use of the emblem and mascot totaled about $135 million, and in

Seoul, they reached approximately $2 billion. However, the licensing of Hodori, the Seoul Olympic mascot (shown in Figure 1.4), was not without incident.

Chosen in April 1984, Hodori was an endearing tiger cub, evoking a strong and positive identification with the tiger as a familiar figure in Korean legends and folk art. He wore the Olympic rings around his neck and a "Sangmo" hat from the traditional farmer's dance. The streamer from the hat formed an S shape, standing for the city of Seoul.[37] Unfortunately, Hodori also bore a resemblance to Tony the Tiger—the trademark character of Kelloggs, the U.S. cereal manufacturer. Claiming that Hodori was an imitation, Kelloggs asked SLOOC to change the mascot or face a lawsuit for copyright infringement.[38] The dispute was resolved when a senior representative of the SLOOC met in Chicago with the senior Kelloggs vice president for legal affairs. The Seoul Olympic Organizing Committee agreed not to sell the rights to Hodori to any of Kelloggs's cereal competitors without its consent.[39]

The Seoul Olympic emblem, shown in Figure 1.3, was derived from the traditional Korean motif called *sam t'aeguk*, which has been used extensively for decorative detail in architecture and handicrafts throughout Korea. The emblem's three swirls represented the harmony of Heaven, Earth, and Man. The outward and upward motion represented progress toward world peace through the realization of the Olympic ideal,[40] and the inward motion stood for the gathering of people from all over the world for the Games. The emblem was designed by Yang Seung-Choon, an associate professor in the Department of Industrial Design at Seoul National University and former president of the Korean Society of Visual Design.[41]

Both Hodori and the Seoul Olympic emblem fused traditional Korean cultural elements with the familiar Olympic rings. As noted earlier, both became common sights in Seoul and throughout Korea during the months leading up to the 1988 Olympics and especially during the immediate period of time surrounding the Games. They also received considerable exposure in other nations around the world, especially those with large consumer markets. They showed up in print, radio, television, and outdoor advertising by Olympic sponsors; as identification on licensed products; and in the form of various souvenir products.

Olympic souvenirs went on sale in Seoul in 1984, just three years after the Summer Games were awarded to the city. Hodori dolls became available in 1985. A variety of souvenir items began to appear in Europe, the United States, and Japan in 1987.[42] At least 86 different types of souvenir items were licensed and produced in Korea bearing the image of Hodori or the Seoul Olympic emblem. They ranged from a $.12 eraser to a $480 teaspoon set with motifs chronicling each Olympics since 1896. Other items included car stickers, lighters, ashtrays, mugs, sportswear, silver goblets, ceramics, brassware, crystal glassware, and figurines.[43]

Hodori dolls were manufactured in 32 varieties, in heights ranging from 4 to 45 inches. They included a judo Hodori, blue jeans Hodori, handpuppet Hodori, pajama bag Hodori, and a Hodori that would wave at you. Hodori adorned posters, plush cushions, towels, and T-shirts, with the latter two items becoming very popular among Korean families.[44] A human-size Hodori under a glass canopy with the slogan "The World to Seoul, Seoul to the World" was placed on display in the international departure lounge at Kimpo Airport during the months preceding the Olympics, and as of early 1993, it remained there. An even larger version of Hodori was displayed in the Seoul Olympic Organizing Committee headquarters building at the Olympic Park.

The SLOOC hired the Japanese advertising agency Dentsu to act as agent for marketing the 1988 Summer Games in Japan. The contract called for Dentsu to turn Hodori into a TV star, and the agency Dentsu made a cartoon series featuring Hodori, for sale to the Japanese networks and overseas.[45]

Other Commercial Activities

Official Theme Song. "Hand-in-Hand," the official theme song of the Seoul Olympics, was inherently global and commercial in its inception. The story of its creation powerfully illustrates the intersection of commercial and political considerations. On the commercial side, there was the interest in having a theme song that could be successfully sold around the world. On the political side, here were the politics of Olympic ceremony planning, in which leading Korean artists and scholars played an important role. Such planning took place amid building pressures toward democratization in South Korea, along with rising hopes for reunification with the North and a broader set of relations with those Socialist bloc nations from which it had been separated by the cold war.

Planning for the Seoul Olympics theme song began in earnest following the 1986 Asian Games. Initially, consideration was given to using entirely Korean resources to compose and promote a song throughout the world. However, the president of SLOOC, Park Seh-Jik, believed that a broader perspective was necessary in creating a theme for this global festival and feared that "too much dependency on national resources might result in wasted money on a failed project."[46] In early 1987, the SLOOC began to make contact with internationally famous recording companies, and it consulted with prominent Korean composers and members of the committee for the opening and closing ceremonies. Several professors registered strong objections on the grounds that a song written by a foreign composer with English verse would provide another avenue of dissent for college students standing against the Olympics. However, Park Seh-Jik held to the view that an Olympic theme song had to be international in character, and a $2.5-million contract signed with Polygram led to the selection of Giorgio Moroder as composer for the music.[47] Polygram's existing contract with the Switzerland-based Korean vocal group Koreana was a factor in the decision. Moroder had written the Los Angeles Olympics theme music, "Reach Out," and had won three Oscars for the scores to the movies *Midnight Express, Flash Dance,* and *Top Gun.*

Moroder suggested Tom Whitlock as lyricist, and the SLOOC agreed on the condition that he "embrace as much Korean imagery as possible into the verse." After the song was completed in October 1987, there were three evaluation meetings with Korean composers and SLOOC opening and closing ceremony committee members at which Polygram accepted suggestions for revisions. "Among them were to add the word 'Arirang' (which is the representative traditional folk song in Korea) and to express Seoul Games' goal of 'Harmony' and the national image of 'Land of the Morning Calm' somewhere in the words of the song."[48]

"Hand-in-Hand," as sung by Koreana, was officially presented to the public on June 21, 1988, in a Seoul press conference with both Korean and foreign press in attendance. The song reached the number 1 spot in the pop charts of 17 countries, including Sweden, West Germany, and Japan. In another 30 nations, the song was listed among the 10 biggest hits, making it the most popular Olympic theme in history. The contract with Polygram called for the SLOOC to receive a royalty of $.05 for each disc, cassette, or CD after 1 million copies were sold. As of the end of 1989, total sales of the theme song in all media stood at 9 million copies.[49]

Of greater significance is the fact that the song entered the repertoire of the Chinese students who demonstrated in Beijing's Tiananmen Square during May 1989. Reportedly, prodemocracy groups in East Germany used the symbol of two joined hands and also sang "Hand-in-Hand" at their demonstrations and rallies prior to the fall of the Berlin Wall. In December 1989, Koreana performed the song in Germany against the backdrop of the crumbled Berlin Wall.[50]

Commemorative Coinage. Seoul followed a practice from prior Olympics by minting and selling commemorative coins. Approximately 11 million gold, silver, and copper coins were issued through the Bank of Korea and sold through the Seoul Olympic Organizing Committee. The coins displayed aspects of Korea's history, with the gold coin showing Admiral Yi Soo Shin's turtle boat and Namdaemun (South Gate), the nation's premier national treasure. Approximately 70 percent of the gold and silver coins were sold overseas, showing popularity in such countries as West Germany, Switzerland, Hong Kong, Taiwan, Japan, and the United States.

Estimated sales of the coins at home and abroad were approximately 100 billion won or $137 million.[51]

Sponsorship as a Communication Process

Whether viewed by corporations and their public relations or advertising agencies, on the one hand, or by scholarly critics of an overly commercialized, television-driven Olympics, on the other, sponsorship is generally acknowledged to be part of a process of persuasive communication.

The entire structure of the advertising and public relations industry across the world mirrors Lasswell's classic model of the communications process, outlined here:[52]

who	Corporate sponsors
says what	Creative directors, copywriters
to whom	Audience research demographics, psychographics
through which channel	Media research, planning
with what effect	Marketing, audience research

In addition, marketing professionals conventionally view the channels of communication very broadly in terms of the marketing communications mix, which until recently has been considered to consist of advertising, public relations, sales promotion (merchandising), and personal selling.

Due to the spread of cable television and the introduction of new media technologies more generally,[53] there has been a steady trend over the past decade or more toward proportionally lower investment in such traditional media as television, radio, and newspapers and a correspondingly higher investment in other areas like sales promotion, direct marketing, and event sponsorship. In this context, the rapid growth of sponsorship has led industry analysts to suggest that it be viewed as an additional medium or channel in the marketing communications mix.

An important reason for seeing commercial sponsorship as an element in the overall marketing communications mix is that corporations, together with their advertising, public relations, or sports consulting firms, plan and conduct their sponsorship activities in relation to each of the other elements. A major corporate goal is to achieve a certain unity of message, a strong media impact, and as much synergy as possible between all elements in the promotional mix. Hence, the entire panoply of television, radio, print, out-of-home advertising, promotions, and personal sales efforts might all seek to exploit the association with the Olympics. Because the building of a corporate or brand image is a long-term effort, one of the most publicly visible indicators of the increased sponsorship of the Games is the growing amount and longer duration of television and other advertising by Olympic sponsors.

The value of integrating sponsorship with advertising and other marketing communications activities was underscored in a study conducted during the Seoul Olympic telecasts by the large U.S. advertising agency Lintas: Campbell-Ewald. One of the major findings was that the largest advertising spenders would be most effective in providing messages that viewers would remember. However, the agency noted several other ways in which the value and memorability of an Olympic sponsorship could be increased. These included category exclusivity, telecast exclusivity, premium pod positions (ad placement within the program), official sponsorship, consumer or trade promotion, and supplement through other media.

Sponsorship as a "Perfect Marriage"

Corporate sponsors also work on the assumption that the effects of sponsorship on corporate or brand image can be maximized when there is a perfect match or "marriage" of:

- the target group of the company and the target group for the event
- the desired image of the company and the image of the event
- the media covering the event and the media used by the corporation's target audience
- the product or corporate characteristics being promoted and the credibility of the event (the Olympics) used to promote them.[54]

If these linkages exist, it is presumably much easier to achieve the desired image effects or associations. Thus, sponsorship might be designed to instill certain connections in viewers' minds, such as:

- "This sport involves running fast; running fast is made possible by Adidas shoes; and Adidas are sponsoring it."
- "This sport is photogenic; good photos are provided by Kodak; and Kodak is sponsoring it."
- "This sport demands refreshment; Coca-Cola provides refreshment; and Coca-Cola is sponsoring it."[55]

The Experience of Visa International

Visa's experience with its TOP sponsorship in 1988 provides an excellent illustration of how a corporation seeks to leverage Olympic sponsorship through all elements of the marketing communications mix; therefore, it will be described at some length here. Visa signed on with TOP in July 1986 after American Express had judged the sponsorship to be too expensive for its purposes. The sponsorship plan became the centerpiece of a three-pronged master marketing program for the company. First, Visa wanted to enhance its image in the upscale travel and entertainment market, long dominated by American Express. Second, the firm wanted to promote an image of international acceptability. Third, Visa was seeking to build a unified, international marketing program for its member banks in 150 countries.[56]

To pursue these goals and maximize the value of being a sponsor, Visa International earmarked half of its entire public relations, marketing, and advertising budget from January 1987 through October 1988 for promotion of its Olympic sponsorship. It retained separate public relations, sports marketing, and advertising agencies to help in developing the program.[57]

As noted by Visa executives, the Olympics provided a perfect match for the three goals of the master marketing plan. There is no more international event to be found, and as shown by an analysis of the U.S. audience for the Seoul Olympics telecast, the Games attract an audience that is "disproportionately upscale." Households earning higher incomes watched more of the Olympic telecasts than the less affluent, as did those with higher educational levels. Especially in prime time, the Olympics "remain one of the most effective showcases for reaching upscale audiences."[58]

Visa's final marketing efforts were tailored to each of five major operating regions of the world. In the United States, for example, its advertising leading up to the Games in Seoul and Calgary used variations on the following message: "If you go, bring your camera and your Visa card, because the Olympics don't take place all the time and this time, they *don't* take American Express. Visa. It's everywhere you want to be." Visa also used a fund-raising promotion entitled "Pull for the team," supported by television, print, and point-of-sale advertising. The company made a donation to the U.S. Olympic team each time customers used their Visa cards or purchased Visa travelers' checks.

In addition, hundreds of member banks in the United States executed their own promotions using a special catalog of Visa Olympic merchandise and package trips to the Games. Member banks were also encouraged to create Olympic editions of the Visa card, and over five million of these were issued.

To strengthen its ties with member banks around the world, the company staged extensive seminars for bank members using specially produced videotapes of past Olympic highlights. Famous ex-Olympians were sent on bank tours to give inspirational talks.

To make sure its 20,000 member banks and financial institutions would know how to take advantage of the sponsorship, Visa developed marketing seminars, Olympic Update memos, and a public relations manual outlining its programs and the ways in which members could use them. It offered first-class tickets and accommodations at the Games to member institutions under an Olympic trips package, to be used as an incentive for employees and for promoting sales by entertaining key customers.

At the Games themselves, in Seoul and in Calgary, ticketsellers and merchandise outlets within the Olympic venues accepted only the Visa card. Moreover, cash machines were installed at venues, and service offices were set up around Seoul.

Visa reported a high level of satisfaction with its Olympic sponsorship, as measured by changes in its image, business volume, and member satisfaction. Tracking studies conducted twice a year among consumers showed gains in three categories: "best card overall," "best card for international travel," and "most appropriate card for use in travel and entertainment."[59]

Currently, it appears that, like Visa, other corporate sponsors are integrating sponsorship into their overall marketing programs and promoting the sponsorship on a more continuous basis over an extended time period. Making future TOP programs and Olympic sponsorships generally more attractive to sponsors was a driving force behind changing the cycle of Winter and Summer Olympic Games so that they would occur every two years beginning in 1994.[60] The corporate interest in longer-term integration of sponsorship into overall marketing activities became evident by August 1990, when eleven companies had already signed up to participate in The Olympic Program II, with global rights to use the Olympic symbols in connection with the Winter Games in Albertville and the Barcelona Olympics. According to an executive of ISL Marketing, "Companies have signed up much earlier so that they can take a more sophisticated and integrated marketing approach to leveraging the global sponsorship."[61]

Critical Perspectives

Critics of the expanding role of commercial sponsorship, both in the Olympics and more generally, also see it as a communication process—but in a very different light than most corporate managers. A representative argument was expressed in this way:

> In industrial societies in this century, national consumer product advertising has become one of the great vehicles of social communication. Regarded individually and superficially, advertisements promote goods and services. Looked at in depth and as a whole, the ways in which messages

are presented in advertising reach deeply into our most serious concerns: interpersonal and family relations, the sense of happiness and contentment, sex roles and stereotyping, the uses of affluence, the fading away of older cultural traditions, influences on younger generations, the role of business in society, persuasion and personal autonomy, and many others.[62]

Such a view suggests that advertising is much more than just a business expenditure. Rather, it is an integral part of modern culture, with the power to appropriate and transform various symbols and ideas. On a global scale, as in Olympic sponsorship, the critique suggests that "the cultural-ideological project of global capitalism is to persuade people to consume above their own perceived needs in order to perpetuate the accumulation of capital for private profit, in other words, to ensure that the global capitalist system goes on for ever. The culture-ideology of consumerism proclaims, literally, that the meaning of life is to be found in the things that we possess."[63]

The expansion of commercial communication on a global scale is seen by many critics as a threat to the autonomy of indigenous culture that operates through processes of cultural imperialism or cultural "synchronization."[64] From the corporate standpoint, the arrival of global television and, with it, "global" or "world" brands is nowhere near so threatening, as the following discussion will show.

Global Television and World Brands

As already discussed, the spread of television technologies around the world during the 1970s and 1980s was accompanied by a growth in the number hours devoted to sports coverage. The range of sports covered by television also increased, and the medium arguably played a role in the cross-cultural transfer of certain sports, such as U.S.-style football to Europe, Asian martial arts to the West, and baseball to South Korea.

A central point in the present analysis is that the arrival of the global television era and the growth of commercial sponsorship around the world were interdependent. It is no coincidence that the increase in commercial sponsorship of sports and other activities paralleled the emergence of the global television era during the 1970s and 1980s. Indeed, television was a major catalyst in the growth of sponsorship. As one industry expert put it in 1987, "Much of the tremendous growth of sponsorship over the last 10 years has been in response to the need for a 'global window' through which companies can offer a clear, strong message to television viewers throughout the world."[65]

An important purpose of the investments in sponsorship made by many large corporations is the creation of global brands, such as Sony,

Panasonic, IBM, Coca-Cola, and others. More generally, the concept of a brand is central to modern marketing, as reflected in the structure of many corporations that gives a central management role to brand managers. Such individuals are responsible for developing and maintaining brands. Those tasks involve product positioning—the creation of a brand "image" or "personality."[66] However, perhaps the most appropriate terminology used in the industry is *brand equity*, which explains why corporations will invest such large sums of money over long periods of time on a brand or will even purchase brand names. For a corporation, the development of a brand is seen as an investment precisely because the brand image is considered to be "owned in the consumer's mind." Accordingly, the largest corporations are willing to make massive, long-term investments in brand equity in order to protect their market share and future sales.

Sport and pop music are seen as good vehicles for global sponsorship activities because they seem to travel well across national, cultural, and linguistic boundaries. However, the Olympics hold a particular attraction for certain large corporate sponsors because of their highly visible nature and the values and meanings associated with them. One of these values is prestige. When undertaken on a large, global scale, sponsorship automatically confirms the prestige of a company in terms of size, financial muscle, and international status. After all, such companies would not be able to sustain such sponsorship activities unless they had adequate financial resources.[67]

In 1985, ISL Marketing conducted a survey in the United States, West Germany, Portugal, and Singapore to explore that visibility and some of those associations. (Some results of that survey were presented in Table 1.3.) Not surprisingly, it showed that the Olympic rings are one of the most widely recognized symbols in the world, with nearly 80 percent of all respondents being able to immediately recognize and identify them. Of the other corporate logos and symbols included in that particular survey, only McDonald's and Shell achieved identification levels at or above those of the Olympic rings.[68] However, it is the unique associations with the Olympic Games that have proven attractive to certain corporate sponsors. As shown in Table 1.3, a high proportion of respondents associated the Olympic Games with the phrases "international co-operation and brotherhood," "worldwide appeal," and "most important sports event." Relatively few respondents, except for those in Germany, associated the Games with "political interference/boycotts."

The ISL Marketing study also found that more than 60 percent of consumers in the four nations thought the Olympic rings mean that a "product is on sale in most parts of the world," and nearly half of all respondents thought the Olympic symbol "indicates that the product is of good quality."[69] A series of questions designed to probe understanding of sponsorship showed that most consumers believe that sports sponsorship is done for commercial reasons but that it provides vital funding for major sporting events and should be a major source of funding for the Olympic Games.

Notably, several of the largest South Korean *chaebol* (business groups consisting of large companies in diverse fields) were contemplating or in the process of developing global branding strategies at the time of the Seoul Olympics. A 1988 survey by the image consulting firm Landor Associates showed that brands from Singapore, Taiwan, and Korea were generally not well known in the United States and that only 4 other brand names among 672 were less recognized in the U.S. market than that of the Korean firm Daewoo. Although Samsung had reportedly launched an effort in 1979 to improve awareness of its corporate and brand name, it also ranked very low when compared with the leading brand names from Europe, Japan, and the United States. Samsung advertised heavily on U.S. television during the Seoul Olympics and in the fall of 1989 took out a nationwide print campaign in publications like *National Geographic* and *Smithsonian* in order to improve perceptions about the quality of its products.[70]

Although the large Korean corporations were active in sponsorship activities, none of them became TOP sponsors. They were criticized for this in an article on sponsorship in the *Japan Economic Journal*, which concluded,

> Nine firms from around the world have been selected as top sponsors for the Seoul Olympics, but Korean company names are not on the list. Korean companies have missed a good chance to display their industrial power before the world. Regardless of who takes home the medals, products from the U.S., Japan and other countries stand to make a lot of gold at the Seoul Olympics.[71]

Sponsorship and Message Control

The International Olympic Committee is attempting to maintain some semblance of control over the amount and kind of commercial activity associated with the Olympic movement, but the effort takes place on a rapidly shifting terrain. On the face of it, the provisions of the Olympic Charter with respect to commercial activity are very strict. No advertising or publicity is allowed in, around, or above the Olympic stadium or other sports arenas. Nor is any advertising permitted on equipment or the uniforms of contestants or officials. Rule 51 states, in part, that

> The display of any clothing or equipment such as shoes, skis, handbags, hats, etc. marked conspicuously for advertising purposes in any Olympic venue (training grounds, Olympic villages or fields of competition), by par-

ticipants whether competitors, coaches, trainers or anyone else associated with an Olympic team in an official capacity, shall normally result in immediate disqualification or withdrawal of credentials.[72]

The rule even goes so far as to specify the maximum height of corporate identification on scoreboards and timing equipment used in the Olympic Games.

If Rule 51 (which became Rule 53 in a subsequent revision of the Charter) is considered the "letter of the law" laid down by the IOC regarding such commercial activity, its spirit is inevitably conditioned by the overall context of commercialization in the Olympics. Even as the IOC sought to strictly limit certain advertising or other promotional display, it simultaneously endeavored to expand its sources of revenue from the Olympic Games through the introduction of TOP in Seoul and TOP II in Barcelona. Consequently, the pressures to allow additional commercial exposure are both enormous and inexorable. As noted by William J. Warren, legal counsel for the organizing committee for the 1988 Winter Games in Calgary,

> It is becoming increasingly apparent that worldwide sponsors and suppliers are prepared to contribute more revenues to the Olympic Movement, provided that they secure additional exposure. The International Olympic Committee will therefore in the future be faced with consideration as to whether or not it wishes to amend the provisions of Rule 53 of the Olympic Charter so as to extend opportunities of site advertising to sponsors, suppliers and licensees in return for greater financial gain.[73]

For Olympic sponsors, exposure equals the creation and maintenance of consumer awareness or attitudes toward a given brand or corporation. Because the corporate concern with building and maintaining a worldwide image involves direct associations with the central symbols of the Olympics, what is at stake is more than simply a legal question or financial gain. In a broad sense, it is control over the meaning of the Olympics.

A related set of questions about the control of Olympic messages have to do with the requirement for exclusivity in sponsorship. *Category exclusivity* in sponsorship means that only one product or service in each product category will be named an Olympic sponsor. "Experience has shown that exclusivity is the most significant inducement for maximizing financial contributions from a wide variety of participants desiring to associate with the Olympics, nationally or internationally."[74]

The issue of exclusivity cuts across all levels of sponsorship, including the related categories of suppliers and licensees. For example, Kang Shin-Joe, president of the Korean Security Printing and Minting Corporation (the state-run organization that minted the commemorative coinage for the Seoul Olympics), expressed in August 1988 concern about the minting of 1 million gold coins and 10 million silver coins by the United States Olympic Committee; he believed this posed a threat to SLOOC's sales of Seoul Olympics commemorative coins.[75] The minting of up to 1 million $5 gold pieces and up to 10 million silver dollars commemorating U.S. participation in the 1988 Olympics was approved by the U.S. Congress in 1987 after testimony that the sale of similar coins for the Los Angeles Olympics had raised $73.5 million, which was split equally between the USOC and the LAOOC. Robert Helmick, president of the United States Olympic Committee, testified that "other governments subsidize their Olympic teams, ours does not. For that reason, the United States has to find innovative ways to finance our ongoing program of training U.S. athletes for the Games. We never could have done it in 1984 without the coinage program."[76]

With the introduction of TOP in 1988, exclusivity surfaced as a major issue between the Olympic movement and television.[77] The issue was one of possible conflict between advertisers who sponsor Olympic telecasts and TOP sponsors of the Olympic Games. As Jurgen Lenz of ISL Marketing put it,

> The obvious conflict is understood and acknowledged: how can, on one side, the networks be expected to commit the extent of dollar figures that they have, whilst being restricted at the same time in the selection of their sales prospects? On the other hand, how can the Olympic Movement expect to continue to receive major funding from the corporate sector for worldwide sponsorship of the Movement in a world of growing television commercialism without the all-important issue of EXCLUSIVITY being satisfactorily resolved?[78]

In other words, under the present arrangement, Visa could become a TOP sponsor at the same time that American Express might sponsor the NBC telecast of the Olympics by purchasing advertising time from the network. Indeed, the stage was set in Seoul and Calgary for the controversy that would erupt between American Express and Visa during the 1992 Olympic Winter Games in Albertville. The claim that "this year, the Olympics don't take American Express" was a very strong one, especially when, in television advertising, it was set against a backdrop of scenes from Seoul, including traditional Korean architecture. As noted previously, it was technically true that only Visa would be accepted *in payment for Olympic tickets or by concessions in Olympic venues*. However, those conditions hardly provided a monopoly for Visa, nor did they represent major difficulties for holders of other credit cards. Competitor American Express was stung by the attack, and in 1992, it decided to fight back against Visa's continuation of the 1988 campaign, using a technique that has come to be known as "ambush marketing." It aired a television campaign around the

Albertville Olympic Winter Games that featured visual images bearing a striking resemblance to the area surrounding the host city and with a message stressing that its card would be honored there.

The question of television versus sponsorship exclusivity is only one example, albeit an important one, of the control issues that arise in the contemporary Olympics as a global media spectacle. On one level, it is important because the Olympic spectacle, with all its political ramifications, is a media-constructed phenomenon. Consequently, the television messages that constitute Olympic reality are more commercial today than they were two decades ago. There is a strong temptation among those who study the Olympics as a communication phenomenon to focus on sports, news, and public affairs coverage by television and the other major media, viewing advertising as merely the "interruptions" or "departures" from programming. The Seoul Olympics and the Calgary Winter Games should have disabused many of this notion. They marked the coming of age of a new era in the financing of the Olympics and, accordingly, in the operations of the media and the content of Olympic television and media coverage generally.

Indeed, this book suggests that the struggle for control of Olympic meanings involves all of the main spectators or "publics" in the Olympic movement. Global television itself has become a much more important actor in constructing the Olympic spectacle, in no small part because of its own commercial basis and its relationship to corporate sponsorship. This chapter lends more support to the notion that television should be treated as a "third protagonist" or independent actor in the Olympics. In a world communications environment increasingly saturated by the moving, visual images of television, this draws attention to the implications of an increased association between the central symbols of the Olympic movement and those of major world corporations whose goals are brand equity, market leadership, and consumption.

However, we do not imply a deterministic model in which commercial sponsors dictate the nature of the global television spectacle. The media spectacle is, in fact, reconstructed through a process of negotiation every four years and in a different host city and national environment. Ultimately, it will be difficult or impossible to pass judgment on the effects of commercialization in the Seoul Olympics without comparing them to the preceding Los Angeles Games and the Barcelona Games that followed for a modicum of both historical and cultural perspective. The process of reconstructing the Olympic television spectacle in each host city allows participation by national Olympic committees, athletes, sports federations, and others with an interest in the outcome. The Seoul experience stands as testimony that the collective effort of a nation and its people can contribute to Olympic success.

Notes

1. Robert R. Prazmark and Nathaniel Frey, "The Winners Play a New Global Game," *Marketing Communications* 14 (January 1989): pp. 18–27.

2. Ibid.

3. The Global Media Commission of the International Advertising Association, *Sponsorship: Its Role and Effects* (New York: International Advertising Association, June 1988) p. 2.

4. "Sponsorship—Marketing's Fourth Medium—Now Worth $2.5 Billion a Year" (Beijing speech by Barry Gill, chairman of CSS International), Business Wire, June 22, 1987.

5. ISL Marketing, Ltd., *Sponsorship: Has the New Medium Come of Age?* (Lucerne, Switzerland: ISL, December 1988).

6. *Mintel Report on Sponsorship 1990* (London: Mintel, 1990).

7. Tony Meenaghan, "Sponsorship—Legitimising the Medium," *European Journal of Marketing* 25 (1991): pp. 5–10.

8. "Q: Why Should Government Take Charge of Sports? A: Because Sports Represent Vital National Interests," interview with Dong-sung Chung, minister of sports, *Koreana* 4 (1990): pp. 2–6.

9. Dong-pyo Cho, "Professional Sports in Korea: What's Needed Tons of Cash," *Koreana* 4 (1990): p. 49.

10. Chung-Woo Suh, "Public Broadcasting and Sports Coverage," *Broadcasting Research* (Summer 1986): pp. 13–14, as cited in Sang Chul Lee "Seoul Olympics: Some Crossed Cultural Communications," *Media Asia* 16 (1989): p. 195.

11. Tony Meenaghan, "The Role of Sponsorship in the Marketing Communications Mix," *International Journal of Advertising* 10 (1991): pp. 35–47.

12. Martin G. Crowley, "Prioritising the Sponsorship Audience," *European Journal of Marketing* 25 (1991): p. 11.

13. The Global Media Commission of the International Advertising Association, *Sponsorship.*

14. Ibid.

15. Richard Espy, *The Politics of the Olympic Games* (Berkeley: University of California Press, 1981), pp. 71, 72.

16. Ibid., p.73.

17. Ibid., pp. 119–120.

18. Rick Gruneau, "Commercialism and the Modern Olympics," in Alan Tomlinson and Garry Whannel, eds., *Five-Ring Circus: Money, Power and Politics at the Olympic Games* (London: Pluto Press, 1984), p. 9.

19. Prazmark and Frey, "The Winners Play a New Global Game," p. 19.

20. Gruneau, "Commercialism and the Modern Olympics," pp. 1–15.

21. Ibid., p. 10.

22. Prazmark and Frey, "The Winners Play a New Global Game," p. 19.

23. Celia Kuperszmid Lehrman, "The Gold Standard," *Public Relations Journal* (July-August 1988): pp. 20–25.

24. Gruneau, "Commercialism and the Modern Olympics," p. 11.

25. "IOC Sounds Themes for Future: Choosing '98 Winter Site Will Be Highlight," *USA Today,* June 13, 1991, p. 1B.

26. William D. Murray, "Sports News," United Press International, February 20, 1989.

27. Stephen Parry, "Olympic Revenue Targeted at 1.84 Billion Dollars," Reuters (Tokyo), September 14, 1990.

28. Prazmark and Frey, "The Winners Play a New Global Game," p. 20.

29. Ibid., p. 18.

30. "Olympic Tiger Ready to Conquer the World," PR Newswire (Seoul, Korea), September 10, 1987.

31. These are based on Lehrman, "The Gold Standard," p. 24, and a personal interview with Kim Bum-Il, marketing director, Seoul Olympic Organizing Committee, Seoul, Korea, November 1988.

32. Personal interview, with Kim Bum-Il, November 1988.

33. Caroline Dewhurst, "Games' Sponsors Cry Foul," *Korea Business World* 4 (September 1988): pp. 12–13.

34. Seoul Olympic Organizing Committee, *Seoul Flame* 18 (September 1987): p. 2.

35. Dewhurst, "Games' Sponsors Cry Foul," pp. 12–13.

36. Ibid., p. 13.

37. Seoul Olympic Organizing Committee, SLOOC information handout SL 87-2, 1987. Hodori was designed by Kim Hyun, a director of the Korean Society of Visual Design who also helped produce the emblem of the 1986 Asian Games.

38. Vincent J. Ricquart, *The Games Within the Games: The Story Behind the* 1988 Seoul Olympics (Seoul, Korea: Hantong Books, 1988), p. 156.

39. Park Seh-Jik, "Hodori Wins His Case," *Chosun Ilbo*, December 23, 1989.

40. This echoes the Seoul Olympic motto, "Harmony and Progress."

41. Seoul Olympic Organizing Committee, SLOOC information handout SL 87-2.

42. "Olympic Tiger Ready to Conquer the World."

43. Ibid.

44. Ibid.

45. Ibid.

46. Park Seh-Jik, "Hand-in-Hand—An Enormous Hit," *Chosun Ilbo*, November 11, 1989.

47. Seoul Olympic Organizing Committee *Seoul Flame* 22 (January 1988).

48. Park, "Hand-in-Hand—An Enormous Hit."

49. Ibid.

50. Park Seh-Jik, "Hot Discussion on 'Breaking Down the Wall' in Olympic Theme Song," *Chosun Ilbo*, January 12, 1990.

51. "Commemorative Coinage," *Korea-Europe Economic Report* 3 (August 1988): p. 12.

52. Harold D. Lasswell, "The Structure and Function of Communication in Society," in Wilbur Schramm and Donald F. Roberts, eds., *The Process and Effects of Mass Communication* (Urbana: University of Illinois Press, 1971), pp. 84–99.

53. This is otherwise referred to as the fragmentation of media or the substitution of "class" media for "mass" media.

54. Ton Otker and Peter Hayes, "Judging the Efficiency of Sponsorship: Experiences from the 1986 Soccer World Cup," paper from ISL Marketing, n.d.

55. Ibid.

56. Prazmark and Frey, "The Winners Play a New Global Game," p. 22.

57. Lehrman, "The Gold Standard," p. 23.

58. Bernard Guggenheim, "Games Advertisers Play," *Marketing & Media Decisions* (August 1989): pp. 128–129.

59. Prazmark and Frey, "The Winners Play a New Global Game," p. 23.

60. Lehrman, "The Gold Standard," pp. 20–25.

61. John McManus, "Grabbing the Rings: Marketers Tie-in Early with Olympics," *Advertising Age* (August 6, 1990).

62. William Leiss, Stephen Kline, and Sut Jhally, *Social Communication in Advertising: Persons, Products and Images of Well-Being* (New York: Methuen, 1986), p. 3.

63. Leslie Sklair, *Sociology of the Global System* (Baltimore, Md.: Johns Hopkins University Press), p. 41.

64. Cees J. Hamelink, *Cultural Autonomy in Global Communications* (New York: Longman, 1983), pp. 5–6.

65. "Sponsorship—Marketing's Fourth Medium—Now Worth $2.5 Billion a Year."

66. Product positioning is most widely understood as consumer perceptions of a product in terms of its attributes and in relation to the attributes of competing products. The concept is broadly similar to image or reputation. See David A. Aaker and John G. Meyers, *Advertising Management*, 3d ed. (Englewood Cliffs, N.J.: Prentice-Hall, 1987), pp. 124–154.

67. Colin McDonald, "Sponsorship and the Image of the Sponsor," *European Journal of Marketing* 25 (1991): pp. 31–38.

68. ISL marketing, *TOP The Consumer View: An International Research Survey into Sponsorship of the Olympic Games,* (Lucerne, Switerland: ISL marketing, 1985).

69. Ibid.

70. Jesus Sanchez, "Asian Firms Hope to Raise Their Profiles Among American Consumers,"*Los Angeles Times*, January 30, 1989, business sec., pt. 4, p. 3.

71. Masayuki Shinoyama, "Win or Lose, Firms Take Home Olympic Gold," *Japan Economic Journal* (August 20, 1988): p. 28.

72. International Olympic Committee, *Olympic Charter* 1990 (Lausanne, Switzerland: Internation Olympic Comittee, 1990), p. 29.

73. William J. Warren, "Television Broadcasting of the Olympic Games from the Perspective of the OCOG" (Presentation at the IOC Television Workshop, Lausanne, Switzerland, April 25–26, 1987), p. 19.

74. Gen. George D. Miller, "Protecting the Marketability of Olympic Designations in the United States" (Presentation at the IOC Television Workshop, Lausanne, Switzerland, April 25–26, 1987), p. 3.

75. "Commemorative Coinage."

76. U.S. Olympic Committee, *U.S. Olympic News* 2 (December 1987).

77. It received extensive discussion at the IOC Television Workshop, Lausanne, Switzerland, April 25–26, 1987.

78. Jurgen Lenz, "Television Versus Sponsorship Exclusivity," discussion paper for the IOC Television Workshop, Lausanne, Switzerland, April 25–26, 1987, pp. 3–4.

5

Korea Enters the Information Age:
The Olympics
and Telecommunications

The media—written, spoken, photographic and electronic—are an integral part of the Olympic Movement and in every sense are a member of the Olympic family.

The International Olympic Committee places the greatest importance on what we now call collectively, the "Media."

As with all great public events, the Games of the Olympiad and the Olympic Winter Games would scarcely exist but for the presence and output of thousands of writers, photographers, commentators, broadcasters and film and television producers with all necessary supporting staff.

—Juan Antonio Samaranch[1]

The contemporary Olympic Games are the television industry's largest regular undertaking, involving more personnel and equipment than any other planned televised event. Judging by their sheer numbers in Seoul, the media already make up the largest branch of the Olympic family. An underlying assumption of this volume is that they are also the most influential part of that family. The Seoul Olympics established a new high water mark for both the number of broadcast personnel and the size of the technical infrastructure involved. In the process, some important questions were posed for the Olympic movement regarding the optimal size of the media contingent required to telecast the Games.

Because the Summer Olympics are held only every four years, they must accommodate changes in broadcasting technology and practices. Furthermore, they must do so each time in the cultural, political, and economic context of another host city. But even within such a context of predictable change, Seoul marked a major departure for the modern Olympic movement because of political and military uncertainties on the divided Korean peninsula and because South Korea was still considered to be a developing nation. Before Seoul, the International Olympic Committee had awarded the Games to cities in industrialized nations with the demonstrated capacity to provide necessary infrastructures. Korea's status in 1981 greatly magnified the challenge that had to be met in order to successfully host the Olympic Games.

The story of the Seoul Olympics as a global television spectacle would hardly be complete without tracing the pan-national efforts and international linkages they required in broadcasting, telecommunications, and electronics. Korea's Olympics elicited a tremendous effort that energized the broadcasting organizations (KBS/SORTO and MBC), along with the Korea Telecommunications Authority, the Data Communications Corporation (DACOM), and leading firms in Korea's electronics industry.

It is widely acknowledged that the two basic infrastructural elements required for economic development in the late twentieth century are transportation and telecommunications. Though the Seoul Olympics involved both of these, this chapter will be devoted to an analysis of the latter, for two important reasons. First, the technical infrastructure put in place for televising the Olympic Games helps explain the production, dissemination, and content of the international telecast. Second, such an analysis addresses the important question of how the effort invested in these particular Olympic endeavors related to Korea's goal of establishing itself as an information-based economy and society.

The Development of Korea's Telecommunications Infrastructure

To address the Olympics project, South Korea assembled a large group of technocrats, many of them educated in electrical engineering and related technical disciplines in the United States. Among the most visible and influential of these individuals was Oh Myung, who served as vice minister and later minister of communications during much of the 1980s. After graduating from South Korea's military academy in 1962, he completed a degree in electrical engineering at Seoul National University, taught the subject for two and a half years, then completed a Ph.D. at the State University of New York at Stony Brook. Upon returning to Korea in 1972, he taught at the military academy for six years and then became a senior research fellow at the Agency for Defense Development. When the government of Gen. Chun Doo Hwan took power under a state of emergency, Oh became a presidential adviser and shortly thereafter, in May 1981, was appointed vice minister of communications.

In considering the important role of Korea's technocrats, two general points must be made. The first is the overriding importance of interpersonal networks among people in the communications field. In the Korean cultural setting, as in other East Asian cultures, these networks are often of paramount importance in getting things accomplished. They may reflect the underlying power structure more accurately than organizational charts and the conventional distinctions between government, industry, academia, and research institutes. They also provide for a certain ease with which some individuals can move from one sector to another. Indeed, during the Seoul Olympics project, many from industry, government, and academia transferred temporarily to the Seoul Olympic Organizing Committee, host broadcaster KBS/SORTO, or many other organizations that were set up to to accomplish Olympic tasks.

A second consideration in explaining the crucial role of Korea's technocrats during the 1980s is the overall approach of the nation in educating its leadership. In contrast to students in Japan, large numbers of South Korean university graduates went to leading universities abroad, principally in the United States, for graduate-level training in many fields, including the technical areas bearing most directly on telecommunications. This has been a sustained pattern from the 1960s to the present, helping South Korea achieve the distinction of having more Ph.D.'s per capita than any other nation in the world. The attractiveness of U.S. institutions of higher education was partly a function of the close military and strategic relationship between South Korea and the United States. Another very important impetus was the extremely high social value placed on education within Korea's Confucian cultural heritage. During the 1960s and early 1970s, many Koreans opted to stay in the United States or elsewhere abroad after earning graduate degrees. However, with economic development, political change, and active recruitment efforts by the Korean government, the pattern began to shift, and more of the nation's best and brightest returned home. Parenthetically, it is appropriate to note here that the large numbers of U.S.-educated Ph.D.'s in Korea's academic, government, research, and private-sector institutions not only distinguishes that nation from the Japanese model but may also be viewed as a major competitive advantage in relation to other contries in the region and elsewhere in the world.

Of most immediate relevance to the present analysis is the manner in which South Korea's technocrats publicly and forcefully seized upon the Asian Games and Olympics as vehicles through which the nation might speed its development in high technology. On the eve of the Seoul Olympics, Minister Oh stated: "Our Korean forefathers failed to ride the surging tide of the Industrial Revolution, consequently failing to modernize, remaining poor and backwards. We've made progress since then, but another revolution is before us and if we fail to adapt ourselves to the changes, future generations will inherit poverty and backwardness just as we did a generation ago."[2] He was referring, of course, to the telecommunications revolution, and he was acutely aware of the impetus that an event like the Olympics could give to Korea's progress toward an information society. Nearly a year earlier, he had written about the "hightech challenge" of Olympic success, summarizing the Asian Games experience with the installation, operation, and maintenance of communication networks; stressing the critical importance of communication management processes; and pointing toward the challenge of the Olympics.[3]

In approximately the two decades preceding the Seoul Olympics, Korea experienced one of the most rapid growth rates in telecommunications of any nation in the world. Development of the telephone system— perhaps the basic infrastructural element—provides a good illustration. In 1969, ownership of a telephone was a status symbol for the rich. The price of a telephone in South Korea was more than $2,000 at a time when the nation's gross national product (GNP) per capita stood at only $400. Moreover, there was a $700 fee to apply for telephone installation, followed by months of waiting before the phone would be in place. Even by the early 1970s, as we both can clearly recall, possession of a telephone was a mark of status, and relatively few private homes had phone service. Even in such large institutions as universities, the service was crude by today's standards. For example, to make a telephone call from Kangwon National University in Chunchon to any destination in Seoul, professors or other staff members had to walk across campus to the main administration building and place the call from the dean's office. Moreover, people often had to shout into telephone receivers whenever making a call, whether local or long distance. Indeed, the Korean people were conditioned through the 1960s and 1970s to expect poor sound quality and inferior telephone service generally. Against such a backdrop, the rapid developments of the 1980s appeared revolutionary. By the end of 1987, South Korea had more than 10 million telephone subscribers, and the country had achieved a penetration rate of one phone per household. Even more striking was the arrival of "same-day service"—telephone customers are now offered installation within a single working day.[4] One important consequence of this late but rapid development of the telephone system, with important implications for Olympic television and media coverage, was that Korea's system consisted of state-of-the-art technologies.

The modern Olympics generate a tremendous demand for satellite transmission capacity. Therefore, it was not surprising that when Korea dedicated its new earth station at Poun in the 1980s, it was announced that the station had been built, in part, to handle the additional demands expected in connection with the forthcoming Seoul Olympics. However, as we will discuss later in this chapter, even that additional capacity would fall short of the unprecedented demand for satellite transmission from Seoul during September 1988.

The national telecommunications infrastructure already in place by the time of the Seoul Olympics provided an important basis for the unprecedented television and media attention that came with the Games. However, Korea was also very conscious that past Olympics had been used to introduce innovations in the world of telecommunications. After noting the use of radio broadcasting at the Tenth Olympics in Los Angeles, the use of new computer techniques in the Tokyo Olympics, and the introduction of an electronic message system in the 1984 Los Angeles Games, Minister of Communications Oh Myung said, "Now we are ready to show the world that the Seoul Olympics can provide advanced systems such as hand phones, trunking radio systems, Group 4 fax and color graphic systems."[5]

As noted earlier, certain individuals from government, industry, academia, and other organizations played key roles in preparing the telecommunications infrastructure required for the Olympics. In Korea, nearly all of them worked directly for or with five major parties:

1. Private Branch Exchange (PBX)—city of Seoul
2. The Korean Broadcasting System (both KBS and KBS/SORTO)
3. The Seoul Olympic Organizing Committee
4. The Korea Telecommunications Authority
5. Press organizations (print media)[6]

The Asian Games as Dress Rehearsal

The Tenth Asian Games, held in Seoul from September 20 through October 5, 1986, were widely viewed, both within Korea and in the international community, as a dress rehearsal for the Seoul Olympics. Virtually all the Olympic venues had been constructed by that time and were used for the sports activities.

It was a particularly important rehearsal for the host broadcaster. In 1982, the year following the decision to award the Olympics to Seoul, the SLOOC asked the Korean Broadcasting System to act as host broadcaster for the games. The role of the host broadcaster is to plan, provide, and install everything necessary for the coverage and worldwide transmission of the Olympics. For purposes of managing such a large project, KBS, in turn, established the Seoul Olympics Radio and Television Operations. KBS/SORTO was also chosen to be the host broadcaster for the Asian Games, marking the first time in the history of those games that the host broadcaster concept had been used.[7]

Although there were some changes in the organizational structure of KBS/SORTO between the Asian Games and the Olympics, its leadership remained remarkably stable, with the major evolution taking place in the overall size of the staff. The Asian Games broadcast operation was small by comparison with that of the Olympics, and SORTO's facilities were located in a temporary broadcast center built next to the KBS headquarters. A total of about 400 foreign broadcasters representing 40 radio and television organizations from 29 countries came to Seoul to cover the Asian Games, figures that would be dwarfed two years later by the 1988 Olympics. However, those broadcasters included representatives from Great Britain, France, Germany, Italy, and Canada, as well as NBC, which sent a crew of 39 observers.[8]

As discussed in Chapter 3, the Western broadcasters attended the Asian Games with an eye toward the Olympics and with attention focused on both the technical and support facilities and the host broadcaster's personnel. NBC Sports wrote a 98-page report entitled "Asian Games Review and 1988 Olympic Suggestions" that pointed out problems and gave advice covering most fields of broadcast operations, ranging from sound, lighting, electrical power, and graphics to the Games operation.[9]

The Olympic Broadcast Infrastructure

The technical infrastructure put in place for the international telecast of the Seoul Olympics was nothing short of massive. It had to serve the needs of 10,360 accredited broadcast personnel—commentators, camera operators, producers, editors, and the like. More than 6,200 of these were employees of international broadcast organizations, including 1,298 local (Korean) staffers who were hired by those organizations.[10] Moreover, the 16 of Olympic competition covered by KBS/SORTO involved 25 sports, in 34 competition sites in Seoul, Pusan, and other Korean cities, as well as the opening and closing ceremonies and all medal presentations and other official ceremonies within the scope of the Games. The Olympic sports schedule included hundreds of individual events, including 110 track and field events, 400 boxing matches, 32 football (soccer) matches, 62 basketball games, about 1,000 individual matches for fencing, and 150 heats for swimming.[11]

The media guide published by the International Olympic Committee in 1985 constituted a bylaw to Rule 51 of the Olympic Charter and was intended as a reference on "all technical matters" related to the Olympic media. Its descriptions of the "television programme" and "international television signal" for the Games were definitive and will be quoted in their entirety.

The television programme of the Games, as it is televised, comprises essentially:

- the international television signal (basic coverage) of all the competitions as produced by the host broadcaster;
- a personalization of the basic coverage (international television signal) made by each foreign broadcaster for the requirements of its national programme. Such personalization begins at the very moment when a journalist begins to comment on an event in his own language and can be extended so as to constitute a complex television programme based on the basic coverage but supplementing this basic coverage with many different programme elements from additional cameras at the sites and other video sources which allow the broadcaster to produce its own final programme at the IBC (International Broadcasting Centre).[12]

The *Media Guide* also defined the international television signal:

The live international television signal (picture and sound), to be produced by the television organization (host broadcaster) having a contract with the IOC and/or the Organising Committee to provide the same, shall consist of a live television picture in the technical standard appropriate to the host country (conforming to specifications of the Consultative Committee for International Regulation [CCIR]) and the necessary related background sound and effects (international sound).

The international television signal should include slow motion, replays, timing, basic graphics such as starting numbers, starting lists, names of competitors, IOC abbreviations for countries, results, World and Olympic records. As a basic rule the graphics should be in Latin characters. However, the possibility should exist for individual broadcasting organizations to substitute their own graphics and to receive "clean feed," i.e., without any of the above information, upon request."[13]

In simplified terms, Olympic television involves getting the television pictures, natural or "ambient" sound, and verbal commentary from each of these venues to the International Broadcast Center for transmission back to each of the 160 nations participating in the Olympics. For most international broadcasters covering most events, this means using the international television signal prepared by the host broadcaster, editing it to their own preferences, and adding their own commentary, then transmitting the result via satellite to their home country. However, the Olympic television infrastructure also provides for "unilateral" coverage that can be purchased by a broadcaster, allowing it to use its own cameras and, in effect, have complete control over its own telecast of a particular event. The amount of unilateral coverage relates directly to the amount paid in rights fees; thus, NBC generated far more unilateral coverage than other international broadcasters.

In actual practice, the construction of a worldwide Olympic telecast involves the sending of pictures, ambient sound, and verbal commentary from the numerous venue locations to the International Broadcast Center, where final editing and preparation is done by the staff of each broadcast organization. Each national telecast is also transmitted from the IBC to the home country. The mixing of verbal commentary with the visual material also takes place at the IBC. Figure 5.1 provides a simplified flow diagram of how the various signals are assembled from the venues, put together into a complete transmission at the IBC, and sent via Intelsat to countries around the world.

In accordance with this basic structure of Olympic television, many of the discussions at the World Broadcasters Meetings the Olympic Broadcast Advisory Committee and other less formal consultations involved one of three topics: venue broadcast operations, operations of the IBC, and the provision of telecommunications circuits.

Venues and Commentary Positions

To facilitate such a massive flow of visual and audio signals, KBS installed and operated a total of 1,173 commentator seats or "positions" at 31 of the sports venues of the Seoul Olympics.[14] Each commentator seat was a box equipped with a television monitor for viewing the international television signal and two headsets and microphones to broadcast the actual commentary and let commentators coordinate with their own producers at the IBC or speak with technicians in the commentary control room. In addition, data monitors, which displayed starters lists and Games progress information, were set up at the more important venues, such as those for swimming, gymnastics, and athletics.[15]

The number and exact location of commentator positions were matters of intense interest to the major international broadcasters, as became abundantly clear in meetings of the Olympic Broadcast Advisory Committee. The June 1987 meeting of OBAC involved a lengthy discussion of proposed commentator positions for a number of different athletic venues—at times becoming a rather heated exchange between international broadcaster representatives and representatives of the SLOOC and SORTO. During the discussion an EBU representatiave commented that "priority of broadcasting commentary positions must not go down, it must rather go up. There are situations where we must seriously discuss whether we should put VIPs in different positions, in order to make the best possible places for commentary positions. We will not demand that as a general

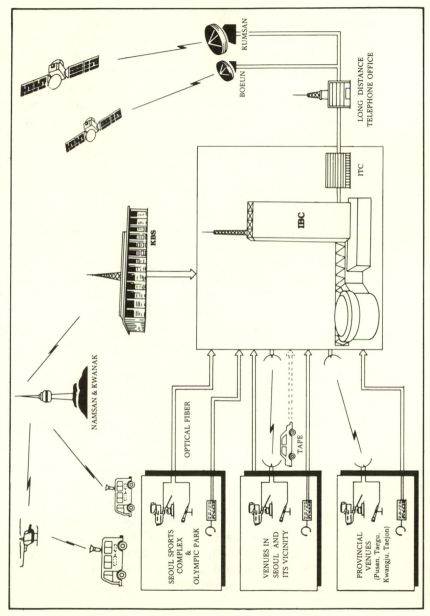

FIGURE 5.1   Simplified flow diagram of the Seoul Olympics broadcasting network. *Source:* KBS/SORTO, press handout, Seoul, Korea, September 1988.

thing, but there are some venues where this should be seriously discussed."[16]

For its part, the Seoul Olympic Organizing Committee, in its final report on television broadcasting operations, singled out the requests by NBC and other major broadcasters for exclusive commentator positions (along with their requests regarding security systems, transportation, and catering) as being "excessive" and suggested reconsideration of this problem for future Games.[17] The clear implication was that the overall size of the broadcasting contingent in Seoul had reached certain limits and that consideration should be given to various forms of pooling and sharing arrangements in the future. The imposition of such changes appears to be a logical and inevitable effect of the burgeoning global television spectacle of the Olympic Games.

The International Broadcast Center

To accommodate the many international broadcasters who came to Seoul to cover the Olympics, Korea constructed a large International Broadcast Center adjacent to the existing KBS headquarters building on Yoido Island. This was also the location of the National Assembly and many large, new corporate headquarters buildings. Sometimes called the Manhattan of Korea, the island had been sandy and barren just two decades earlier. As with other Olympic facilities, the new IBC was built with a view toward its use following the Games, in this case as an expansion and upgrading of KBS facilities.

The new IBC consisted of three main structures, with a total of 34,880 square meters of floor space. It cost approximately $58 million to construct, with an additional $105 million going toward the purchase of equipment. The largest, most architecturally innovative, and most visible of these structures—the first suspension structure in Korea—stood next to the main KBS building, facing Yoido Plaza, an expansive parade ground offering high visibility to the buildings on either side of it. To the north and opposite the KBS complex stand the twin office towers of the Lucky-Goldstar group.

Although the architecture of the International Broadcast Center was unique to Korea, the basic technical facilities it housed are common from one Olympics to the next, evolving in conjunction with television technologies and practices. Accordingly, several components of the IBC in Seoul have become necessary organizational elements for the global Olympic telecast.

- Distribution center, where all the international signals from each competition site are coordinated and distributed to each broadcaster;

- Commentary distribution center, where signals from each of the commentary positions are gathered before being sent to the technical areas occupied by each of the broadcasters in the IBC;
- Transmission control room, where the signals produced by each of the broadcasters for transmission to their home countries are coordinated;
- Central VTR room, where all international signals from the various competition sites are recorded; and
- Summary production room, where the highlights of the Games are produced and sent to the distribution center.

In addition to these facilities, each of the international broadcasters had technical and office space in the IBC for its own operations, with the location and amount of space varying based on the size of the organization and the rights fee paid. For example, the EBU/OIRT (West/East European Broadcasters) operation included a master control room with an audio routing and recording system capable of handling the 28 languages in which commentary was provided to accompany the video feed.[18]

There were also a number of studios, and editing and viewing rooms available to be booked in advance by international broadcasters for a specified time at a designated cost. Finally, the IBC contained a range of hosting services, including information on accreditation, results, transportation, a CATV (cable television) information service, express delivery service, banking, a post office, and several food services.[19] Pizza Hut, for instance, operated a concession in the outdoor walkway connecting two buildings of the IBC complex, and hamburgers from Wendy's, the official snack food sponsor of the Seoul Olympics, were readily available.

NBC, by far the largest of the rightsholding broadcasters, occupied most of one wing of the new IBC. Its equipment for the Games included 15 mobile production units, 100 cameras (7 at the IBC and 93 at the venues), 96 tape machines at the IBC and 58 at the venues, 1,000 monitors, and 7,500 videotapes. The cost of the equipment was part of the $40 million NBC reportedly incurred in capital expenses. Its production costs were approximately $100 million.[20] The NBC wing of the IBC had its own U.S.-style cafeteria, whose food and service was no doubt indistinguishable from that in the large NBC operations in New York, Los Angeles, or Chicago. In fact, much of the technical equipment NBC used in Seoul was shipped to the network's Chicago studios for permanent use after the Olympics.

In addition to using the official Olympic accreditation cards described in Chapter 3, NBC also operated a separate security system with special identification badges for its own employees. Concerns over security were so great that at one point, even the director-general for broadcasting operations of the Seoul Olympic Organizing Committee was asked to obtain an

NBC security badge in order to enter the network's section of the IBC, a request that he refused.[21]

Information and Results Systems

With the growth in size of the Olympics and the concomitant dramatic increase in the number of broadcasting, press, and support personnel involved came mounting demands for the rapid dissemination of Games results and other Olympic information to media representatives. Indeed, this development was partly spurred by the more generalized computerization of television operations, whether in news, sports or other production and programming. The demand for Games information and results reached an all-time high at Seoul because these Olympics involved the largest number of nations, athletes, and other members of the Olympic family in history.

Computers were first used for simple statistics during the 1960 Olympic Winter Games in Squaw Valley.[22] Four years later, during the Tokyo Summer Olympics, a simple computer system was again used for calculations and statistics. There was no major computer system used in Mexico City in 1968, but in 1972, the Siemens system was utilized to provide Games results.

The 1976 Olympics in Montreal were the first to possess a full-scale computerized results system, comparable to the basic functions of the Games Information On-line Network (GIONS), the results system used for the Seoul Olympics. The system from Montreal was adapted to Russian circumstances for the 1980 Moscow Olympics. In 1984, a new computer system, the Electronic Message System (EMS), was introduced, which added a message system to the Games results system and was made accessible to the people of Los Angeles through a larger communication network.

When Seoul was awarded the Olympic Games in 1981, one of the first questions to be asked was whether Korea would be able to develop satisfactory information systems. At that early date, even the nation's telephone system was facing a growing backlog, despite a series of investments in it, and the country's electronics and computer industries were still in embryonic stages. However, the government resolved to use the Olympics as an opportunity to foster Korea's information industries, and it set three general goals from the outset. First, it would carry out preparations for the Olympics in conjunction with its Telecommunications Modernization Plan. Second, it would provide state-of-the-art information services for the Games. Finally, it would seek to spread the benefits of the Olympics project across all relevant industries and users.

In the initial stages of the project, from 1982 through mid-1984, the Systems Engineering Research Institute (SERI) of the Korean Advanced Institute of Science and Technology (KAIST) worked with the Technology Section of the Seoul Olympic Organizing Committee. A major question was whether Korea should even attempt to develop its own software systems. In an effort to assess the domestic technical capacity, SERI was asked to prepare a results system for the 1983 National Games held in Inchon. Despite only three months of preparation, this field trial of a prototype information system was a major turning point for it convinced people that a computerized information system was absolutely necessary for a large-scale event like the Olympics and that such a system could be developed with domestic expertise. In February 1984, the Seoul Olympic Organizing Committee decided to develop its own systems instead of adopting the system from Montreal.[23] Once that decision was made, various delegations of experts were sent around the world to gather information in various locations, including the host cities of several prior Olympics—Munich, Montreal, Los Angeles, Sarajevo, and Calgary. Upon returning from Los Angeles in June 1984, a group led by Vice Minister of Communications Oh Myung issued a report that was highly influential in establishing the overall direction of Korea's planning for telecommunications and information systems. Its key recommendations were:

1. To expand the information and telecommunications groups in the Ministry of Communications, Korea Telecom, and the Seoul Olympic Organizing Committee;
2. To expand facilities for international television broadcasting, including additional earth stations and portable earth stations;
3. To provide of new services that drew attention in Los Angeles, including an electronic messaging system, electronic mailbox, and card telephones;
4. To integrate computer and communications systems;
5. To foster domestic manufacture of telecommunications equipment for the Olympics; and
6. To set up a fully computerized support system for management of the Games.[24]

Ultimately, four different organizations developed four computer systems that were integral to the Seoul Olympics. First, DACOM developed Integrated Network System (INS), which was tested during the Asian Games in 1986. This service was then improved and became the Wide Information Network Services (WINS) for the Seoul Olympics. Second, the Systems Engineering Research Institute, a department of KAIST, developed the Games results system called GIONS. GIONS also provided athletes' profiles and game schedule information. Third, Ssang-Yong Software and Data Corporation developed the Seoul Olympic Management System (SOMS) to assist the SLOOC in processing accreditations, managing the Olympic Village, controlling VIP protocol, recruiting volunteers, and printing tickets. Fourth and finally, the Korean Information Computing Corporation (KICO) developed the Seoul Olympic Support System (SOSS) to handle accommodations for the Olympic family, room reservations, logistics, transportation, and training site management.

The Wide Information Network System, developed by DACOM and tested in an earlier and more limited version during the 1986 Asian Games, provided both electronic mail and information retrieval services in four languages: Korean, Spanish, English, and French. The information retrieval service of WINS provided both general information and information about the Games themselves. The former included past Olympic records, a sightseeing guide, a list of cultural events, an accommodations guide, and information on shopping. The latter part of the service provided Games results; athlete profiles; medal status by countries, by sport, or by day; and new records by sport or by day. Much of the Games information came through a link with GIONS, which transferred results as soon as they were available as well as other information to WINS.

To meet the needs of broadcasters and other members of the Olympic family, the WINS service was made available in four ways. First, 1,000 WINS terminals with 500 printers were set up at the IBC, venues, the Main Press Center, designated hotels, and other locations in Seoul. Second, some users accessed the system through private, leased lines and dedicated terminals with WINS emulation software. This option would operate like the public terminals, except that the lines were leased or paid for privately. Third, the service was made available worldwide through 52 overseas Public Switched Packet Data Networks (PSPDN) such as Telenet in the United States, Transpac in France, Venus-P in Japan, and so forth. This option allowed users around the world to log into the system using their personal computers. Finally, WINS was made accessible through local telex networks around the world.[25]

In the United Kingdom, the BBC used a dedicated leased line to link a WINS terminal at its Television Center in west London with Seoul. This allowed results to be displayed on the computer in London within seconds of being announced in Korea. In case the dedicated line failed, the BBC planned to use British Telecom's public data network, the Packet Switch-Stream (PSS). ITV Sport, which handled the broadcasts of both ITV channels and Channel 4, used three IBM personal computers in London and accessed WINS from Seoul through the Dialcom UK electronic mail service.[26]

Sixty-four of the 1,000 public WINS terminals and 40 printers were installed in the International Broadcast Center. This relatively small proportion of terminals became an issue in the OBAC meetings, as the following exchange between a representative of the European Broadcasting Union and a top SLOOC official indicated:

> SLOOC Official: The total number of WINS that SLOOC is providing including venue commentator position and the number of CRT's is 1000. Printers are 451. Within this total number of WINS we have to secure quota for the broadcasters. And next time we are going to give you the exact number allocated for the broadcaster. If you wish to have it by tomorrow we'll let you know by tomorrow. If you want to compare it with press allocation, I'll give you the data. Is that agreeable to you, if I give you the data tomorrow?

> EBU Representative: It's no problem. The point we are trying to make is that we don't want to have the data just to have the data. Because we believe there's a big confusion here. The WINS terminals according to this table is 700 to the written press. We have discussed it many times in the previous OBAC meetings that the information for commentators and for the people who are working in the broadcasting center is much more important than the written press. I'd like to say that this is a proof that the press gets everything they want and we have to fight for the facilities that we need.[27]

Data compiled on actual usage of the WINS terminals in the IBC showed that nearly half (47.6 percent) of all information retrieved by broadcast personnel was competition results, which together with the retrieval of information about competition schedules (13.7 percent), accounted for more than 60 percent of all usage. Only 21.1 percent of the usage was for general information retrieval.[28]

WINS and GIONS jointly set at least three new standards for Olympic information systems. First, they were the first full-scale integration of computer and communications systems, making both the information retrieval service and E-mail available to domestic and overseas users in more than 70 countries. Second, GIONS was built around distributed processing architecture, with a pair of microcomputers at each of 24 venues connected to the host computer. (Distributed processing architecture features a computer network in which linked personal or microcomputers, rather that a single large computer, do the information processing.) If one unit failed, the other could serve as a backup, and the venue systems were designed to operate independently should the host system fail. Third, there was a direct interface between the information systems and timing or measurement devices for seven sports, including swimming, cycling, shooting, archery, gymnastics, and some track and field events. A mobile computer center was introduced to provide up-to-the-second information on such events as the marathon, racewalking, and road cycling.[29]

NBC set up its own local area network in Seoul, linking 120 personal computers that used Novell, Inc., system software called NetWare to support its coverage of the Seoul Olympics. The network linked computers at the IBC in Seoul with additional connections to remote sites in Seoul, as well as networks at NBC in New York and a Minneapolis-based travel agency. The network handled over a dozen applications, including:

- a library system allowing users to track down any one of NBC's 15,000 videotapes with Olympic footage in less than ten seconds. Information about each tape was entered into a database; the videotapes were identified with bar code stickers affixed to each tape and entered into the database using a bar code scanner;
- a research system to give assistants to on-air announcers instantaneous access to athlete biographies and histories, results of recent athletic events, and Olympic rules;
- a manpower system to track the wherebouts and schedules for the 3,500 employees working at the Games;
- a logistical support system that contained personnel and financial information to help manage and track travel and accommodations information; and
- a teleprompter link that enabled an on-air script entered on a personal computer (PC) to be transmitted to teleprompter display within seconds.[30]

Telecommunications Circuits

Responsibility for the provision and operation of all telecommunications circuits required for the Olympic telecast fell to the Korea Telecommunications Authority within Korea, working with Intelsat internationally. In 1982, KTA set up an Olympic Telecommunications Group, dedicating 60 of its 53,000 permanent personnel to the operation. By early 1988, the size of that group had grown to 3,000 staff members, providing some indication of the scope of the effort.[31]

KTA's responsibilities included the provision of various types of circuits for getting the international television signal and audio signals from 31 venues to the IBC, along with circuits required for talkback, feedback, mobile telephone service, and the like. For the highest quality circuits—those connecting the IBC to satellite earth stations and connecting major venues to the IBC—fiber-optic cable was used. For certain venues and in moving competitions such as the marathon, racewalking, and the cycling road race, microwave systems were used.[32]

KTA also participated with KBS/SORTO and the SLOOC in the joint operation of the IBC Booking Office, through which international broadcasters could make arrangements for overseas transmission of Olympic television. Two terminals were set up in Seoul to link with the main computer at the Intelsat headquarters office in Washington, D.C.[33] In addition, Intelsat sent personnel to the IBC in Seoul to provide on-site technical and operational assistance with transmissions and to assist with last-minute questions and concerns about access to the satellite system.[34] Intelsat is the largest international satellite service, with 115 member nations. It provides services either on short-term (three-month) leases (in which case the broadcaster has use of a channel 24 hours a day) or on an occasional-use basis. For an event like the Olympics, new television requirements and changes to existing orders are received throughout the competition because the results of each event alter the complexion of the coverage. This pattern of activity is reflected most directly in the booking of occasional-use satellite channels through Intelsat, as shown in Figure 1.1.

Because it is the only organization capable of providing service on such a global scale, Intelsat has become the hub for planning and organizing the international component of Olympic television coverage. That planning begins years in advance. Intelsat received the first television orders for the 1988 Olympic Games three years before the opening ceremonies for the 1984 Games in Los Angeles. In fact, the orders were received the day after Calgary and Seoul were designated as the 1988 Olympic host cities.[35]

To ensure the availability of the required satellite space-segment capacity, Intelsat was involved in regular meetings with KTA representatives from Korea and with individuals from countries interested in receiving transmissions. Based on such meetings, a detailed operating plan was developed that covered uplink and downlink countries, satellites, frequencies, and capacity to be used.

Indeed, international broadcaster demand for television circuits did become an issue at the June 1987 OBAC meeting. There, an EBU representative who also served as a member of the IOC Television Commission questioned KTA's provision of only six leased and one occasional satellite channel instead of the seven channels requested by the European Broadcasting Union. The following exchange took place with a senior representative of KTA:

> KTA Representative: KTA's situation is that the earth station capacity is not enough to provide additional leased circuits.
>
> EBU Representative: Then, I'm afraid we will have to ask SLOOC to press on this, because according to the contract we have made with SLOOC, we are supposed to have seven channels. We want them permanent and leased. If you have up-link capability, I don't understand why the up-link doesn't work for 24 hours a day, which is what we are requesting.[36]

Intelsat eventually used a total of 9 satellites to broadcast the Seoul Olympic events—4 in the Atlantic Ocean region, 3 in the Indian Ocean region, and 2 in the Pacific Ocean region. Demand for television transmission of the Summer Games was so great that a near-saturation level was reached on the Indian and Pacific Ocean television channels.

By the time September 1988 arrived, Intelsat had orders for 32 simultaneous television channels for the Games. During peak periods of the global telecast, all of these channels were used simultaneously. Full-time coverage was provided through 19 short-term leases—8 channels in the Indian Ocean region to Europe and Japan, 10 channels in the Pacific Ocean region to Australia, Canada, Japan, Mexico, and the United States, and 1 channel in the Atlantic Ocean region to Spain via a double-hop through Canada.[37] Prior to the Seoul Olympics, the usual practice was for broadcasters to prebook satellite time in the form of 2-, 3-, or 4-hour blocks. According to an Intelsat spokesman, the previous precedent for short-term leases was 2 or 3 for coverage of 1986 World Cup Soccer in Mexico.[38]

To meet the additional TV requirements that developed as the Games approached, an agreement was reached for the Korea Telecommunication Authority to lease a transportable K-band antenna from Teleglobe Canada. This earth station, situated at the IBC in Seoul, was used to accommodate 6 additional TV channels between Korea and Canada, Mexico and Spain.[39] The overwhelming demand for satellite transmission services out of Seoul during the Olympics also led KTA to call in IDB Communications, a Los Angeles–based transmission service, to fly two 4.5-meter and one 3.5-meter Ku-band earth stations to Seoul for use in radio transmissions.[40]

As of September 7, 1988, more than 7,500 television hours had been booked on Intelsat's 13 occasional-use TV channels. This figure did not include the 19 short-term leased channels. This was 2,000 hours more than were carried for the 1984 Los Angeles Games.[41]

There are two important factors that explain the extensive demand for satellite time to cover the Seoul Olympics. The first is the large number of countries represented at the Games. Even so, the 38 nations that directly used Intelsat made up a far from exhaustive list of those receiving Olympic telecasts because many of the Intelsat users were regional broadcasting organizations, including the European Broadcasting Union, the Soviet Intersputnik system, and the Asian Broadcasting Union—all of which used non-Intelsat satellites to further distribute their coverage to member countries.[42] The second factor accounting for the extensive demand was the continued increase in the number of international earth stations capable of using the Intelsat satellites, an important reflection of the expansion of global television. That number was 200 in 1980, 300 in 1984, and 500 by September 1988.[43] The general trend is toward increasingly powerful satellites, allowing more countries to afford earth stations and, hence, satellite coverage.

The Burgeoning Olympic Spectacle: Questions of Size and Control

With 160 of 167 national Olympic committees participating, the Seoul Olympics underscored the problems that accompanied growth in the size of the Games. According to IOC President Samaranch, "The size of the Olympic Games is reaching a peak where we cannot go higher. We had nearly 10,000 athletes in Seoul. We have to find a formula that will work for both the IOC and its members because we would like all 167 NOCs taking part in the games."[44] Samaranch, who is concerned about providing housing for athletes and officials, has repeatedly expressed this idea since the Seoul Olympics. "An Olympic village for more than 15,000 people would represent an excessive burden on the host city," he noted.[45]

As shown in Seoul, concerns about the size of the Olympics extend as well to the optimum size and makeup of the international media contingent and, therefore, the technical and support infrastructure required to serve their needs. As noted in Chapter 3, the number of accredited broadcast and press personnel exceeded the number of athletes and officials. Another measure of the sheer size of the television Olympics is provided in Figure 5.2, which compares the major types of television equipment and circuits provided in Seoul with those that were available in Los Angeles four years earlier. By every measure, Seoul was substantially larger.

The size of the broadcast and print media contingents arose repeatedly as an issue underlying the more specific concerns discussed at meetings of the Olympic Broadcast Advisory Committee. For example, the Olympic Charter limits the number of media personnel who may visit the Athletes' Village to 200 at any one time. At a certain stage of planning, consideration was given to placing an injection point (the technical term for a place from which broadcasters can feed videotapes to the International Broadcast Center) inside the Athletes' Village, but with more than 8,000 media personnel entitled to visit the village, that idea proved unworkable.[46]

The question of size was addressed in the Seoul Olympic Organizing Committee's final report on television broadcasting operations. It noted that requests by major broadcasters for exclusive commentator positions, security systems, transportation, and catering were excessive. At the same time, it commended the role of the European Broadcasting Union in solving many of its members' problems, relieving the SLOOC of those burdens, and it suggested that such regional broadcasting unions should be given a greater role as coordinators in future Olympics.[47]

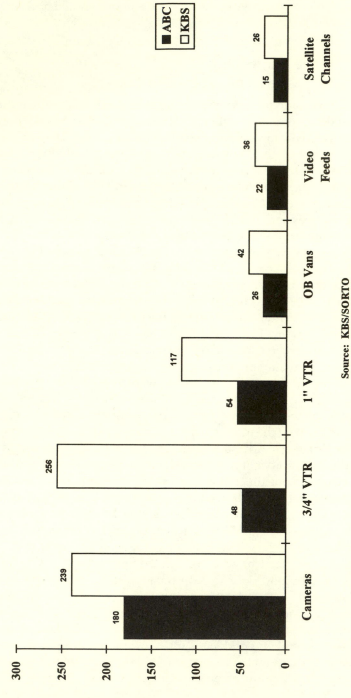

Source: KBS/SORTO

FIGURE 5.2   Television equipment in Seoul (1988) versus Los Angeles (1984). *Source:* KBS/SORTO, Korea.

The Olympics and Korea's Information Society

Questions about the nature and degree to which the Olympics influenced South Korea's progress toward an information society are indeed complex and admit no simple answers. However, as the world's largest planned television and media event, the Olympics, with the years of planning and preparation they entail, wield a great potential influence not only on broadcasting but also on other information-related industries. Such influence affects the hardware components of the technologies, the information inputs (programming or "software"), and the skills required of people in the various information industries. There are multiple indications that, for Korea, both the Olympic television and overall telecommunications requirements of the Seoul Olympics gave an across-the-board impetus to such developments.

The overall impact of meeting the responsibilities of host broadcaster was hinted at in a presentation of SORTO's philosophy at the November 10–13, 1986, World Broadcasters Meeting in Seoul. After stating that SORTO would observe the relevant parts of the 1982 Olympic Charter, respect the operational practices of former Olympic host broadcasters, and support the unilateral activities of international broadcasters, the organization's representatives made two important assertions.

First, they said that "SORTO pursues the Olympic spirit and retains the KBS standpoint as the public broadcast organization representing the image of Korea" in determining the range of services to be provided and their cost. Second, they stated that "SORTO seeks to achieve a balance between the promotion of national prestige and the nation's situation as a developing country."[48]

That notion of balance was perhaps best illustrated by the massive task of assembling production crews for the entire range of Olympic sports—in a country where many of these sports did not exist or had only recently been introduced, let alone televised. Accordingly, in its own description of the Seoul Olympics Radio and Television Operations, KBS stated that

> SORTO identified production crew experience as the most crucial element for success. To achieve that expertise, the SORTO team has received countless hours of training and practice in sports broadcasting. In particular, they have covered Olympics in Calgary, Sarajevo and Los Angeles; the Seoul Asian Games; and the Universiade in Kobe, Japan. To complement this on-the-job training, individuals have been sent around the world to consult experts in many fields.[49]

Even with this substantial effort, SORTO found it necessary to assign the production of certain sports to international teams. According to KBS, these measures were taken "in order to enhance the quality of its coverage and to preclude the surplus of domestic personnel and equipment after the Games." The partial or total production of seven sports was assigned to foreign broadcasting organizations: the equestrian sports to Great Britain's BBC, gymnastics to Japan's NHK, yachting to Net-10 of Australia, cycling to NOB of the Netherlands, weightlifting to TV-Asahi of Japan, athletics to Finland's YLE, and all diving and water polo preliminary events to Maximum TV, Inc., of the United States.[50]

The Seoul Olympics gave impetus to the development of several broadcast-specific technologies, including graphics, character generators known as PRISM units, and the inauguration of the first Korean teletext service using equipment developed by the KBS technical laboratories. In addition, Korean electronics manufacturers supplied KBS with 45 percent of all the electronic equipment used at the Games. This included such items as audio tape recorders, turntables, mixers, audio consoles, all audio and video cables (including fiber-optic ones), video distribution amplifier fiber terminal gear (modulators/demodulators), color monitors, and VCRs.[51]

In describing indirect investment projects completed before the Seoul Olympics, a report by the Korea Development Institute noted that

> investment in broadcasting and communications support required the procurement of advanced technology. While preparing for the Olympics, considerable technology was accumulated, creating an opportunity to advance the domestic electronics industry. In particular, WINS (Wide Information Network System Service), which was developed by a domestic technological team, proved a great success and showcased domestic technology to the world. WINS will be the base from which ISDN (Integrated System Digital Network) will be built, establishing Korea as an information society.[52]

The same report grew even more emphatic, declaring that the "Wide Information Network Services developed by a domestic research group successfully met the needs for information and laid the foundation for the establishment of an ISDN, the first step in realizing an information society."[53]

In short, all the evidence strongly suggests that Korea made a forceful, broad, and long-term effort to further develop its own indigenous television production capabilities in order to host the global Olympic telecast. The same observation applies to the development of the computer systems necessary to manage and produce Olympic television. Although difficult, if not impossible, to quantify, it would appear that the Olympic effort gave a boost to a variety of activities generally associated with the term *informa-*

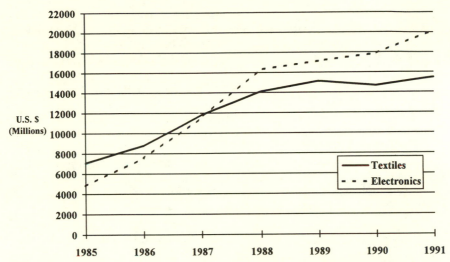

FIGURE 5.3 Korea's export of textiles versus electronics, 1985–1991. *Source:* "Economic and Industry Trends," *Korea Trade & Business* 10 (October 1992): p. 11.

tion society. These included television program production, telecommunications, computer system hardware and software design, and management information systems, to name a few.

Perhaps more convincing are the data regarding the growth of Korea's electronics industry. Forecasts for mid- and long-term growth of that industry issued by the Korea Electronics Association in 1986 were exceeded within just a few months. By 1987, their production estimates for 1990 had already been achieved, with total production of $17.4 billion. In 1988, the electronics industry, including both consumer and industrial electronics, overtook the textile industry as Korea's leading exporter, as shown graphically in Figure 5.3.[54] Analysts have attributed such growth to publicity associated with the Olympics and the promotion of technological growth in electronics and telecommunications necessitated by the Olympics.[55]

Notes

1. Juan Antonio Samaranch, "General Introduction," *Media Guide* (Lausanne, Switzerland: International Olympic Comittee, 1985).

2. "With the Blink of an Eye: Will Korea Hitch Its Future to the Telecommunications Revolution?" *Korea Business World* 4 (September 1988): p. 25.

3. Myung Oh, "Olympic Success: A Hightech Challenge," *Korea Business World* (January 1988): p. 25.

4. "With the Blink of an Eye."

5. Ibid., p. 26.

6. Personal interview with Yang Seungtaik, president, Korea Telecommunications Authority International, Seoul, Korea, September 17, 1991.

7. "Role of Host Broadcaster KBS & SORTO," *SORTO Courier* 1 (August 1986): p. 6.

8. "Seoul Olympics Radio and Television Operations (SORTO)," *SORTO Courier* 1 (August 1986): p. 18.

9. Seoul Olympic Organizing Committee, "Report on Television Broadcasting Operations for the Games of the XXIVTH Olympiad," April 1989, p. 35.

10. Ibid., p. 20.

11. Korean Broadcasting System, "Coverage of the XXIVTH Olympiad: A Description" KBS/SORTO press release, Seoul, Korea, September 1988, p. B-2.

12. Seoul Olympic Organizing Committee, *Media Guide* (Seoul, Korea: Seoul Olympic Organizing Committee, 1985), p. 43.

13. Ibid., p. 43.

14. Seoul Olympic Organizing Committee, "Report on Television Broadcasting Operations," p. 36.

15. *KBS Courier* 7 (March 1988): pp. 22–25.

16. Korean Broadcasting System/SORTO, "2nd OBAC Meeting Transcript," June 10–12, 1987, p. 55.

17. Seoul Olympic Organizing Committee, "Report on Television Broadcasting Operations" p. 19.

18. Joe Roizen, "Pre-Olympic Update from Seoul," TELEGEN (A Television Industry Report), September 2, 1988: p. 5

19. *KBS Courier* 8 (June 1988): pp. 14–17.

20. "NBC Warms Up for Summer Olympics in Seoul," *Broadcasting* 115 (August 29, 1988): p. 28.

21. Personal interview with Cho Sung Min, director-general for broadcasting, Seoul Olympic Organizing Committee, Seoul, Korea, November 1988.

22. The following historical information is taken from WINS (Wide Information Network Services), a background document prepared by Data Communications Corporation of Korea, Seoul, Korea, n.d.

23. Oh Sung-baik, "The Development Process for the Seoul Olympic Information Network" (Paper presented at the First International Workshop on a World Olympic Academic Network, Seoul, Korea, November 28–30, 1991), pp. 4–6.

24. Ibid., p. 7.

25. WINS (Wide Information Network Services).

26. Della Bradshaw, "All Lined Up for the Great Data Race," *Financial Times*, September 16, 1988, p. 16.

27. Korean Broadcasting System/SORTO, "OBAC Meeting Transcript," April 6–8, 1988, p. 172.

28. Seoul Olympic Organizing Committee, "Report on Television Broadcasting Operations," p. 30.

29. Sung-Baik Oh, "The Development Process," pp. 2–3.

30. "Novell NetWare Joins NBC in the 1988 Summer Olympic Games," Business Wire, August 22, 1988.

31. Chung Kyong-Jin, "KTA Telecommunications Plan for the XXIVth Olympic Games," *KBS Courier* 8 (June 1988): pp. 8–13.

32. Ibid., p. 9.

33. Ibid., p. 10.

34. "Intelsat to Provide Record Coverage of 1988 Summer Olympics," PR Newswire (Washington, D.C.), September 12, 1988.

35. Susan L. Gordon and Arnold W. Meyers, "INTELSAT Goes for the Gold in '88," *Telephony* 215 (September 26, 1988): p. 44.

36. Korean Broadcasting System/SORTO, "2nd OBAC Meeting Transcript," p. 56.

37. INTELSAT (International Telecommunications Satellite Organization), news release (Washington, D.C.), September 12, 1988, p. 2.

38. "TV Coverage to Set Records at Olympics," *Broadcasting* (September 9, 1988): pp. 73, 74.

39. Gordon and Meyers, "INTELSAT Goes for the Gold in '88."

40. "NBC Warms Up for Summer Olympics in Seoul."

41. "Intelsat to Provide Record Coverage of 1988 Summer Olympics."

42. "TV Coverage to Set Records at Olympics," p. 74.

43. Ibid.

44. William D. Murray, "Sports News," United Press International, February 20, 1989.

45. Morley Myers, "Sports News," United Press International, August 29, 1989.

46. Korean Broadcasting System/SORTO, "OBAC Meeting Transcript," p. 83.

47. Seoul Olympic Organizing Committee, "Report on Television Broadcasting Operations," p. 19.

48. Seoul Olympics Radio and Television Operations, p. 9.

49. Korean Broadcasting System, "The Host Broadcasting Role," news release, September 1988, p. A-2.

50. Ibid., p. B-3.

51. Joseph Roizen, "KBS Television Coverage Largest in Olympic History," *KBS Courier* 9, (November 1988: pp. 47–48.

52. Kim Jong-gie, Rhee Sang-Woo, Yu Jae-cheon, Koo Kwang-mo, and Hong Jong-duck, *Impact of the Seoul Olympic Games on National Development* (Seoul: Korea Development Institute, 1989), pp. 41–42.

53. Ibid., p. 56.

54. "Economic and Industry Trends," *Korea Trade & Business* 10 (October 1992): p. 11.

55. Kim, et al., *Impact of the Seoul Olympic Games*, pp. 56–57.

6

The 1988 Olympics and the Transformation of Korea

Introduction

The decade of Korea's engagement with the 1988 Olympics, from the inception of the idea to bid for the Games through their successful conclusion, framed a tumultuous period of political change and liberalization within the nation. The Olympic experience began in the midst of the political turmoil that followed the October 1979 assassination of President Park Chung Hee, whose government had, only months earlier, decided to bid for the 1988 Olympics. In the aftermath of Park's assassination, there were widespread public hopes for a return to civilian government after years of military dictatorship. However, a sequence of events in 1980 and 1981 were to confer extraordinary political importance on the Seoul Olympics. The following were some of the key occurrences:

- By April 1980, Gen. Chun Doo Hwan had consolidated his power by a staged military coup.
- In May 1980, the government of General Chun dispatched troops to quell demonstrations in the city of Kwangju, leading to massive bloodshed and what is now known as the Kwangju prodemocracy uprising.
- In December 1980, the Chun government decided to proceed with the bid for the Olympics, as initiated under the Park government.
- In February 1981, newly inaugurated U.S. President Ronald Reagan conferred public approval on the Chun government by inviting President Chun to be the first foreign head of state to visit the White House in Washington, D.C.

- In September 1981, the International Olympic Committee, meeting in Baden-Baden, voted to award the 1988 Olympics to Seoul.

Such developments at the beginning of the Olympic period helped to make the Seoul Games both an important new criterion in Korean politics and also a project of more than passing interest to the Olympic movement and international community. The Games helped to make otherwise domestic political considerations inseparable from the character of the Olympics as a global media spectacle. Accordingly, an underlying theme throughout this chapter is how the prospect or actual experience of massive international media attention on South Korea affected ongoing political, social, and economic changes in that nation.

The timing of preparations for the Olympics, on the one hand, and progress toward democratization in South Korea, on the other, reached another crucial juncture in the spring of 1987. The deepening political crisis at home led to widespread international media attention and open discussion about whether it placed the Seoul Olympics in jeopardy. Several other cities around the world offered to host the 1988 Games should Seoul be unable to fulfill its obligation. The now-famous June 29 declaration by ruling party leader and presidential candidate Roh Tae Woo broke the logjam and opened the way for a successful hosting of the Olympics. However, an important part of that solution was an agreement with the political opposition to postpone public inquiry into the Kwangju uprising and the activities of the Fifth Republic under Chun Doo Hwan until after the Olympics. Consequently, the nationally televised hearings of the National Assembly on Kwangju and the Chun government were—from a political communication standpoint—integrally part of the Olympic experience and will be discussed in this chapter.

That such momentous political evolution should occur within South Korea at a time of East Asian dynamism, change in the worldwide political structure, and the global communications revolution make Seoul an important case study in which to explore several more generally discussed or hypothesized relationships between the Olympics and politics. Therefore, this chapter will examine how the Olympics related to Korea's national development, national pride, the development and popularization of sport, and the role of television and the media in sport and politics.

The Olympics and National Development

From its very inception, the decision to bid for the Seoul Olympics was intertwined in the minds of key government officials with the potential impact of the Games on Korea's national development. Moreover, it was explicitly linked in their minds to Japan's experience with the 1964 Tokyo Olympics.

Before Korea first broached the idea of bidding for the Olympics in international circles, Park Jong-kyue, president of the Korean Olympic Committee, had discussed the idea with President Park Chung Hee and had received his approval. There were three major reasons given for hosting the Olympics in Seoul. First, a turning point had been reached in Korea because of high economic growth, and the Japanese experience with the Olympics could be a model for Korea. Second, South Korea might be able to seize a very practical opportunity through the Games to terminate the state of confrontation with North Korea. And third, staging the Olympics in Seoul would provide an opportunity for Korea to join the ranks of the advanced nations.[1]

With respect to the first goal, it should be noted that the leaders of Korea undoubtedly wished to emulate Japan's success with the 1964 Olympics but in a distinctively Korean manner. Among top leadership in government, industry, and academia, there remained a significant reservoir of negative feeling toward Japan—a legacy of the colonial era from 1905 through the end of World War II. In a persuasive analysis, Professor Choe Chungho argued that Japan, unlike Germany, embarked on no systematic and public effort to "surmount its past" following the war. Instead, he suggested, the atomic bombing of Hiroshima and Nagasaki near the end of World War II transformed Japan in the eyes of world public opinion from an aggressor nation that had pursued a "scorched earth" policy in Asia to a victim.[2] Because they carry implications for the future of the Olympic movement in Asia, his views will be treated at greater length in Chapter 7.

In keeping with the nature of Korean politics generally and the Park government in particular, the decision to bid for the Olympics was a top-down, bureaucratic one, initially involving only a few high-level members of the government and sports community. Yet even among these men, there were doubts about whether Korea, as a developing country, could afford such an effort. Those involved in the deliberations were acutely aware that Korea had lost face in 1971 when it had to forfeit its plan to host the 1976 Asian Games in Seoul because it could not afford the estimated $34 million required for facilities.[3]

In terms of the overall goal of using the Olympics as a boost to national development, the argument was made from the start that ongoing development projects could be adapted to the requirements of hosting the Olympics, thereby avoiding large outlays on infrastructures for the Games per se that could not be used later.

Public Campaigns to Prepare for the Games

East Asia boasts a long tradition of using mass campaigns to further various political and development goals. In South Korea during the years leading up to the Seoul Olympics, they came in rapid-fire succession as the nation engaged in a massive national mobilization aimed at ensuring success in hosting the Games. Taken together, such mobilizations need to be understood as contemporary and peculiarly Korean manifestations of the long East Asian tradition.

Because the Tenth Asiad in 1986 was the first international sporting event of such scope to be hosted by the Republic of Korea, the government took a keen interest in it, providing many forms of direct and indirect support through various ministries.[4] In addition, the private sector and citizens organizations joined in the effort.

The direct government support included construction of the sports venues, the Athletes' Village, the Olympic Park, the International Broadcast Center, the Main Press Center, and other Olympic facilities. In addition, there was a massive effort to train Korea's Olympic athletes, to popularize Olympic sports, and to develop sport more generally in Korea.

Over and above these direct efforts to prepare for the Asian Games and the Olympics, there were a large number of indirect programs, many sponsored by government ministries and others involving broader citizen or corporate support. In February 1982, the Ministry of Home Affairs issued guidelines for organizing and managing a pan-national civilian cooperative body to support the Olympics. It was to involve dignitaries from virtually all administrative units in the country. In March 1985, this movement established a Central Council for Pan-national Olympic Promotion, and in the following year, it expanded its membership to include representatives from various vocational and social organizations. More than 60,000 people became involved with local chapters of the council, joined by 70 groups of Korean residents from 54 countries around the world.[5] Within Korea, the council undertook a drive to raise the people's consciousness and initiated several programs in the area of public relations, education, and environmental improvement.

Most of the government-supported projects had highly visible results. The indirect projects and campaigns included efforts to improve the living environment, to beautify the host city of Seoul and provincial areas throughout the country, and to eliminate "public nuisances." The following description of the major projects and campaigns is intended to provide some idea of the scope and duration of Korea's mobilization for the Seoul Olympics.[6]

The Han River Development Project. This massive project, requiring an investment of 387.5 billion won, was at once a flood control and antipollution project and a program to beautify Seoul. The Han River is legendary as the lifeline of the Korean nation and site of its capital. However, as the city burgeoned around the river during the 1960s and 1970s, the water became foul and polluted, to the extent that fish could no longer live in those lower reaches that flowed through Seoul. Accordingly, the Han River Project involved drainage work, dredging, and the construction of raised embankments on both sides of the river within the city. These were developed into public parks, gardens, and athletic fields. A new, 37-kilometer Olympic Expressway was built on the south side of the river.

Of special relevance to the present study is the impact of the Han River Project on the telecast of the Seoul Olympics. The clean-flowing river became the location for the beginning of the Seoul Olympic opening ceremony, with the Han River boat parade. It was also the site of the Han River festival accompanying the Olympic Games and one of the most frequently televised backdrops as Seoul presented itself to the world through television.

Subway Construction. The three newest lines of the Seoul subway system were completed simultaneously in 1985. Consequently, the city was able to utilize one of the most modern subway systems in the world for both the Asian Games and the Seoul Olympics. The system included stops at the Olympic sports complex south of the Han River, near the Olympic Park and, of course, near most major hotels and shopping areas.

International Transportation. The infrastructure for international transportation also received attention in the years leading up to the Olympics. The government built a new international terminal at Kimpo Airport outside of Seoul, constructed new runways, negotiated new aviation agreements with a number of countries that increased the number of international flights connecting with Seoul, and approved new routes for the national flag carrier, Korean Air. It also increased the number of ferryboat lines linking Korea and Japan.

Roadside Improvement and Beautification. Within the city of Seoul and throughout the provinces, programs were undertaken to expand and beautify roads and highways. These efforts included the paving of roads or sidewalks and the planting of trees, shrubs, and flowers alongside. Beginning in 1982, Seoul began a large-scale program to remove aboveground electric power and telephone lines and replace them with underground distribution. Also, administrative units throughout the country waged a campaign to remove "unrefined signboards and other advertisement posters which detracted from the beauty of the streets."[7] The governments of Seoul and provincial cities encouraged residents to clear the rooftops of their streetside buildings of ugly or makeshift structures, TV antennas, and other objects that were considered damaging to the beauty of the streets.

Special effort was put forth to give a new look to the upscale shopping area of Myong-dong, a thriving center within easy walking distance of several major international hotels in downtown Seoul. The arrival of ultra-modern neon lights on a large scale gave the city of Seoul a distinctly new look at night.

Railway and Torch Relay Course Beautification. Beautification efforts were also focused on major railway routes in Seoul and throughout the country and on portions of the torch relay course. Poor quality roofs were replaced with new ones, small streams were cleaned, and flower gardens or miniparks were created.

Public Gardens and Reforestation. Three large parks were newly dedicated in Seoul, and six public gardens were renovated before the start of the Asian Games. In a complementary effort, Seoul and provincial government units carried out an ongoing program of planting street trees and reforestation. Many mountainsides in Korea, especially those surrounding the larger cities, had been deforested during the first half of the century, largely to provide wood fuel for the traditional *ondol* floor heating system but also due to logging during the Japanese occupation. In the 1960s and into the 1970s, the nation mounted an intensive reforestation effort that yielded results that were clearly visible from satellite photographs.

During the immediate pre-Olympic period of August and September 1988, Seoul and other major cities mounted an unprecedented program of planting flowers, placing potted plants, and forming flower roads and flower towers around the city.

Prevention of Noise. Local governments in Seoul, Pusan, Taegu, Taejon, Kwangju, and Inchon conducted educational campaigns to remind the public of the harmful effects of noise generated by loudspeakers, car horns, and industrial or construction machinery. They sought the cooperation of concerned parties to control noise during the Asiad period.

Guidance for Restaurants. The Korean government arranged loans of 19 billion won from the National Citizen's Bank for the owners of 7,765 food stalls and restaurants to support their plans to improve kitchen equipment and facilities, toilet facilities, and service tables. A major emphasis was also placed on encouraging à la carte ordering and restaurant service. Nationwide, more than 2,000 restaurants were designated as "exemplary" and were encouraged to develop Korean, Japanese, Chinese, Western, and instant dishes that were designated as "Olympic food."

Improvement of Public Toilets. Beginning in 1984, a nationwide program converted traditional lavatories to flush toilets in selected schools, expressway rest stops, sports venues, and sight-seeing stops.

Production of Western Vegetables. By the 1980s, hothouse agriculture had already provided South Korea with an indigenous and plentiful supply of fruits and vegetables, but the Olympics offered the challenge of providing Western vegetables for consumption by athletes and other visitors from around the world. Moreover, the demand for such foods would be on a scale far above the normal requirements of the tourism industry.

Beginning in 1982, the Rural Development Administration conducted a two-year field experiment to produce 23 species of 8 vegetables, such as cabbage, parsley, and lettuce, anticipating increased demand for Western vegetables during the Asian Games and the Olympics. The government provided financial support for greenhouses and other facilities, and two farmers cooperatives in the eastern part of the country produced 44.9 tons of Western vegetables that were consumed during the Asian Games.[8]

Participation Drive. The Central Council for Pan-national Olympic Promotion launched a nationwide participation drive in March 1985 along with its chapters in cities, provinces, and social organizations. The drive included massive rallies, foreign language education programs, organization of cheering squads for each participating nation, publicity to encourage desirable behavior by sports spectators, and campaigns calling for kindness and cleanness. The results were quantified. A total of 161 schools and business firms—15 construction firms, 40 trading companies, 20 sponsors and suppliers, 50 middle schools, and 36 high schools—organized cheering squads and visited athletes from the 26 participating nations to offer encouragment. The press carried a total of 939 stories, and the nation's two television networks broadcast a total of 3,800 programs. In addition, the campaign involved the distribution and display of 8.9 million stickers, 3.6 million slogan placards, 8.4 million leaflets, 2.9 million pamphlets, 3,280 banners, 99,900 ribbons, 540,000 matches, 520 slides, and 200 videotapes.

Public Order. One of the national campaigns before the Olympics was a movement to "make public order a part of daily life." The Ministry of Home Affairs and the Social Purification Committee led this campaign to reemphasize public order in the streets, in sports venues, and in commercial transactions. Government officials and members of the committee went out on the street to make sure that citizens crossed within the crosswalks, queued at bus and taxi stops, and placed cigarette butts and trash in trash containers. During the 1981–1986 campaign period, traffic control education programs were arranged for a total of 9.9 million drivers who worked in public transportation. To ensure a more pleasant time at athletic events, alcoholic beverages were banned from stadiums, and facilities were improved.

In an effort to introduce new commercial practices in commercial transactions, the government required businesses to post price tags and set up consumer protection centers. Also, 7.6 million merchants participated in seminars, symposiums, and talks designed to promote commercial ethics.

Beginning in 1982, the government conducted educational programs for the general public. These were directed at parents, workers, and members of social organizations. A chapter on the Olympics was placed in the textbooks of primary, middle, and high school students.

The foregoing summary of projects and campaigns undertaken in South Korea during the 1980s helps to show the scope and pervasive character of the national mobilization for the Asian Games and Seoul Olympics. It is not, however, meant to imply that the measures met with the full approval of citizens. To the contrary, some of them met with disapproval, that at times was broadly based, especially in the early years when the Olympics were seen as the project of a military government. The negative reactions persisted right up to the beginning of the Games. As one long-time Western resident of Seoul wrote at the start of the Games, "The press reports for some time have been speaking of the enthusiasm and eagerness of the public about the Games. Such reports have derived largely from the wishful thinking of the planners and organizers in government and business, while the reaction of most 'ordinary people' has been quite lukewarm, even negative."[9] He went on to observe that, although almost everyone wanted the Olympics to succeed for the sake of Seoul's reputation, many individuals had not felt identified with the preparations and "have remained indifferent, even annoyed by the demands and inconveniences."[10] Though public reaction to the succession of campaigns and mobilizations leading up to the Olympics was mixed, it is nevertheless true that through these campaigns, the Olympic experience touched virtually every citizen of South Korea in a very immediate and concrete fashion.

Development and Popularization of Sport

When the Olympics were awarded to Seoul in September 1981, South Korea had no ministerial-level government body in charge of sports, and many Olympic sports had not yet been introduced to the Korean public. Consequently, the Olympic experience drew the government and industry more directly into sports in ways that would contribute to the ongoing processes of political, social, and economic change within the nation.

South Korea established the Ministry of Sports in 1982, largely in response to the demands of hosting the Asian Games and the Olympics, as the sports minister noted:

> One thing must never be forgotten. It is that when the degree of sophistication climbs in any country, the opportunity dwindles for its people to undergo enough physical exercise. The outcome is damaging in terms of physical and mental health.

In the wake of our spectacular economic development, this fact, along with the mounting pressure to get set for the Seoul Olympics, made itself felt. So much so that this ministry came into being eight years ago.[11]

One of the first priorities of the Ministry of Sports was to help identify promising athletes and to train them with the best methods that sports science had to offer. A nationwide scouting drive was launched in which 6.2 million young people were put through athletic aptitude tests. Out of these tests, 4,300 athletes were identified as promising. They were given intensive training under the supervision of the Korea Sports Science Institute, beginning in elementary school. Some were sent overseas for training.

The goal of this effort was to achieve success in competition, and by that measure, the results were impressive. In the 1986 Asian Games, Korea finished second to China, winning 93 gold medals versus China's 94 and Japan's 58. In overall medals won, Korea came out ahead of China, with 224 versus 222. Earning 12 gold medals in the 1988 Olympics, Korea placed fourth after the Soviet Union, East Germany, and the United States.[12] Moreover, 16 of the 33 Olympic medals won by Korean athletes went to those who had gone through the government scouting and training program. In the words of the minister of sports, the role played by the government in these competition successes "was massive and comprehensive."[13]

These efforts also involved financing on a scale that only the government could afford. Beginning in 1972, with the establishment of a National Sports Promotion Foundation, Korea adopted a pension system for top athletes to provide a financial incentive for more victories. According to one longtime journalist and sports editor in Seoul,

> The pension system for sportsmen brought forth a turning point for sports nationalism in Korea. For better or for worse, excellence in sports meant a lot of cash for athletes. Inevitably the system led to extra-hard work in training among athletes and solidified their will to win. The outcome was telling. Koreans began copping honors right and left at international meets.[14]

Under this system, athletes are given points according to their performance. An Olympic gold medal counts for 90 points and provides the medalist with a monthly pension payment of $850. A silver medal counts for 30 points and a monthly payment of $426, and a bronze medal earns 20 points and a payment of $280. As of 1990, Kim Soo-nyung, who earned top honors in the single and group archery competition in the 1988 Olympics, rated a monthly pension of $1,570.[15] In that same year, the Seoul Olympic Sports Promotion Foundation (originally the National Sports Promotion

Foundation) paid as much as $118,570 a month to 253 "pensioners" in 22 sports.[16]

The effort to recruit and train athletes for competition in the Asian Games and the Olympics built on historical precedents in which sport had served overtly political purposes. In 1920, after ten years of Japanese colonial rule, the Choson Sports Association, predecessor to the Korea Amateur Sports Association, was founded by a large group of prominent citizens, only a small minority of whom were sports figures. According to one account, "This sports association was not a mere grouping of sports fans. It was in fact a front for a fraternity of patriots."[17] In those days, Chon Yuryang, a patriarchal figure in Korea's rugby circles, told a group of Korean ruggers who were about to play against a Japanese team that "what you are about to do is not a sport but an independence movement. You must win—no matter what."[18] The Korean team won its match with the Japanese, but this was only the first of several incidents in which athletes used sport to assert Korea's independence.

The most famous such episode of this kind was the victory of Korean marathon star Sohn Kee Chung in the 1936 Berlin Olympics. His victory sparked a burning desire for independence among the Korean people. In a courageous defiance of Japanese rule, for which they were imprisoned, journalists at the *Dong-A Ilbo* carried a photo of the victorious Sohn after erasing the Japanese national flag from his uniform. Other vernacular papers made similar gestures, including the women's monthly *New Home*, which ran a photo showing only Sohn's legs to avoid displaying the Japanese flag on his uniform.[19] The story of Sohn Kee Chung became a centerpiece of the Seoul Olympics and its global telecast.

The government of President Chun Doo Hwan found it very advantageous to make use of sport, both to improve its image overseas and to enhance harmony among people at home. As already noted, it even came to be known in Korea as the "Sports Republic." In particular, his government was helped by two epochal developments. One was the International Olympic Committee's decision to award the 1988 Summer Games to Seoul. The other was the launching of professional sports in South Korea.[20]

If governments around the world had concerns about the legitimacy of Chun Doo Hwan's military-led government, the IOC's decision to award the Olympics to Seoul diminished those concerns in one fell swoop. Especially for Eastern bloc countries and many other nations of the world for whom South Korea was virtually an unknown entity, the decision to award the games automatically and almost immediately conferred the sort of international legitimacy that could hardly have been gained in any other way. For the North American public, the action likely reinforced whatever legitimacy had already been conferred by the February 1981 White House meeting between Chun and President Reagan.

The introduction of professional sports into South Korea, their popularization, and their increasing presence on television and in the media (as discussed in Chapter 4) also influenced the social and political climate of the nation during the buildup to the Olympics. Most notable was the introduction of professional baseball. As a prominent journalist and sportswriter noted, "If the IOC decision to allow Seoul to host the Games in 1988 played a dramatic role in enhancing Korea's image throughout the world, the start of pro baseball in the country did much towards diverting the public's interest from politics to sports. Indeed the pro ball game has succeeded in drawing huge crowds of spectators. It has contributed to diversifying the leisure activities of Koreans across the country."[21]

The Olympics and the Politics of Military Dictatorship

The division of Korea by outside powers following World War II remains the central political reality in that nation to this day. It underlies both the appropriateness and the poignancy of the Seoul Olympic opening ceremony theme, "Toward One World, Beyond All Barriers." With the events of 1991 in Eastern Europe and the Soviet Union, the continued presence of U.S. military forces in South Korea is perhaps the world's most prominent vestige of the cold war.

For the citizens of South Korea, two of the most pervasive consequences of national division and the cold war confrontation with North Korea were that stability was valued over all else and that the nation lived under military dictatorships that were at least tacitly supported by its major patron, the United States. The military-led governments of President Park Chung Hee, who assumed power in a 1961 military coup, and Chun Doo Hwan compiled a record of human rights abuses that included the arrest, jailing, and occasionally torture of dissidents and heavy-handed measures to control the media. Such abuses, together with growing public restiveness with the large role of military in national politics, led to the bloody Kwangju uprising in May 1980.

It is difficult to identify incidents in other nations that are exactly analogous to Kwangju, but Beijing's Tiananmen Square massacre is probably the closest, occurring as it did in Korea's East Asian neighbor and leading to bloodshed when the military cracked down on prodemocratic students and citizens. As Bruce Cumings noted in 1982, Kwangju "made the suppression of Solidarity in Poland seem like child's play."[22] The real bloodshed began when the military government sent in Black Beret troops, untrained in crowd control, to put down demonstrations in the capital city of South Cholla Province, a stronghold of opposition politics located near the hometown of opposition leader Kim Dae Jung. Enraged by the bloodletting, the citizens of Kwangju threw out those military forces and held their city for more than one week before armed forces led by Gen. Chun Doo Hwan ordered an early morning assault to retake it. Official government estimates acknowledge that close to 300 people died in Kwangju, but opposition political groups claim that 2,000 or more were killed.

What is most important for the present study is that Kwangju became a central reality of South Korean politics and a principal source of contention between the government and opposition groups during the years leading up to the Seoul Olympics. The uprising became a symbol and rallying cry that was inextricably related to the question of democratization, which, in the Korean context, meant ridding the government of military influence. Students, labor, intellectuals, and the opposition political parties generally agreed that a first step toward a more broadly based and democratic government would be a return to direct, popular election of the president—a procedure that had been outlawed with the imposition of the Yushin system by President Park Chung Hee in 1972.

As the Olympics approached, the whole question of elections and constitutional reform became more and more urgent, with the political opposition pushing for democratic change prior to the Seoul Olympics and the ruling party favoring the existing system or some variation on it. On April 13, 1987, President Chun, in a nationwide television address, announced plans to suspend the debate over constitutional reform until after the Olympic Games. This announcement sparked weeks of protests in the streets of Seoul and in dozens of other Korean cities, in which growing numbers of middle-class citizens joined with students and other opposition forces.

The June 29 Declaration

By June 1987, the political crisis in South Korea had deepened and was receiving considerable attention from the international media. This led several cities, including Berlin, Los Angeles, and New York, to publicly express their interest in staging the 1988 Games if Seoul was unable to host them because of the unrest.[23] IOC President Samaranch was repeatedly asked about the possibility of moving the Games from Seoul. On July 9, he stated,

> It will be Seoul only. I don't know any other solution. If there will be no games in Seoul, there will be no games at all next year. We are not considering any other city as an organizing post. They've had outstanding preparations in Seoul and I can say that never has any city showed such a degree of preparation. They do have some internal problems in South Korea, but I

think that situation is improving. We have received some very good news recently.[24]

Press accounts at the time indicated that Samaranch may have played a direct role in bringing about the resolution of the political standoff in Seoul. On a visit to that city, Romanian IOC member Alexandru Sipercu carried a letter from Samaranch "expressing the IOC's concern at the civil unrest." The letter was said to be for a high-ranking government official. Two days later, Roh Tae Woo, former SLOOC president, proposed his package of democratic reforms—the now-famous June 29 declaration. Samaranch would not elaborate on his involvement beyond saying, "I know the candidate for the presidency of the republic who has made the eight-point plan for reform and, since his statements, the situation is improving all the time."[25]

June 1987 also marked a period of new openness for the media in Korea. Late in the month, the *Hanguk Ilbo* published a front-page photograph of opposition politician Kim Dae Jung, who met with reporters after being released from two and one-half months of house arrest. For years, the government had forbidden the use of his picture, although editors had sometimes published pictures of Kim conducting political business with his back to the camera. Moreover, despite objections from the government, South Korean newspapers carried prominent stories reporting that other cities would seek to host the 1988 Summer Olympics if Seoul proved unable to hold them.[26]

All evidence suggests that the possibility of jeopardizing the Olympics was a decisive factor in the June 29 declaration. Roh Tae Woo's nationally televised speech came as a political bombshell. In it, he accepted virtually all of the opposition demands, point by point, including direct presidential elections and political amnesty for opposition leader Kim Dae Jung. He also made the following comments on the Seoul Olympics: "At a time when the Olympics are around the corner, all of us should be responsible for preventing the national disgrace of being mocked and derided by the international community because of a division in the national consensus."[27]

The declaration had an immediate effect across the political spectrum in Korea. It even moved opposition politician Kim Young Sam to declare that he "would like to see the Olympic Games successfully carried out" under a new government in the fall of the following year.[28]

An excerpt from a *Los Angeles Times* report was representative of an outpouring of press attention worldwide: "But most of all there was the matter of the 1988 Olympic Games, which could give this nation its finest moment in the world spotlight. Chun and Roh Tae Woo, chairman of the ruling party, joined South Korean and foreign analysts in citing the Olympics as an important reason for their overnight change of heart. To Roh, loss of the Games would have brought national humiliation to a nation that looks on 'saving face' as vital."[29]

In his television speech accepting the recommendations of the June 29 declaration, President Chun mentioned the Seoul Olympics twice. In one of those references he stated, "It will be the consistent hope of not only myself but also of you, the people, that we should carry out successfully by every means the continuous economic development, the peaceful transition of government, and the 1988 Seoul Olympics which will be a golden opportunity for national prosperity, thereby placing the country on the road towards becoming an advanced country."[30]

When asked how important the Olympics were as a factor in the decision for political change at the end of June, Chyun Sang Jim, deputy secretary-general of the Seoul Olympic Organizing Committee, replied, "Certainly they were a great factor in making the decision. President Chun and Mr. Roh were both very involved in getting the Olympic Games into Seoul. They both have a very strong personal commitment, obligation and attachment to hosting the Olympics."[31]

During the unrest in the spring of 1987, *Newsweek* magazine reported that NBC was also among those concerned. "NBC executives are taking no chances. *Newsweek* has learned that network officials have quietly contacted South Korean opposition leaders. The activists gave assurances that they have no objections to the Seoul Games—and that they would feel the same should they somehow come to power in the next year. Still, NBC is waiting for the turmoil to cool before opening a permanent office in Seoul.[32]

The June 29 declaration defused the volatile political situation and paved the way for elections later in the year, reassuring not only Koreans but also representatives from all branches of the Olympic family internationally. However, it actually postponed, rather than solved, the central political problems facing the nation. Among the most important agreements reached by the ruling party and political opposition prior to the Olympics was the decision to suspend inquiry into the Kwangju uprising and activities of President Chun's Fifth Republic until after the Olympics. These were taken up in hearings by the National Assembly in November 1988.

Televised Hearings on the Fifth Republic and Kwangju

With the Olympics successfully completed, political leaders once again turned their attention to unfinished business. Nationwide television coverage of the National Assembly hearings in November showed a procession of former ministers and confidants submitting to hostile questions from opposition lawmakers who probed allegations of massive abuse of power during President Chun's eight-year rule. Topics included the 1980 Kwangju uprising, the deaths of at least 54 inmates in military "reeduca-tion" camps, and the tactics used by Chun's aides in pressuring industrial-ists for political funds.

Although these hearings did not attract the global television audience of the Olympic Games, they set a precedent within South Korea. Portions of these hearings attracted the highest viewership ever recorded for a nationwide telecast by the Korean Broadcasting System.

As noted in Chapter 8, an estimated 22.2 million people, or 60 percent of the total potential audience of South Koreans, viewed the opening cere-monies of the Seoul Olympics.[33] By comparison, during the most crucial portions of the nationally televised hearings on Kwangju, when generals responsible for crucial decisions testified, citizens from all walks of life were pulled toward the television at home and at work. In Seoul, crowds gathered in shops, restaurants, offices, and bus stations to watch the testi-mony. Those who could not view television listened by radio and presum-ably viewed televised summaries of the testimony later. In the provincial capital of Kwangju, many companies gave employees the day off.

The hearings enjoyed the highest audience ratings ever, peaking at 62 percent during the daytime and exceeding even the Seoul Olympic Games as a TV spectacle. The state-run Korea Broadcasting System had planned to resume normal broadcasting at 5:30 P.M. on the first day of the hearings but canceled them after receiving a barrage of phone calls from citizens de-manding that the network stay with the assembly hearings.[34]

The Public Response

Public opinion polling in Korea before and during the Olympics provides some indication of the public response. Such survey results are of interest not only in the narrow sense of how the Koreans responded to the Seoul Olympics per se but also as a measure of the nature of Korea's new civic-mindedness and of the changes in public attitudes in a newly urbanized and industrialized nation in the midst of political liberalization.[35]

The Asian Games

Of particular interest are the results of a nationwide survey conducted be-fore and after the 1986 Asian Games.[36] The general purpose of that re-search was to measure public attitudes on a variety of political, economic, social, and cultural issues to see how they might be affected by the Asian Games experience. Major findings from the study bear on public use of the media and reflect the impact of the Asian Games on national development and pride, politics, sport, and the efficacy of the public campaigns discussed earlier. The following sections discuss each of these in turn.

Patterns of Interest and Media Usage. The 1986 Asian Games were the first major international sports event to be held in South Korea. As such, they generated a large amount of television coverage and attracted a great deal of public interest. The number of survey respondents who said they were "very" or "quite" interested in the Asian Games increased from 70.2 percent before the Games to 83.2 percent after. Television was cited as the principal source of information about the Games by 75 percent of respondents before the Games began, compared with only 12 percent who cited newspapers, the next most frequently mentioned source of information. However, perceived reliance on television shot up as a result of exposure to the Games, with 90 percent of all respondents citing it as their primary source of information in the survey following the Games, compared with only 7.4 percent who cited newspapers.[37]

National Development. The survey showed rather dramatically how an event like the Asian Games can affect the self-perception of a public. One of the survey questions asked whether respondents considered Korea to be "developed," "between developed and developing," "developing," "between developing and underdeveloped," or "underdeveloped." The proportion of respondents who considered the nation to be either developed or between developed and developing increased from 44.6 percent before the Asian Games to 59.4 percent following them.

Politics. The research included a battery of questions to measure the public's attitudes about the influence of the Asian Games on the nation's politics. Several of these deserve mention. First, the percentage of respondents who thought that "the '86 Asian Games will aid Korea's search for democracy" dropped from 50.9 percent in the pre-Games survey to 46.3 percent following the Games. Such a finding reflects the fact that the Asian Games preceded the decisive political change that began in June 1987 and were characterized by the prominent role of President Chun Doo Hwan and his military government. Quite simply, the Asian Games were organized and exploited in a highly visual fashion by a military regime that was not accorded a high level of legitimacy by the Korean public. John MacAloon and Kang Shin-Pyo, in an extensive analysis, attributed major changes in the ritual practices of the torch relay and opening ceremonies between the 1986 Asian Games and the 1988 Olympics to the underlying processes of political change taking place in Korea. Part of their analysis focused on the behavior of politicians who played a prominent role in the torch relay. In 1986, that behavior exuded political domination and tended to be addressed toward the party hierarchy in Seoul; in 1988, by contrast, there seemed to be a greater civic-mindedness, political politeness, and compliments to all constituencies assembled along the torch route.[38]

Another survey question asked if respondents felt that "the '86 Asian Games will be of help in the North-South dialogue." The proportion of respondents who answered affirmatively dropped from 36.2 percent before the Games to 25.4 percent after. The before-Games level probably reflected the lack of any North Korean participation in the Asian Games, along with a lack of any other public movement toward unification. The sharp drop undoubtedly was occasioned by the bombing at Kimpo Airport on the eve of the Games, attributed by authorities in Seoul to North Korean attempts to disrupt the hosting of the Games. The bomb killed five South Korean citizens and wounded thirty others.[39]

Two other related questions on the survey touch on the question of how an event such as the Asian Games might contribute to national pride. In the first, the number of respondents who thought that "the '86 Asian Games will be of help in creating a sense of unity in the nation" increased from 71 percent before the Games to 81.5 percent after them. In the second, responses indicating that "the '86 Asian Games are a good opportunity to promote patriotism" increased from 76.2 percent to 81.5 percent across the two surveys.

The research also addressed the Korean public's own view of the impact of the Asian Games on the nation's international prestige. The number of respondents who thought that the Games would "help boost Korea's international image and status" rose from 79.8 percent to 82.5 percent.

Sports in Korea. The number of respondents nationally who agreed that the Asian Games promoted the Korean people's "interest in sports" increased from 83.7 percent before the Games to 91.5 percent following. The public also thought that the Games helped to promote the standards or level of competition in various events, with the proportion who thought so increasing from 84.1 percent before the Games to 87.5 percent after. The researchers attributed this finding, in part, to the unexpectedly successful, medal-winning performance of Korean athletes.

Response to Public Campaigns. To measure the success of the various public campaigns undertaken by the government and social organizations, the research included a battery of questions on each of these efforts. The results showed large and positive changes for almost all of the campaigns:

- The number of respondents who thought traffic order was "very well kept" increased from 51.8 percent to 78.2 percent.
- Respondents who thought pedestrian behavior was "very well kept" increased from 48.3 percent to 70.4 percent.

- Those who thought sanitation in public restaurants was "satisfactory" increased from 35.9 percent to 59.6 percent.
- The proportion who thought taxi drivers were "polite" increased from 48.4 percent to 62.4 percent.
- The proportion who thought public order was "well kept" in queues increased from 47.1 percent to 70.1 percent.
- Those who thought the marked-price system was "well executed" increased from 22.5 percent to 33.7 percent.
- The proportion of people who thought public facilities were "used with care" increased from 36.6 percent to 52.1 percent.
- One of the largest changes occurred in perceptions of spectator behavior, with the proportion who thought spectators were "well behaved" increasing from 40.2 percent to 78.2 percent.

This last change illustrates an effect of the television broadcasting of the Games. Korean spectators knew very well that the Asian Games would be televised to many other nations in the region. Coupled with the traditional cultural value of showing one's best face to a guest, this awareness of television's larger audience was the principal reason for the large increase in the proportion of people who thought spectators were "well behaved." Indeed, they likely were, at least in comparison to the general behavior at sports contests before the scrutiny of international television.

The Seoul Olympics

Several public opinion polls were also conducted in South Korea during or immediately following the Olympics. One nationwide poll in early October 1988, immediately after the Olympics, obtained results generally in line with those of the earlier Asian Games study. It showed that, in the short term, the Olympic Games contributed to a burst of national pride. Approximately 88 percent of those surveyed felt that the Korean people had a strong response to the Games and that the Olympics had helped engender a sense of solidarity among the Korean people. On the related question of national prestige, about 91 percent of respondents believed that the Seoul Olympic Games had enhanced the international standing of Korea.[40]

A national survey conducted on October 1, 1988, near the end of the Olympic Games, corroborated their immediate influence on the public. When asked to name the most direct and largest influence of the Olympics, there were only two responses given by a large number of respondents. The first, given by 44.9 percent of respondents, was that the Olympics increased national pride. The other, coming from 22.5 percent of respondents, was that the Olympics had broadened the Korean public's view of the world. Both of these responses showed differences across age cohorts, with only 37.4 percent of people in their twenties naming an increase in national pride, compared with 54.3 percent of those age fifty or over. Conversely, 24 percent of respondents in their twenties thought that the Olympics had broadened their worldview, compared with only 18.5 percent of those over fifty.[41]

The post-Olympics survey also found that 79.1 percent of respondents thought the Olympic Games served to broaden international horizons, especially among the youth. This finding was interpreted by some analysts as contributing to political liberalization by helping to develop a pluralistic spirit of understanding.[42] The response to several questions about the impact of the Olympics on democratization showed that the public generally felt the Games had a positive effect, but there was also considerable wariness about the post-Olympic period. Approximately 56 percent of respondents thought the Olympics stimulated democratization, 53 percent agreed that they helped improve human rights, and 50 percent said that they contributed to freedom and fairness of the press. However, more than one-quarter of the public had negative responses to these same questions, and about 44 percent predicted that the political situation would become more unstable after the Games.[43] These findings reflect quite clearly the unresolved status of the central political issues facing the country. Although such events as the June 29 declaration in 1987 and the direct elections later that year represented progress, there had also been an agreement to postpone consideration of the underlying issues of Kwangju and the Fifth Republic of President Chun Doo Hwan. The October survey no doubt reflected public apprehension about this forthcoming political confrontation and inquiry.

The October 1988 survey also provided some corroboration for other estimates of the audience for Olympic television within Korea. It showed that 55 percent of respondents actively watched the Olympic telecasts and that 86 percent had seen at least some of the broadcasts.[44]

Taken as a whole, the information presented in this chapter demonstrates convincingly that the Seoul Olympics involved a massive mobilization that could never be completely separated in the public mind from the military dictatorship of Gen. Chun Doo Hwan and the unresolved issue of his government's involvement in Kwangju and related abuses. For many Koreans, the Seoul Olympics had a bad taste from the very beginning: People thought it was a military show. However, during the two years preceding the Games, mainstream opinion shifted toward the view that everyone should work for a successful Olympics out of national pride, regardless of how the Games came about. The survey findings reported here are consistent with this broad analysis. They also suggest a number of positive influences on the Korean public, such as the new awareness of other nations, especially among the young, and a strong belief shared by many that the Olympics had helped Korea's development. However, such influences mingled in the public mind with a pervasive awareness of the progress yet to be made toward democratization and removal of military influence in government. Consequently, the nationally televised hearings of the National Assembly added a strong punctuation mark to the successful conclusion of the Seoul Olympics and helped to explain why press and public discussion of the Olympics virtually disappeared in the weeks and months following the Games. Even to this day, Koreans who travel abroad are frequently greeted with discussions of the Olympics as seen on television or experienced through other media. In South Korea itself, except for formal anniversaries and official Olympic or sports-related activities, the success of the Seoul Olympics takes a back seat to other, more urgent matters on the public agenda.

Notes

1. Park Seh-Jik, "The Seoul Olympics: A People's Masterpiece (The Inside Story)," manuscript, 1991, pp. 1–11.

2. Choe Chungho, "Surmounting the Past: A Korean View of Japan and Germany," *Koreana* 4 (1990): pp. 99–105.

3. Vincent J. Ricquart, *The Games Within the Games: The Story Behind the 1988 Seoul Olympics* (Seoul, Korea: Hantong Books, 1988), p. 15.

4. Lee Dong Wook, *How to Prepare for the Olympics and Its Task* (Seoul, Korea: Lee Dong Wook, 1988), pp. 45–54.

5. Seoul Asian Games Organizing Committee, *10th Asian Games—Official Report: Organization and Planning* (Seoul, Korea: Seoul Asian Games Organizing Committee, December 31, 1987), p. 102.

6. Ibid., pp. 100–123.

7. Ibid., pp. 104–105.

8. Ibid., p. 119.

9. Edward W. Poitras, "Olympic Questions," *Korea Times*, September 18, 1988, p. 2.

10. Ibid.

11. Chung Dong-sung, "Q: Why Should Government Take Charge of Sports? A: Because Sports Represent Vital National Interests," *Koreana* 4 (1990): p. 2.

12. Koh Too-hyon, "Korea's 'Secret' Base for Sports: Taenung Athletes' Village," *Koreana* 4 (1990): p. 33.

13. Chung, "Q: Why Should Government Take Charge of Sports?" p.5.

14. Lee Bang-won, "Sports Nationalism in Korea: Decline Has Set in After Seoul Games," *Koreana* 4 (1990): p. 58.

15. Ibid., pp. 59–60.

16. Ibid., p. 60.

17. Koh, "Korea's 'Secret' Base for Sports," p. 35.

18. Ibid.

19. Ibid., p. 36.

20. Lee, "Sports Nationalism in Korea," p. 60.

21. Ibid., p. 61.

22. Bruce Cumings, "Devil to Pay in Seoul," *New York Times*, July 6, 1982, p. A17.

23. Mladen Jergovic, "Samaranch Says More Changes Possible in North Korean Offer," Reuters (Zagreb, Yugoslavia), July 9, 1987.

24. Ibid.

25. Morley Myers, "Sports News," United Press International (London), July 9, 1987.

26. John Burgess, "S. Korean Media's Brave News World; Demonstrations Started Cautious Flowering of a Restricted Press," *Washington Post*, July 6, 1987, p. A18.

27. *Hanguk Ilbo*, special edition, June 29, 1987.

28. Nick B. Williams and Mark Fineman, "Chun Party Chief Agrees to Reforms; Roh Backs Korea Protest Demands, Including Direct Vote for President," *Los Angeles Times*, June 29, 1987, pt. 1, p. 1.

29. Sam Jameson, "U.S. Reportedly Had Little Influence in South Korean Policy Turnabout," *Los Angeles Times*, July 3, 1987, pt. 1, p. 12.

30. The British Broadcasting Corporation, *Summary of World Broadcasts* (London: British Broadcasting Corporation, July 2, 1987), p. FE/8609/B/1.

31. Mark Fineman, "Future of Olympics Called 'Great Factor' in Regime's New Policy," *Los Angeles Times*, July 2, 1987, pt. 1, p. 10.

32. Nancy Cooper, "High-Stakes Games: Are the Olympics at Risk?" *Newsweek*, U.S. edition (June 29, 1987): p. 32.

33. ISL Marketing, *TOP: The Olympic Program*, handbook, ed. 2.90 (Lucerne, Switzerland: ISL Marketing, 1989), p. 5.13.

34. Karl Schoenberger, "Millions Captivated by Televised Probe into Bloody 1980 Uprising; Kwangju Hearings Have South Koreans Spellbound," *Los Angeles Times*, November 19, 1988, pt. 1, p. 3. Sonya Hepinstall, "TV Hearings Making, Breaking South Korean Political Careers," Reuters, November 17, 1988.

35. Lim Hysup, "Social Impact of the Asian Games and Seoul Olympiad in Korea," in Shin-pyo Kang, John MacAloon, and Roberto Da Matta, eds. *The Olympics and East/West and South/North Cultural Exchange* (Seoul, Korea: Institute for Ethnological Studies, Hanyang University, 1987), pp. 649–654.

36. Lee Sang Hwe, "The Survey on the Attitudes of the Korean People on the '86 Asian Games," Final report of the Korea Institute for Policy Studies, 1987.

37. Lee Sang Hwe, "The Survey on the Attitudes of the Korean People on the Xth Asian Games," in Shin-pyo Kang, John MacAloon, and Roberto Da Matta, eds., *The Olympics and East/West and South/North Cultural Exchange* (Seoul, Korea: Institute for Ethnological Studies, Hanyang University, 1987), p. 665.

38. John J. MacAloon and Kang Shin-Pyo, "*Uri Nara:* Korean Nationalism, the Seoul Olympics, and Contemporary Anthropology," in *Toward One World Beyond All Barriers*, proceedings of the Seoul Olympiad Anniversary Conference, vol. 1, (Seoul, Korea: Poong Nam Publishing, 1990), pp. 117–159.

39. Clyde Haberman, "From Conciliatory Talk to a Bitter Accusation," *New York Times*, September 21, 1986, Sec. 4, p. 2.

40. Kim Jong-gie, Rhee Sang-woo, Yu Jae-cheon, Ku Kwang-mo, and Hong Jong-duck, *Impact of the Seoul Olympic Games on National Development* (Seoul: Korea Development Institute, 1989), pp. 27–28.

41. National survey conducted by professors Kim Hak Soo, Department of Mass Communication, Sogang University, and Park Yong Shin, Department of Sociology, Yonsei University, October 1, 1988. Survey results were provided by the researchers.

42. Kim et al., *Impact of the Seoul Olympic Games on National Development*, p. 78.

43. Ibid., pp. 28–29.

44. Ibid., p. 34.

7

"Toward One World, Beyond All Barriers": Olympic Diplomacy and Korea's New International Relations

Introduction

When the Olympics were awarded to Seoul, South Korea's lack of diplomatic relations with the Socialist bloc nations of the world was thought by many to pose a serious obstacle to their success. However, for Korea, this potential obstacle presented a unique opportunity to pursue a new, more independent foreign policy, built around the establishment of relations with the Soviet Union, China, and other nations of the Socialist bloc. A central goal of such a policy would be to create an international climate more conducive to eventual Korean reunification. Moreover, given Korea's recent economic growth and its export-led economy, establishing relations with as many countries in the world community as possible suited its national interests.

In the pursuit of these goals South Korea saw the Olympics as an ideal vehicle, in no small part because of the attendant television and media coverage they would generate. However, actual research on the image of Korea conveyed by television and the other media, along with the effects on public attitudes, was conducted in only a few of the 160 nations that participated in the Seoul Olympics. The purpose here is to outline major aspects of the relationship between the Seoul Olympics and South Korea's international relations, pointing when possible to the role that actual or prospective television and media coverage played.

The Seoul Olympics also catapulted South Korea into a highly visible and important place within the Olympic movement, especially with respect to the future place of Asian nations in that movement. The manner in which Korea assumed this role sheds light on both the Olympics as a transnational actor in the world system and on how one nation participates in such transnational activity. Therefore, this chapter will discuss the growing influence of South Korea within the Olympic movement and the IOC. Also discussed is the extensive involvement of Korean industry in the Beijing Asian Games, which assumed particular importance given that city's bid to host the Olympics in the year 2000.

The Seoul Olympics and Nordpolitik

A report of the Korea Development Institute offered a succinct description of the origins and purposes of Nordpolitik.

> The Korean people having lived for forty years as a divided nation have as their greatest desire the reunification of their homeland, and the most urgent matter at hand is to overcome the suffering resulting from this division. From a more realistic point of view, Koreans aspire toward a daily life without the fear of a constant threat to security from the North Korean communist regime, to mitigate the suicidal competition of national struggle carried out against North Korea in international relations and to act freely in the international arena.
>
> To create an atmosphere conducive to improved South-North relations, Korea is interested in establishing friendly relations with socialist countries such as the Soviet Union and China, supporters of North Korea.[1]

Of the 160 countries that eventually participated in the Seoul Olympics, there were 144 sovereign states and 15 territories without sovereign status. Of those, 24 had no diplomatic relations with South Korea.[2] The most important of these were the Soviet Union and China because of their leadership positions within the Socialist bloc and their special geopolitical relationship with Korea.

The Soviet Union

The participation of the Soviet Union was of immense importance because of its role in the division of Korea, its close cold war relationship with North Korea, and its boycott of the Los Angeles Olympics in response to the U.S.-led boycott of the 1980 Moscow Olympics. Moreover, the Soviet Union wielded considerable influence over the Socialist bloc nations of

Eastern Europe and their possible participation in the Seoul Olympics. Kim Un-Yong reported that in many meetings with his colleagues from international sports federations during the years leading up to 1988, those from Eastern Europe would frequently allude to the Soviet Union. In Kim's words, "For them, the Kremlin was everything."[3]

From the very start of its planning for the Olympics, South Korea aggressively sought to utilize every possible contact with representatives of the Soviet Union to ensure their participation in the Olympics and to work toward the longer-term goal of fostering a broad and stable relationship. Although the Soviet Union proceeded more slowly, it took the same path. Of course, the shooting down of KAL flight 007 in 1983 slowed the early process of establishing Korean-Soviet contacts. The very first contact between planners of the Seoul Olympics and any representative of the Soviet Sports Ministry took place during the Los Angeles Olympics and involved a Soviet official who was attending the Games, despite the boycott, in his capacity as president of the Cycling Federation. The meeting was arranged with the help of Horst Dassler of Adidas.[4]

The contrast between South Korea's eagerness to improve ties with the Soviet Union and the USSR's cautious but steady approach was nowhere more apparent than in the activities of the media in the two nations during the buildup to the Olympics. In South Korea, the media put on a strong push to carry as much news and commentary from the Socialist nations as possible. For example, *Chosun Ilbo*, South Korea's largest circulation daily newspaper, solicited and carried a series of front-page articles on the Seoul Olympics written by prominent scholars or journalists in the Socialist nations, including the Soviet Union. The behavior of Soviet media contrasted sharply. In the words of James Riordan, a longtime student of sport in the Soviet Union,

> Throughout the run-up to the Olympics *no informative material* (beyond current political events) on the Olympic host appeared in the Soviet media. The silence was truly deafening. Even during the Games, despite the presence of 91 journalists from the USSR, many from non-sports periodicals like *Ogonyok* and *Literaturnaya Gazeta* (both popular literary weeklies), there was no attempt to educate or even inform the Soviet public in regard to Korean culture, everyday life, sports amenities or the developing relations between the host and Eastern Europe. For example, as he confirmed to me, the *Literaturnaya Gazeta* correspondent, Vladimir Sharov, wrote two short pieces—one on the arrival of the Soviet ship in Inchon (on which he stayed) and one on Gorbachev's Krasnoyarsk proposals—on 14 and 21 September, and *nothing subsequently*. Other reporters confined themselves to sport, as did the Soviet TV coverage (190 hours in total, including the Opening and Closing ceremonies).[5]

For the Soviet Union, the decision to attend the Seoul Olympics—let alone engage in a series of contacts with South Korea—marked a reversal of its position in 1981, when it had voted with other Communist nations against awarding the Olympics to Seoul. Riordan suggested that several major factors led to the changed Soviet view.

- To a significant degree, the political changes under way in South Korea opened the way for the USSR and its allies to compete in Seoul. "For Soviet leaders, themselves contemplating a transition from a totalitarian to a pluralist society, the experience of the South Korean regime's dealing with opposition parties was of particular import."[6]
- A breeze of change had swept through the USSR since 1985 and Gorbachev's *realpolitik* of moving away from confrontation internationally.
- The USSR could not be sure of receiving full support from its allies if it had chosen to stay away from Seoul. Indeed, in 1987, Hungary and Poland unilaterally declared their intention to attend the Seoul Olympics.
- The USSR would have forfeited political prestige with a boycott of Seoul.
- Soviet leaders may well have felt that their participation in Seoul might help Korea move toward reunification.
- The economic performance and skillful diplomacy of South Korea itself were important. Soviet periodicals had given a great deal of attention to economic growth rates in South Korea, as one of the four East Asian "tigers."
- Nearly half a million Koreans lived in the USSR, mainly in Uzbekistan, Kazakhastan, Turkmenia, and on the island of Sakhalin.[7]

On September 16, 1988—the day before the Seoul Olympic opening ceremony—Soviet leader Mikhail Gorbachev made a speech at Krasnoyarsk in Siberia in which he declared, "There is a possibility that economic exchanges with Korea could be established."[8] His choice of those words on that date and in that place were certainly no accident. *Asiaweek* referred to the speech as a "Siberian serenade." The underlying economic reality was that the Soviet Union needed industrial and technological assistance from nations like Korea and Japan if it was to develop the resource-rich region of Siberia. By giving the speech in Krasnoyarsk when he did, Ghorbachev was using the international media to send a positive signal to South Korea, while simultaneously putting North Korea and the other major political actors in the region on notice of Soviet intentions.

The South Korean contact with the Soviet Union involved not only sports officials and athletes but also trade and business delegations and cultural and academic exchanges. A number of concrete steps were taken by the two countries—short of opening up formal diplomatic relations but nevertheless significant. For example, Korean Air, the national flag carrier of South Korea, was given permission to fly over Soviet territory, initially in connection with the Olympic Games. The Korean government permitted the 12,800-ton ship *Mikhail Sholokov* to berth at Inchon Harbor from September 3 through October 6, 1988. The ship transported, housed, and fed nearly 200 Soviet athletes and officials for the duration of the Games and transported Soviet Olympic yachts and medical and technical equipment.[9] To see a ship flying the Soviet flag and with the hammer and sickle emblazoned on its smokestack in Inchon Harbor—site of U.S. Gen. Douglas MacArthur's landing during the Korean War—was a dramatic reminder of the already changed relationship between South Korea and the Soviet Union.

The Soviets were very responsive to the Seoul Olympic planners' emphasis on cultural programs and sent the Moscow Philharmonic Orchestra, the Bolshoi Ballet, and the Moscow State Radio and TV Choir to the Games. The latter group included two Soviet-Korean vocalists, soprano Nelli Lee and mezzo-soprano Ludmilla Nam. The Olympic gymnastics champion from the 1976 and 1980 Games, Nelli Kim, born in the USSR of a Korean father and a Russian mother, gave televised classes in Seoul under the aegis of the Korean Gymnastics Association.[10] Virtually all the cultural exchanges and other activities involving the Soviet Union received extensive coverage on television and in the other media of South Korea.

China

South Korea's relationship with the People's Republic of China also changed during the Olympic period but not in such a public way as did its contacts with the USSR. In part because of its relationship with North Korea, China engaged in very little public discussion of improving its ties with South Korea. However, on a practical level, the so-called back door or indirect trade continued to increase. In 1988, it reached approximately $3 billion. From January through October of the Olympic year, 3,105 South Korean business representatives visited China, twenty times the number in that period during the previous year.[11] By 1991, the overall level of trade between the two nations had reached more than $5.8 billion, and with the establishment of formal diplomatic relations in 1992, many observers predicted that trade would nearly double to about $10 billion that year.[12] Such a level would have made China the third largest trading partner with Korea.

The growing trade between South Korea and China was based on the underlying economic logic that one country, China, possessed energy and resources while the other country, Korea, could provide technology and capital investment. In addition, the two nations shared a strong interest in Olympic sport. Indeed, China sought and Korea eagerly provided assistance with the Asian Games in Beijing, coming on the heels of the 1988 Olympics. Such collaboration would have implications for the success of Beijing's bid to host the Olympic Games in the year 2000, as we will discuss.

Other Socialist Nations

Korea's activities with respect to the Soviet Union and China were also aimed, by extension, at the Socialist nations of Eastern Europe. Efforts to establish ties with those countries were hindered by a lack of contact in the past. Koreans had worked with Americans, Japanese, or Germans in one way or another during most of the twentieth century, but there was no common experience or language with nations like Poland, Hungary, or Czechoslovakia. In practical terms, this made it extremely difficult to communicate with those countries, whether on a personal or an institutional level.

Given the lack of past contact, the Seoul Olympics served as a large, multifaceted vehicle for communication, helping to establish sound relations with the Socialist bloc nations and laying the groundwork for Korea's northern diplomacy. Sports authorities from all participating nations had to deal directly with the South Koreans regarding the many details of Olympic participation. As Kim Un-Yong put it when describing his own efforts on behalf of the Seoul Olympic Organizing Committee, "I started to use the phrase 'Olympic relations' instead of diplomatic relations in my discussions. Our common language was sports. Sports could surpass many barriers."[13]

Furthermore, it should be stressed that the organizers of the Olympics in Seoul put together a program that extended far beyond sports coverage and arrangements for the media. Activities involving the arts and cultural exchange, for example, were extensive. However, the scholarly activities promoted by the Seoul Olympic Organizing Committee provide the best single example of a uniquely Korean addition to the normal Olympic program; they also served the important purpose of expanding contact with individuals from the Socialist nations. Prior to Seoul, the major scholarly undertaking associated with the Games had been the Olympic Scientific Congress, which, though it involved many academics, was traditionally focused rather narrowly on such areas as sports science and the physiology of sport. The SLOOC broke sharply from that tradition by convening scholars from around the world to address and discuss a broad range of topics. The World Academic Conference of the Seoul Olympiad, held during the weeks immediately preceding the Games in 1988, and the Seoul Olympiad Anniversary Conference were two major efforts. Scholars from the Soviet Union, China, and other Socialist countries were well represented at these gatherings. Because the organization of these conferences was placed in the hands of professors from some of the leading universities in Seoul, the meetings served as an invaluable means for Seoul's academic organizations and individuals to establish direct contact with their counterparts in the Socialist nations.

A major breakthrough toward full participation of the Socialist bloc nations in the Seoul Olympics came when Korea hosted the fifth Association of National Olympic Committees (ANOC) convention in April 1986. The meeting was attended by 150 nations, including 30 with whom Korea did not, at the time, have diplomatic relations. Among those 30 were the Soviet Union and many countries of Eastern Europe. At the close of the convention in Seoul, IOC President Samaranch congratulated Roh Tae Woo, then chairman of the ruling Democratic Justice Party, and stressed the significance of such full attendance by Socialist bloc nations. His congratulatory comment underscored a consideration that is central to this study: "Because of distorted reports in the world press, people thought some sort of revolution was going on in Korea. But when they actually came here and saw this country, they must have realized that those news stories were total fabrications. They also found out that there were absolutely no terrorist incidents occurring in Korea."[14]

The point to be underscored here is a powerful one. For many Socialist nations *prior to about 1986*, the press may have offered up a stereotypical picture of South Korea that stressed political unrest and violence. Such a finding would not be surprising in view of what we know about the mainstream media treatment of Korea even in a country like the United States.

To the extent that communication between South Korea and Socialist nations prior to the Seoul Olympics was either nonexistent or mediated through fragmented and stereotyped press coverage, the concept of *disintermediation* helps explain what occurred during the Olympics project. Dayan and Katz borrowed the term from the world of finance to describe the process in which media events allow their principals to bypass a traditional intermediary and talk directly to a new public. Examples would include Egyptian President Sadat talking directly to the Israelis, over the heads of their leaders, or the Pope talking directly to the people of Poland, bypassing Communist dignitaries and local prelates on his visit to that country.[15]

Schematically, the phenomenon of disintermediation as it occurred through the Seoul Olympics can be thought of as follows.

- Korea using multiple opportunities offered by the Olympics to
- talk with the public in Socialist nations
- over the head of traditional intermediaries (press, friendly nations)

Simply put, the Seoul Olympics offered South Korea an opportunity for direct, rather than mediated, communication with people in many of the Socialist nations.

In summary, the Seoul Olympics gave worldwide exposure to Korea's Northern policy and simultaneously put leaders of South Korea's key institutions in direct contact with their counterparts in the Socialist nations. The success of that policy is now a matter of historical record. In February 1989, Korea established diplomatic relations with Hungary, then with Poland in November and Yugoslavia in December. Ties were established with Czechoslovakia, Bulgaria, and Romania in March 1990 and with the Soviet Union six months later.[16] In the fall of 1992, formal relations were established with the People's Republic of China.

The Negotiations with North Korea

Among the cruel ironies of the Seoul Olympics was that, despite the participation of more nations than ever in the past, Korea remained divided against itself and negotiations aimed at securing North Korea's participation ultimately failed. The history of sports talks between North and South Korea dates from 1963 and involves twenty-four rounds of talks since that time. In 1957, the IOC had tentatively recognized the North Korean Olympic Committee as a regional representative, with the consent of the (South) Korean Olympic Committee (KOC). The talks between South and North Korean officials began after the IOC, during its fifty-ninth general session in Moscow in 1962, urged the two Koreas to send a unified delegation to the 1964 Tokyo Olympics.[17]

The awarding of the Olympic Games to Seoul offered a chance to renew the off-and-on sports contacts between North and South Korea. It was three months after Seoul's bid had been successful that the people of North Korea learned about it through an article in the *Rodong-sinmun*. According to that article,

Recently South Korean military fascists have been mobilizing high-ranking officials and related staff of the puppet government as well as pro-government trumpeters to raise a ridiculous hullabaloo every day about the Olympics, which are said to be going to be held in Seoul in 1988. Now the puppets of South Korea are approaching Socialist nations and non-aligned countries in the hope of establishing diplomatic and official relations in order to have their "state" recognized as a legitimate one.[18]

During the years leading up to the Seoul Olympics, several incidents complicated efforts at South-North cooperation. One was the bombing during President Chun's October 1983 visit to Burma that killed seventeen South Korean government officials, including Deputy Prime Minister Suh Seuk-jun. In the immediate aftermath of the bombing, rumors circulated that the perpetrators might have been South Korean. Park Seh-Jik, who was dispatched to Burma in his capacity as a senior official of the National Security Planning Agency, held a press conference at the Korean Embassy because, as he later described it, he "thought it necessary to prevent overseas public opinion from turning against us at an early stage when rumor might be turned into 'fact.'"[19] Eventually, evidence pointed toward North Korean involvement in the bombing and led Burmese leaders to sever diplomatic relations and order all North Korean diplomats in their country to leave within forty-eight hours.[20]

A second incident was the November 1987 bombing of KAL flight 858, in which 115 passengers lost their lives. The arrest of Kim Hyon-hi by South Korean officials and her public confession to involvement in the bombing once again focused public attention on the North Korean threat to the Olympics. Later, reflecting on the incident, Seoul Olympic Organizing Committee President Park Seh-Jik wrote, "I believe it is owing above all to the sacrifice of the lives of the 115 victims of the KAL 858 bombing that the Seoul Olympics were carried out safely. Even Kim Il-sung could not risk any more propaganda failures of that magnitude."[21]

Beginning in 1984, suggestions began to surface that some form of cohosting arrangement should be considered for the 1988 Olympics. The Soviet Union played a key role by suggesting to South Korea that its own participation might be made more difficult if North Korea continued to object and that it would be advisable for Seoul to share several events with North Korea. By late 1984, an agreement had been reached for direct talks between representatives of North and South Korea under the supervision of the International Olympic Committee in Lausanne, Switzerland. Subsequently, several meetings and a series of negotiations were held. Although a comprehensive summary of the talks is beyond the scope and purpose of this chapter, it is worth noting that at the very first meeting (in Lausanne during October 1985), North Korea proposed that "profits from telecast rights shall be shared equally."[22] North Korea maintained that demand through the fourth and final North-South meeting, which took place on July 14 and 15 in Lausanne. According to Korea's IOC member, Kim Un-Yong, "It would have been very difficult to break up Seoul's TV rights for

Pyongyang at that time because all TV rights were based on contracts, but the IOC was considering giving $20 million to Pyongyang for TV installations assistance and the OIRT was investigating the technical feasibility of providing technical assistance to Pyongyang."[23]

The question of possible television coverage of the Olympics in North Korea arose again only days before the start of the Games. On September 12, 1988, Michele Verdier, information director of the International Olympic Committee, said that the IOC had offered North Korea free television coverage of the Seoul Games. She told a news conference that the offer was made by IOC President Juan Antonio Samaranch after North Korean officials were quoted as saying in Pyongyang that they had been unable to reach an agreement over live TV coverage of the Games. She said the IOC had sent a message to North Korea, stating that the country would be able to receive live broadcasts through the OIRT, (the Eastern bloc broadcasters' organization) free of charge, if it so desired. North Korea is a member of the OIRT, which had signed a Seoul Olympic TV rights contract with the Seoul Olympic Organizing Committee.[24]

The unrest in South Korea during the spring of 1987 posed a threat to the ongoing negotiations with North Korea and powerfully illustrated how the spotlight of television and world media coverage affected the principals in the negotiations. Kim Chong Ha, president of South Korea's National Olympic Committee and the chief negotiator in meetings with North Korean sports officials, stated in an interview published on June 29 that he had been troubled by the antigovernment protests that had raged since June 10. "I went through a lot of agony. If the turbulence continued, North Korea would raise more unreasonable demands concerning the Olympics, and then communist-bloc nations would support the North Koreans," he said. Kim added that he was ashamed when continuing political turmoil at home led cities like Indianapolis and West Berlin to say they were ready to host the 1988 Games in South Korea's stead. "I was worried because if that sort of thing continued the Seoul Olympics would be a failure. In that case we would suffer an irrecoverable loss of prestige in the world community."[25]

Several aspects of the North-South negotiations about the Seoul Olympics bear on central themes of our research. First, although the actual negotiations were held behind closed doors, they were shaped by considerations of highly public diplomacy. The tone was set with the initial decision to bid for the Seoul Olympics, which made the important assumption that the Games would help South Korea in its propaganda battle with the North. Accordingly, representatives from Seoul viewed the negotiations in the context of how events like the Burma bombing or domestic political unrest might affect world public opinion. If Seoul were not viewed as a safe location for the Games, the participation of key nations could easily be lost.

Second, it was apparent that the key parties to these negotiations all recognized the centrality of television and other media to any possible cohosting of the 1988 Olympics. North Korea, the International Olympic Committee, and South Korea all demonstrated such an awareness in concrete ways. The North was explicit from the beginning in asking for a share of television rights revenues.

Concerns over television and other media point to a third and final consideration, the inherent conflict between a closed and government-directed media system like North Korea's and an Olympics in which television and the press have arguably become the single most important members of the Olympic family. During the waning years of the cold war, much has been made about North Korea's status as the lone surviving Communist state, under the leadership of Kim Il-Sung. The core concept of North Korean ideology under Kim is *Juche*, a philosophy of self-reliance and independence. The term was first used in a 1955 speech in which Kim castigated some colleagues for being too pro-Soviet. It is virtually impossible to read a newspaper or listen to a speech in North Korea without hearing references to Juche. It takes Korean ideas as basic and foreign ideas as secondary, while calling for absolute unity at home and self-reliance and independence vis-à-vis the rest of the world.[26] Under the ironclad rule of Kim Il-Sung, North Korea has had no concept of an independent press, and the government has maintained total control over the flow of information. Given this historical context, North Korea was caught on the horns of a dilemma, however attractive the prospect of sharing the 1988 Olympics with the South may have been.

A strong clue about the conflict North Korea must have felt came in May 1987 when it denied passage from North to South Korea through Panmunjom for an IOC inspection team led by Alexandru Sipercu, president of the Romanian National Olympic Committee. The denial prompted IOC President Samaranch to send a protest letter, pointedly asking, "How can mass traffic through Panmunjom be possible, if North Korea cannot even approve the symbolic passage by the IOC delegation?"[27] A high proportion of the "mass traffic" referred to by Samaranch would have been television and media personnel. This was directly acknowledged later by Kim Un-Yong, who wrote that "Pyongyang was not really ready to accept 25,000 accredited athletes, officials and press and TV, especially those from the West."[28]

The failure to achieve success in the North-South talks over some form of participation in the 1988 Olympics provided one more example, if such were needed, of the depth and intransigence of Korea's national division. At the same time, it clearly suggested the important role that telecommunications and travel will have to play in Korea's reunification. The modern Olympics are so intrinsically a television and media phenomenon that any agreement by North and South Korea to share hosting of the 1988 Olympics would necessarily have meant a significant opening of the sealed border at the DMZ. Notably, as of this writing, the two Koreas reached formal agreement in 1992 on a number of exchanges, one of which was to establish a telephone link between military headquarters in Pyongyang and those in Seoul. This step, reminiscent of the old "hot line" between Washington, D.C., and Moscow during the early cold war years, contrasts sharply with the global focus of television and press on Seoul in 1988. Although highly symbolic and positive, it indicates how much remains to be done before any semblance of free communication between North and South will be possible.

Korean-U.S. Relations

While South Korea's relations with countries in the Socialist bloc and beyond generally improved in connection with the Olympics, its relationship with the United States—already on a rocky road—suffered a pronounced setback as the Games became what Donald Clark appropriately termed "an arena for anti-Americanism."[29] He argued convincingly that the roots of Korean anti-Americanism are found in several basic, stereotypical, and sometimes contradictory images of the United States held by most Koreans born after 1945.

The first of these stereotypes casts the United States as a protector and benefactor. It is disillusioning to Koreans who hold such a view to learn that, even after five decades of military, political, and economic involvement with Korea, most U.S. citizens can hardly find it on a map. In the second view, the United States is seen as a "careless colossus." According to this view, a great deal of U.S. policy toward Korea is inadvertent because so much policy-relevant information filters back to Washington, D.C., from only a few key places in Seoul. As Clark put it, "In a pattern reminiscent of Chungking and Saigon, cultivating key Americans becomes an art, based on the knowledge that the American side isn't really paying attention."[30] The third stereotype is that of the United States as an "ailing giant," an image fostered by the "loss" of the Vietnam War, the fall of the Shah in Iran, and the oil shocks and subsequent economic difficulties. Finally, there is a fourth, highly ideological stereotype that sees the United States as a "ruthless hegemon." In this view, most popular among radical students and some intellectuals, the United States is pictured as having sought only to dominate and exploit Korea, without ever considering the best interests of the Korean people.

These Korean views of the United States did not arise in a historical vacuum. For hundreds of years before contact with the West, Korea "practiced a form of calculated submission to China called *sadaejuui*, in which the Koreans paid copious amounts of tribute to obtain Chinese protection."[31] In Confucian terms, this could be considered an ethical arrangement similar to the older brother-younger brother relationship. However, it also involved an element of abasement or humiliation, memories of which were aggravated for many educated Koreans during the period of Japanese colonial rule between 1910 and 1945. Against this backdrop, U.S. influence in South Korea since 1945 assumes a degree of historic meaning not intended by the U.S. side. Moreover, expressions of anti-Americanism, such as those that occurred during the Seoul Olympics, can be viewed in this historical context as a "mirror of Korean pride" and a genuine effort on the part of the Korean people to put an end to sadaejuui forever.[32]

In recent years, trade issues, the U.S. military presence in Korea, and Korean perceptions about the U.S. role in relation to the 1980 Kwangju uprising have all helped to shape public views of the United States. Moreover, they are also the product of schooling and political socialization. In that light, as Clark observed, the textbook treatment of the United States in Korean schools is outdone by the mass media treatment—the barrage of movies, television programs, music, and printed media to which Koreans have been exposed during the cold war years. In this regard, the U.S. Armed Forces Korea Network has been a particularly strong influence for more than thirty years, televising an authentic mix of U.S. television fare.

As these comments make clear, the sources of difficulty in U.S.-Korean relations are not to be found in the Olympics alone, nor in television coverage of the Games per se. Nevertheless, it was NBC Television's reporting in Seoul that provided the major spark igniting a wave of public antagonism toward the United States. The controversy even provoked the following broadcast comment from North Korea's Central News Agency, KCNA, under a headline that read, "American Athletes Insult Korean National Dignity at Seoul Olympics":

> Some athletes of the U.S. Olympic team marched, wearing the mock ears of the Mickey Mouse at the opening ceremony of the single-hosted Olympic games in Seoul on September 17. The South Korean [words indistinct] this as another insult of the U.S. imperialist aggressors [words indistinct]. Last year U.S. ambassador to Seoul Lilley uttered the insulting words "King Kong Korea," implying that the South Korean patriotic students and people involved in the anti-U.S. struggle for independence are like "King Kong" in a motion picture. It is not fortuitous that indignation was expressed in copies of a literature scattered on campuses in Seoul on September 20, which said: "The ugly looks of the Yankees were clearly seen at the march of the opening ceremony."[33]

The North Korean broadcast comment was one more small but somehow telling sign of the growing prominence of the media, especially television, in relations among nations. Because the media and the images they convey are so central to contemporary international relations, the origins and nature of the NBC controversy and the turn for the worse in U.S.-Korean relations will be treated in considerable detail in the following chapter.

The Future of Olympic Television in Asia

The Seoul Olympics greatly increased South Korea's influence within the Olympic movement, with direct implications for the future of the movement in Asia. In part, this was a natural consequence of hosting the 1988 Games. The various requirements of infrastructure, organization, and planning for the modern Olympic Games ensure that each successive host city assumes a prominent role in the movement for a period of years. However, in the case of Seoul, the geopolitical and historical circumstances were especially favorable.

Seoul marked the return of the Summer Olympics to East Asia nearly a quarter century after Japan's success with the 1964 Games in Tokyo. However, it was a new and rapidly transforming East Asia to which the Olympics had returned. Not only was the end of the cold war in sight but the region was also in the midst of a sustained period of economic growth, symbolized by the experience of South Korea and the other "tigers" of the region—Hong Kong, Taiwan, and Singapore. Clearly, the Olympic movement would require a strong future presence in this region for its very survival. Both its universalistic ideals and the practical, commercial realities of maintaining a dependable stream of income from worldwide television rights and sponsorship seemed to demand no less.

A strong future presence in Asia would appear to dictate that the Olympic movement expand its presence beyond Japan. Regional concerns about the Japanese economic juggernaut or Japan as an "economic animal" undoubtedly translated into some concerns about an overreliance on the Japanese for the technology and expertise to host the Olympics. In a broad historical context, Korea's role as Olympic host took on added importance and gave it increased stature within the Olympic movement because of the unresolved legacy of Japan's regional role during and before World War II. As this volume goes to press, the issue of Japan's activities in World War II, including the recruitment of "comfort women" by the Japanese Army, is being widely discussed from the Philippines to China to Korea.

Professor Choe Chungho's analysis, mentioned briefly in the preceding chapter, contrasted the postwar behavior of Japan with that of Germany. Although both nations are widely acknowledged to have committed horrendous war crimes, they differed profoundly, he argued, in their internal attitude toward the past. German scholars and politicians took up the question of guilt and the problem of "surmounting the past" immediately after the war. They were also under the watchful eye of both Socialist bloc and Western nations for any sign of a resurgence of neo-Nazism.

For Japan, on the other hand, the bombing of Hiroshima and Nagasaki helped to liberate the country from any sense of moral guilt over its past. Almost overnight, Japan came to regard itself as a pitiable victim of the war. It became a leader in the world peace movement and, according to Choe, pursued a "gigantic nationwide public relations strategy" to rally people in all walks of life and across the whole political spectrum. This campaign succeeded in encouraging a kind of "Hiroshima sentimentalism" among intellectuals all over the world. He argued further that "the position of Japan as defendant against war crimes charges and war responsibility in the Pacific was reversed to that of plaintiff to denounce the United States to the world. Thus, Japan is obliterating the moral responsibility of the past for the mass massacre of Koreans with bamboo spears in the wake of the great earthquake in the 'Kanto' region and for the mass murder of 10 million Chinese people in mainland China."[34]

When China's turn came to host the 1990 Asian Games in Beijing, South Korea lavished every manner of assistance on the Chinese hosts. Having successfully hosted both the Asian Games and the Olympics, Seoul was eager to provide technical, financial, and other assistance. Business took a leading role in these efforts, as China brought in about $15 million in revenue from commercial billboards rented by South Korean corporations. In addition, Hyundai and other automobile manufacturers donated 400 cars to help transport athletes and officials during the Games.[35]

Looking to the future, two other elements may strongly influence the course of the Olympics in Asia and, by extension, globally. One was the 1992 election in Barcelona of Kim Un-Yong, South Korea's representative on the International Olympic Committee, as IOC vice president. Both he and South Korea as a nation are well positioned for future activities in Asia. The second major element, Beijing's bid to host the Olympics in the year 2000, could have a transforming effect on Olympic sport in East Asia. If Beijing should be successful, the effects will undoubtedly extend to international relations. In any event, the historical precedent is there. The International Olympic Committee awarded the 1988 Olympic Games to Korea when its government was widely understood to have a strong-arm military government. Concerns about human rights and domestic politics in China after Tiananmen Square may likewise have little bearing on the choice of a host city for the historic year 2000.

Notes

1. Kim Jong-gie, Rhee Sang-woo, Yu Jae-cheon, Koo Kwang-mo, Hung Jong-duck, *Impact of the Seoul Olympic Games on National Development* (Seoul: Korea Development Institute, 1989), p. 4.

2. Ibid., pp. 16–17.

3. Kim Un-Yong, *The Greatest Olympics: From Baden-Baden to Seoul* (Seoul, Korea: Si-sa-yong-o-sa, 1990), p. 116.

4. Ibid., p. 117.

5. James Riordan, "The Tiger and the Bear: Korean-Soviet Relationship in Light of the Olympic Games," in *Toward One World Beyond All Barriers*, proceedings of the Seoul Olympiad Anniversary Conference (Seoul, Korea: Poong Nam Publishing, 1990), pp. 340–341.

6. Ibid., p. 333.

7. Ibid., pp. 334–337.

8. FBIS Daily Report: Soviet Union, September 20, 1988, pp. 29–41.

9. Riordan, "The Tiger and the Bear," p. 338.

10. Ibid., pp. 338–339.

11. Kim et al., *Impact of the Seoul Olympic Games*, p. 14.

12. "Quick Off the Mark," *Korea Trade & Business* (October 1992): p. 12.

13. Kim, *The Greatest Olympics*, p. 119.

14. Park Seh-Jik, *The Seoul Olympics: The Inside Story* (London: Bellew Publishing, 1991), p. 24.

15. Daniel Dayan and Elihu Katz, *Media Events: The Live Broadcasting of History* (Cambridge, Mass.: Harvard University Press, 1992).

16. Young Whan Kihl, "Foreign Relations: Diplomatic Activism and Policy Dilemmas," in Donald N. Clark, ed., *Korea Briefing 1991* (Boulder, Colo.: Westview Press, 1991), p. 59.

17. Lee Tae-young, "World's Longest Sports Talks: Thirty Years Spent Talking, and No Goals in Sight," *Koreana* 4 (1990): pp. 68–74.

18. Park, *The Seoul Olympics*, p. 8.

19. Ibid., p. 12.

20. Ibid., p. 14.

21. Ibid., p. 21.

22. Ibid., p. 17.

23. Kim, *The Greatest Olympics*, p. 141.

24. James Kim, *Korea Times*, September 13, 1988, p. 12.

25. James Kim, "Sports Official Says Reform Proposals Show Hope for Olympic Success," United Press International (Seoul, Korea), June 29, 1987.

26. Bruce Cumings, *The Two Koreas*, Headline Series 269 (New York: Foreign Policy Association, 1984), p. 54.

27. Park, *The Seoul Olympics*, p. 19.

28. Kim, *The Greatest Olympics*, p. 144.

29. Donald N. Clark, "Bitter Friendship: Understanding Anti-Americanism in South Korea," in Donald N. Clark, ed., *Korea Briefing 1991* (Boulder, Colo.: Westview Press, 1991), p. 163.

30. Ibid., p. 153.

31. Ibid., p. 157.

32. Ibid., p. 157.

33. FBIS East Asia Daily Report, September 23, 1988, p. 4.

34. Chungho Choe, "Surmounting the Past: A Korean View of Japan and Germany," *Koreana* 4 (1990): p. 101.

35. *Far Eastern Economic Review* (October 4, 1990): p. 26.

8

National Images in Telecasts from Seoul

It deserves to be called the broadcast Olympics. We are ready, we will do our best.
—Lee Jung Suk, managing director, KBS/SORTO, interviewed on
NBC Television's "Today Show," September 12, 1988

On the eve of the Seoul Olympics, those who had worked so intensively over a period of years to prepare for the global telecast were self-consciously aware of the central role that television would play in constructing the Olympic experience. And well they should have been. For many of the managers, producers, engineers, and others within KBS/SORTO, the Olympic project marked the culmination of long careers in broadcasting. Those who produce television, in this case Olympic television, come to know it intimately and over an extended period of time. Although such experience does not automatically translate into insight, it frequently does, as was illustrated when Hwang Kil-Woong, the host broadcaster's director of planning and development, spoke in October 1986 to a congress of the General Association of International Sports Federations in Monte Carlo. He noted that those who experience the Olympics through television can have a more profound experience than people actually present in the sports venues. He continued:

> The image rendered by television is not the raw material, the raw image which venue attendants perceive. It is an image processed by the manipulation of television. Television provides not only a space domain processing by enlarging or squeezing the visual dimension, but also time domain processing by replaying the past events of interest in slow-motion. Therefore

what television presents is not merely a communication function, but another world recreated and reproduced through its image processing mechanism.[1]

In other words, television is not just a communication medium to cover
the Olympic Games but a *part* of the Games. Olympic television is a media
event, and one of its most important effects is to create what Katz and
Dayan referred to as an *electronic monument*.[2] Such monuments are built by
television and exist in the collective memory of the millions who viewed
the event, rather than in the memories of those few who were privileged to
attend. Although the character of the Seoul Olympics as an electronic monument was the subject of years of planning by the host broadcaster, international television organizations, and representatives of the Olympic
movement, it ultimately required the participation of viewers to take
shape.

From the beginning, Korea profoundly hoped that the television experience would change the nation's image in some countries and make it visible in others where little information had previously been available. On
the first anniversary of the Games, Park Seh-Jik, president of the Seoul
Olympic Organizing Committee, expressed that hope and his view that it
had been fulfilled.

> The Games changed the Korean people's view of the world and the world's
> view of Korea. The world's view of Korea had been mostly formed by the
> dark days of war-torn Korea. The Seoul Olympics and the 9,000 hours of TV
> coverage that came with it wiped the image away. Television showed a
> pearl of a city—modern, active, prosperous and peaceful. Since the Seoul
> Olympics the Korean people have been treated with more respect and so
> have Korean-made products.[3]

Assertions like these regarding the influential role of television in the
modern Olympics are now commonplace. The purpose of this chapter is to
explore and elaborate the general assertion of influence by looking more
specifically at the image of Korea conveyed through global television and
attendant media coverage. The analysis of television content is crucial. Different content implies differences in the highly political process of negotiating and producing a telecast. Equally as important, it speaks volumes
about the political impact of the Seoul Olympics. As the following section
of this chapter will show, that political impact is created by the whole
Olympic telecast and, in the larger historical perspective, by all Olympics-
related television. On commercial television, such programming may be
categorized into messages that emphasize Olympic, corporate, or nation-
al/cultural messages, respectively.

Given the sheer volume of television coverage beamed around the world from Seoul, television's multidimensional character, and the number of countries and broadcasting systems involved, it is well beyond the scope of this volume to provide a comprehensive analysis of content. Inevitably, what follows emphasizes our own interests and the data we have collected or information gathered by several colleagues who recognized the significant role of television in the Seoul experience and sought to address it through research. This chapter gives priority to the question of how television coverage relating to the Seoul Olympics affected the image of Korea in the United States and, by extension, in certain other countries. Accordingly, it focuses predominantly—but not exclusively—on television content dealing with Korea as a nation and culture. Such analysis deals with the "symbolic suggestion" component of images, rather than the feelings or responses people bring to that suggestion,[4] and it implies the probable direction of Olympics-induced change in public images of Korea.

The analysis is based in large part on a review and examination of NBC Television's coverage in the United States and less so on the comparative study of Olympic television and media coverage in other nations. The importance of such in-depth study in one nation stems from several considerations that are worth reemphasizing at the outset. First, U.S. television has heavily influenced the development of television internationally and Olympic television more specifically. Hence, at least some of the production patterns reflected in U.S. television tend to be found to a significant extent in other nations as well. Second, the Seoul Olympics played an important, if somewhat unexpected, role in the transition in U.S.-Korean relations. NBC Television's coverage of the boxing incident and other activities by the network's personnel made it a lightning rod for the surge of anti-American sentiment that swept the Korean public during the Games. Because NBC was at the center of this episode, this chapter provides a more detailed analysis of how television relates to change in public opinion and politics. Finally, the Seoul Olympics were the first in history in which the population of a host nation had immediate access to the entire Olympic telecast of another country. This availability of an international telecast is of particular interest because the other country was at once Korea's patron and partner, as well as a nation in which mainstream media coverage during the 1970s and 1980s had helped to create an "image problem." Coverage of Korea by network television and the *New York Times* over those decades focused predominantly on student demonstrations, other forms of violent political unrest, and visits or statements by U.S. presidents or other high officials.[5]

Major Categories of Olympic Television Content

As explained in earlier chapters, this study approaches the contemporary Olympics as a communication process that revolves centrally around the activities and messages of television and the other media. That process extends over time, and with the growing influence of television and commercial sponsorship, it is becoming more continuous and more global. In the Seoul Olympics, because of the infrastructure buildup required, the all-out national mobilization, and the prior hosting of the 1986 Asian Games, the whole process spanned nearly a decade. If its effects are considered, the process extends over an even longer period.

Altogether, the massive amount of publicity generated for Seoul and for South Korea by the Olympics during the 1980s may be categorized using the six types of television programs or segments discussed hereafter. Within each program or segment category, three types of meaning or symbolism deserve scrutiny. One set concerns the Olympics, another nations or cultures, and the final group are corporate and commercial symbols. Although these content categories are by no means mutually exclusive, they represent the basic set that must be dealt with, whether by researchers conducting content analyses or by Olympic officials, athletes, sports federations, and other parties interested in the role of television and the other media in the contemporary Olympics.

Sports

Olympic sports coverage falls mostly within the 16 days of Olympic competition themselves, when the medals are being won or lost, records are set, and athletic heroes are created. However, in a broader conceptualization, sports coverage includes the many Olympic qualifying competitions held in different locations around the world. Some of these, especially as the Games approach, generate publicity for the host city and nation.

In the case of the Seoul Olympics, the most prominent of such pre-Olympic sports competitions were the Asian Games, whose timing made them an ideal dress rehearsal for the Olympics. Given their status as a regional competition, they received the most intensive coverage within the Asian region and especially in participating nations. As with coverage of the Olympic Games themselves, television coverage of major international sports competitions preceding the Olympics illustrated the difficulty of separating sports and news in the media. At this level of international sport, the media covering competitions inevitably engage in some discussion of whatever geopolitical circumstances impinge on the competition at the time. For example, during the Asian Games in Seoul, the international media engaged in considerable discussion not only of South Korea's preparations for the Olympics but also about whether North Korea would participate or seek to disrupt the Games and whether Socialist bloc nations would take part.

Torch Relay

The quadrennial lighting of the Olympic flame in Greece and the torch relay that culminates in the lighting of the flame in the main stadium during the opening ceremony characteristically attract some news attention. However, the Seoul Olympics illustrated the now-conventional pattern in which the international media largely ignore the torch relay, although it may be a major media focus in the Olympic host city and nation. Massive worldwide attention to the Olympics begins closer to the opening ceremony and falls off sharply after the closing ceremony. This pattern contrasted sharply with coverage inside South Korea, where the torch relay received massive television and press attention and was an important final stage in the buildup to the Games.

The Olympic flame for Seoul was lit in the Temple of Hera in Olympia, Greece, on August 23, 1988, in accordance with rules of the Olympic Charter. A series of Greek runners carried the torch 380 kilometers to the Panathenian Stadium, where, on August 25, it was formally transferred to representatives of the Seoul Olympic Organizing Committee. The same day, these representatives departed by charter plane, arriving with the torch at Cheju International Airport on August 27, 1988.

During the next three weeks, the torch was carried through all the provinces and major cities of South Korea, with folk festivals held in each to welcome the Olympic flame. The entire torch relay received extensive national coverage by both KBS and MBC television, with considerable emphasis on the ceremonials and folk festivals in each of the cities along the route. Among those carrying or receiving the torch were a large number of provincial and municipal officials. The level of public involvement and enthusiasm demonstrated in these ceremonies began a crescendo as the Games approached and as each succeeding village or city sought to outdo the preceding one. In this process of mobilizing public enthusiasm, television and media coverage quite obviously played a key role.

Ceremonies

The opening and closing ceremonies of the Olympics, as well as the medal ceremonies, also constitute a distinct category of television content. Of these, the opening ceremony is accorded a special status by all involved with the Olympic movement. From a political communication point of view, it is the single most important episode in Olympic television, for several related reasons. As recognized by Pierre de Coubertin, founder of the modern Olympics, it is primarily through the ceremonies that Olympic ideals are performed and communicated; therefore, they are responsible for distinguishing the Olympics from mere "athleticism."[6]

The opening ceremony perennially attracts the largest audience of any Olympic event; in Seoul, that was estimated to exceed one billion viewers.[7] For commercial broadcasters and Olympic sponsors, it is an important lead-in to the Olympic telecast, with a crucial impact on viewership as measured by audience ratings and, hence, commercial income during the ensuing days of the telecast. The concept of "audience flow" in commercial television dictates that, to be successful, programming must attract audience interest and hold it. It refers to the manner in which the overall size of an audience tuned in to one channel changes over time as viewers switch channels between or even during programs. The same general concept can be applied across the hours and days of the Olympic telecast.

The opening ceremony is the principal vehicle for what Dayan and Katz called the "self-presentation of a society."[8] The entire ceremony juxtaposes national symbols with the symbols of a transnational, Olympic community,[9] granting central prominence to the national identity of the host city. Consider the following characteristics of the opening ceremony, all mandated by the Olympic Charter, as they appeared in Seoul. A substantial portion of the ceremony was devoted to cultural performances in which Korea could display its heritage to the world. The president of South Korea, Roh Tae Woo, formally declared the Games open. The Korean national anthem was sung. Korean athletes marched into the main stadium last, passing through the teams from all other nations of the world who had preceded them. The president of the Seoul Olympic Organizing Committee, Park Seh-Jik, gave a welcoming speech, as did IOC President Juan Antonio Samaranch. Finally, the Seoul Olympic emblem and mascot were prominently displayed in different ways throughout the ceremony.

Margaret Dilling's study of the music in the opening and closing ceremonies showed the central priority planners gave to the presentation of Korea and its culture to the world.[10] Early in the planning process, they established three guidelines by which music would be commissioned, composed, and selected for the ceremonies: It should be universal, distinctively Korean, and new. The actual ceremonies made extensive use of traditional Korean music, but it was re-created and composed for a contemporary and international audience. The music was a strong and essential component of the cultural nationalism expressed through the ceremonies.

Due, in part, to the preceding considerations, both the Olympic host and organizing committee and the international broadcasters spend a disproportionate amount of time, money, and effort in planning and rehearsing the opening ceremony, in comparison with other Olympic ceremonies and events. In July 1986, two months before the Asian Games, Seoul Olympic Organizing Committee President Park Seh-Jik organized a 13-member planning board for the exclusive purpose of preparing the opening and closing ceremonies of the Seoul Olympics. The board consisted mostly of professors and included leading national experts on Korean culture and the performing arts. Well-known professors Lee O-young and Choe Chungho led the decisionmaking on themes for the ceremonies, while others worked on scenarios, music, and other aspects of the project. In the words of Park Seh-Jik, "The reason we started our preparations so early for the opening and closing ceremonies was that we had long been aware of their importance, especially of the opening ceremony. In the past, success in gaining publicity and the success of the Games themselves had often appeared to be dependent upon public reaction to the opening ceremonies."[11]

Cultural Features

In addition to the opening and closing ceremonies, television systems produce their own cultural programming, focusing on the host city, nation, culture, or people. The U.S. networks have traditionally done more of such programming than other systems around the world because they could afford to. During more than 170 hours of Olympic coverage from Seoul, NBC Television aired a total of 41 such feature reports.[12] In addition, the network aired numerous spots prior to the Olympics, primarily during the week preceding the Games, when it hosted its 2-hour, morning "Today" show from Seoul. Among international broadcasters, the Japanese pool and German television were also active in producing material about Korea to supplement the international television signal provided by the host broadcaster.

News and Public Affairs

The Olympics are themselves considered news, as implied by conceiving of them as both actor and stage in the international system. Accordingly, both the Olympic Charter and the more extensive *Media Guide* take explicit note of the importance of news and public affairs coverage to the Olympic movement. Rule 59 of the Olympic Charter states, in part, "In order to ensure the fullest news coverage by the different media and widest possible audience for the Olympic Games, all necessary steps shall be determined by the IOC Executive Board and implemented by the OCOG."[13]

There is generally a buildup of news attention to the forthcoming Olympics or the city in which they are hosted for a year or more preceding the Games. The amount and nature of such coverage varies, depending on the location of the Games and the international context surrounding each Olympiad. The U.S.- and Soviet-led boycotts of the 1980 and 1984 Olympics, respectively, provide good examples of how international circumstances sometimes generate more news coverage for the Olympics at an earlier date than it might otherwise begin. Coming on the heels of those boycotts, Seoul provides an equally instructive example. As discussed in earlier chapters, it posed questions for the international media on several issues: the possible cohosting of events with North Korea, the North Korean military threat, participation by the Socialist bloc nations, and whether domestic political unrest was a threat to successfully hosting the Games.

The news value of the Olympics is also manifest at the time of the competition, as illustrated by coverage from Seoul in the United States. In addition to the NBC Sports team, led by Bryant Gumbel and a corps of commentators, NBC broadcast its "Today" show from Seoul during the week preceding the Games, and the "NBC Nightly News" with Tom Brokaw was broadcast from Seoul for seven days, beginning Thursday, September 15, just one day before the opening ceremony telecast. Also, a number of local television stations from the United States, such as KING-5 television (the NBC affiliate in Seattle) and KNBC (the network's affiliate in Los Angeles), hosted their news broadcasts and other features from Seoul during the Games.

Commercials

Commercial messages from advertisers and sponsors of the Olympic Games are another important type of Olympic communication. As already discussed, especially in Chapter 4, the Olympic Charter itself recognizes the significance of commercial messages, whether by official Olympic sponsors or by sponsors of Olympic telecasts. They provide the principal vehicle through which those corporations associate their names or products with the central symbols of the Olympics. Precisely because the purpose of many commercials and sponsorship messages is to establish or strengthen such an association, the analysis of such messages must deal with Olympic, national-cultural, and corporate meanings. Although not a primary focus of the present analysis, such associations were sprinkled throughout NBC's telecasts of the Seoul Olympics. During most of its programming—including the opening ceremony, "Nightly News" broadcasts, and the "Today" show—NBC rather consistently used live or taped visuals of Olympic action or scenery and activity in Seoul as a transition *to and from* commercial breaks. One effect of such a technique is to increase the frequency with which certain visual elements may be seen. Such transitional visuals may be particularly attention-getting because viewers who use a remote control to "zap" commercials might be anticipating the return to normal programming and would take the initial visual as a cue that the commercial has ended. Possible effects like that may have been even more pronounced for viewers in Korea who saw the AFKN version with the commercials excised. AFKN often (but not always) inserted station identifications or public service announcements when the U.S. networks took breaks for commercials.

The Existing Story Line and the Re-creation of News

As the preceding discussion makes clear, Olympic communication pervades television and other media and consists of various kinds of content. Although this argues against facile attribution of changes in Korea's image to one form of content or medium of communication, some priority should be given to the news media, especially television. One reason for this emphasis is the inexorable, worldwide trend toward greater public reliance on television. In the United States, periodic industry-sponsored surveys, beginning about 1960, have documented the shift from public dependence on newspapers to a reliance on television for news, particularly news of international affairs.[14] Furthermore, the medium plays a dominant role in creating the massive focus of international attention on the host city and country of the Olympics, and radio and print media clearly occupy a secondary and supporting position, however important they may be. With phenomena like the contemporary Olympics, the process of getting "attention in world society" as discussed by Lasswell has begun to approach a more truly global scale.[15]

Numerous studies of the news media over the years have established the importance of the media themselves as a source for news accounts. For a long time, the wire services were thought to set the agenda for television news and for many newspapers. More recently, it has become apparent that for coverage of war and other crises—as in the Gulf War or the abortive coup against the government of President Gorbachev in the Soviet Union—members of the print media may turn to television for a significant portion of their information. Also well established in the research literature is the importance of routine organizational practices and media formats in determining what is covered by the news media and how it is covered. Such considerations imply that representatives of television and other media would have come to Seoul with a certain story line in mind and with a set of newsgathering routines that would influence how events in Seoul were shaped into news.

News coverage of South Korea during the years and months preceding the 1988 Olympics suggested the expectations many media representatives likely brought with them to Seoul and the nature of the story line they might have anticipated. The following passages discuss the amount and nature of coverage given Korea, with special emphasis on U.S. television and NBC, but in the context of overall mainstream media coverage. Findings from an earlier study of U.S. network television coverage of Korea during the 1970s and 1980s are supplemented with a look at two critical periods in 1987 and the pre-Olympic buildup of attention in 1988.

The consistent pattern in U.S. television and mainstream media coverage of South Korea during the 1970s and 1980s displayed low and intermittent levels of attention. A study of evening network television news between 1972 and 1981 showed that more than 20 other nations ranked above South Korea in terms of overall coverage.[16] European nations like Great Britain, France, West Germany, and Italy all received greater and more consistent attention, as did both the People's Republic of China and Japan in Asia.

A more detailed analysis of coverage in the *New York Times* and on "The CBS Evening News" for the years 1979, 1983, and 1987 showed that the news narrative about Korea had several prominent features. First, student demonstrations were the dominant symbol of protest in both television and the print media. Through television visuals or news photographs, the U.S. public became familiar with masked students hurling firebombs and helmeted combat police firing rounds of tear gas. Second, other forms of political violence formed a related theme in Korean coverage, including assassinations, bombings, and the bloody Kwangju uprising in May 1980. Third, coverage of South Korea showed the tendency of television to "presidentialize" its international affairs coverage. State visits to Korea, such as those by President Jimmy Carter in June 1979 and President Reagan in 1983, received extensive coverage by the accompanying pool of White House reporters. When the Soviet Union shot down KAL flight 007 in 1983, the incident became a prolonged subject of news attention, not because it involved Korea per se but rather because President Reagan decided to use it as a battering ram of sorts in a propaganda campaign. He and other members of his administration repeatedly alluded publicly to KAL 007 in an effort to trigger international condemnation of the Soviets. A fourth characteristic of the narrative about Korea points up a contrast between television and newspaper news. Coverage of the South Korean economy and its growing trade relationship with the United States received very little treatment on television. By contrast, it was a staple of coverage in the *New York Times*, accounting for 14 percent of all Korean coverage during the three years examined.[17]

The process through which the world media turned their attention to Seoul and South Korea took place over a period of months. Although it would be impossible to measure or estimate it on a global level, Figure 8.1

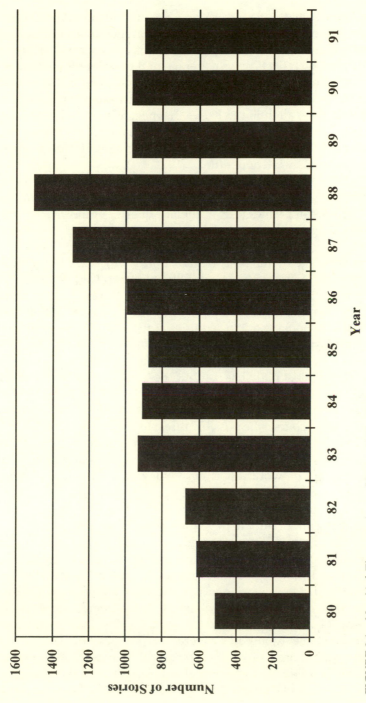

FIGURE 8.1 *New York Times* stories on Korea, 1980–1991.

begins to suggest what coverage of Korea might have looked like. It shows the number of stories in the *New York Times* that mentioned Korea for the years 1980 through 1991. It should be noted that the increase in attention during 1983 largely reflects news coverage of the Soviet downing of KAL flight 007 and subsequent references to it in numerous official speeches by President Reagan and members of his administration. Figure 8.1 also shows the increased attention to Korea that began in 1986, the year of the Asian Games in Seoul—an increase that was sustained through the Olympics. During the post-Olympics year of 1989, coverage of Korea by the *New York Times* dropped by fully one-third.

Although the Olympic Games themselves were undoubtedly the primary factor influencing the extent of coverage in 1988, the "unfinished business" of Korean politics during the last quarter of the year—notably the televised National Assembly hearings on the Kwangju uprising and the Fifth Republic—also accounted for some of the coverage. Similarly, the increase in coverage by the *New York Times* from 1986 to 1987 cannot be completely explained simply as pre-Olympics publicity. Instead, there was an interaction between the currents of South Korean politics and the forthcoming Olympic Games. Here, the pattern of news attention can be best illustrated by looking at the activities of the U.S. television networks. The political crisis in South Korea during June 1987 led the three New York-based television networks to dispatch correspondents to Seoul. They reported on an almost daily basis about the antigovernment demonstrations, the growing involvement of the middle class in opposition to President Chun's government, the stand taken by the church and opposition politicians, and, of course, the possible threat to the Seoul Olympics.

The 2-minute, 30-second report by CBS correspondent Barry Peterson that aired on June 29, after Roh Tae Woo's now-famous declaration, illustrated the tenor of network reporting. It showed the reaction of citizens and included statements by opposition leader Kim Young Sam, a skeptical student, and ruling party National Assembly member Hyun Hong Choo, who spoke of the importance to the nation of the Seoul Olympics.[18]

In December 1987, U.S. network television again turned its attention to South Korea, to cover the presidential elections and the bombing of a KAL plane in Thailand. Coverage of each event had a clear tie-in to the Olympics. The latter incident was laden with political significance because it suggested that North Korea had embarked on a systematic effort to sabotage the Seoul Games.

During 1988, television news coverage of Korea in the United States placed the greatest emphasis on two recurrent themes, student unrest in Seoul and the possible North Korean threat to a successful hosting of the Olympics. A review of the *Television News Index and Abstracts* for January through August 1988 showed the pattern of attention to Korea on the network early evening newscasts.[19]

- January: A total of fifteen stories were aired during the month by ABC, CBS, and NBC. All but three were short anchor reports dealing with announcements that the Soviets would attend the Seoul Olympics and that North Korea and Cuba would not. The major story, reported from Seoul by NBC and CBS, dealt with a televised interview in which Kim Hyon Hui admitted to being a North Korean agent responsible for the bombing of a KAL plane.
- February: The Winter Games in Calgary generated considerable news attention during this month. However, very little attention was paid to South Korea and the Summer Olympics. In a total of five stories, three featured correspondents covering the U.S. presidential campaign who picked up on Congressman Richard Gephardt's criticism of Korea and other Asian countries for their trade practices. The longest report was a 4-minute, 20-second story by CBS's Morley Safer on the possibility of North Korean terrorism disrupting the Seoul Olympics.
- March: There were no stories relating to the Seoul Olympics aired in March. Of the total of nine stories on Korea generally, seven dealt with allegations by former U.S. Representative Pete McCloskey that evangelist Pat Robertson's father had used his influence to prevent his son from serving on active duty in the Korean War. All but one of these reports were short anchor items.
- April: In April, there were also nine stories about Korea. They included short anchor reports on student demonstrations against President Roh Tae Woo's government and on gains made in National Assembly elections by Kim Dae Jung's opposition party. Several other stories contained incidental mention of Korea in connection with news on Larry Speakes's book about the Reagan White House, which mentioned the KAL 007 downing, and Ford Motor Company's economic outlook. One long correspondent report from Seoul by Mark Littke dealt with preparations for the Seoul Olympics. It also focused on the possibility of a North Korean invasion as a threat to the Olympics.
- May: The number of stories about Korea doubled in May to eighteen, largely because the month marked the eighth anniversary of the Kwangju uprising. Indeed, on May 18—the anniversary of the bloodshed—both ABC and CBS carried correspondent reports on the unrest that featured videotaped coverage of the massacre and of students burning an effigy of Uncle Sam. Another CBS correspondent's report, on May 19, showed students burning the U.S. flag and sug-

gested that such gestures by radical students might be designed to take advantage of Olympic publicity. On the same day, NBC aired a report on the funeral of a dissident student who had committed suicide. It included scenes of his self-immolation and jump from a building, and the report quoted University of California-Berkeley Asia scholar Robert Scalapino as saying that the protest leaders were trying to disrupt the Olympics. Several other reports aired during the remainder of the month focused on the violently anti-American demonstrations. This theme was visually supported with scenes of students attacking the U.S. Embassy or burning the U.S. flag.

Student unrest on the anniversary of the Kwangju uprising, coming one year after the unrest that led to the June 29 declaration in 1987, was to be expected and did not surprise experienced observers of Korea. However, television coverage of the demonstrations just four months before the Seoul Olympics again aroused public concerns in the United States. An excerpt from a *Washington Post* story from Seoul illustrated those concerns. According to that story, South Korean government spokesman Park Shin Il

acknowledged that reports from abroad since June 10, when 10,000 leftist students battled riot police in Seoul's streets, have been "a little depressing." Australian officials disclosed emergency evacuation plans for their delegation; U.S. athletes talked about shunning Seoul's shiny new Olympic village for the safer haven of Japan, flying to Seoul only for their events.

"To say the television coverage is distorted is not enough," Park said. "What can we do? We suffer from it so much, every time."

U.S. Ambassador to South Korea James R. Lilley said the embassy has received anxious calls from "athletes, relatives, government people, all kinds of people. The response from the States has been way overblown," he said. "People have canceled trips. It's very unfair," Lilley said. "I tell them Seoul is a very safe town. There's absolutely no thought of putting out a travel advisory."

A senior ruling party official, Choi Chang Yoon, agreed. "My friends in the U.S. told me that it looked like Vietnam, or the Philippines," Choi said. "But once you are here in Seoul, it's quite different."[20]

- June: The level of coverage remained about the same during the month of June and continued to focus on unrest, but the anti-American theme shifted to a dual emphasis on North Korea: first, student demands for cohosting as a move toward reunification of the nation and second, the possible threat of military action or terrorism to disrupt the Olympics. On June 9, NBC led its newscast with a report on the student demonstrations. The next day, it was a major, although not lead, news story on all three network newscasts as radical students attempted to carry out a planned march to the DMZ to meet with their North Korean counterparts and discuss reunification.

- July: Levels of attention to Korea per se decreased in July. The month began with the shooting down of an Iranian civilian airliner by the U.S. Navy in the Persian Gulf, which received heavy news attention and was compared by all three networks to the Soviet downing of the KAL 007 plane—thus, amounting to an incidental mention of Korea. Indeed, more than half of the stories involved this incidental association. On July 16, ABC aired a 20-second anchor report stating that visiting Secretary of State George Schultz had declared Seoul secure for the Olympics. On July 26, NBC had an anchor report of similar length noting North Korea's letter to South Korea expressing a desire to discuss participation in the Seoul Olympics.

- August: Overall coverage levels remained about the same in August, as attention to the efforts of students to march to the DMZ for a meeting with their counterparts in the North continued. On August 28, NBC aired a 5-minute "Sunday Journal" report that looked at Korea's history, preparations for the Olympics, politics, and North-South relations, among other topics. On August 23, it had devoted 4 minutes, 10 seconds to a report by a BBC reporter who had posed as a tourist and filmed scenes from inside North Korea. On August 26, the network aired another 3-minute segment of the same story. Only NBC followed the last-minute exchanges between North and South Korea on cohosting possibilities with short reports. There were also a few stories on Olympics security. On Saturday, August 27, only CBS carried scenes of the arrival of the Olympic torch in Cheju Island, in a 10-second anchor report. NBC, the rightsholding broadcaster, did not carry even a short item on it.

Coverage Surrounding the Olympics as an Event

As the preceding review shows, the storyline about Korea had been rather clearly established for NBC, the other U.S. television networks, and, indeed, for most major international media by the time the Olympics arrived. The opening 2 minutes, 18 seconds of the very first "Today Show" broadcast originating from Seoul in September gave one indication of how NBC intended to frame its treatment of the Olympics. The visuals showed a city putting the final touches on its Olympic preparation, while host Bryant Gumbel's commentary suggested some major themes to be touched on in the forthcoming "Today Show" telecasts.[21]

Commentary: Bryant Gumbel (BG): Good Morning. In Seoul, Korea, workers and officials are applying the finishing touches to seven years of effort since being awarded the Games of the 24th Olympiad in September of '81. Seoul has invested countless hours and three and one half billion dollars preparing for not only a great international sports competition, but also a great exercise of national pride. Once known as the "Hermit Kingdom," Korea's games represent a kind of coming out party, for which Seoul's final countdown is already in progress today, Monday, September the 12th, 1988.

Visual: Scenes in Seoul of Olympic banners being hung, flowers being placed on a pedestal, and a view of main Olympic stadium from the air. Scenes from ceremony inside the stadium. Scenes of Olympic Rings, Seoul Olympic Emblem, and City Hall Plaza.

Commentary: Announcer: From NBC News, this is "Today" with Bryant Gumbel and Jane Pauley.

Visual: Scene of City Hall Plaza, traffic and pedestrians, with "TODAY, Sept. 12, 1988" graphic superimposed. Camera pans toward Toksu Palace.

Commentary: BG: Located on the Han River in the heart of the Korean peninsula, Seoul is a city of ten million people. Long the capital of the Republic of Korea, this city is set to become the temporary capital of a world with no borders, as it hosts the Games of the 24th Olympiad. The world is coming to Seoul.

Visual: Gate of Toksu Palace. Shot of the Palace from the air.

Commentary: BG: And good morning. Welcome to Seoul, or should I say "Anyonghashimnikka?" We're going to be spending all of our week ... our base of operations this week in Seoul, as we prepare for the Summer Games, the Games of the 24th Olympiad. The Opening Ceremonies are set for Friday night where you are, but we'll be telling you more about that as the week progresses. I'm on the grounds this morning of Toksu Palace, or Toksu Gong, as they might say here. It's called the palace of virtuous longevity. It's a fifteenth century structure, surrounded now by the gleaming monuments to Korean commerce. A war-ravaged nation, just, oh ... just about thirty years ago, Korea today is an Asian power with a booming economy, and a reform-minded president. As we begin our week in Korea this morning, we'll have the first-ever network television interview with President Roh Tae Woo. We'll be talking about the Olympics, about U.S. relations, and about reunification attempts with the North. We'll also look at the radical student movement confronting Roh's government, we'll see how the popular images of the real MASH units of the Korean war days compare to the TV show and the images they left behind, and we'll go behind the scenes of the massive TV coverage planned for these Olympics. There is lots more to come, of course, but before we go any further, we're going to send you back to New York and bid a good morning there to Deborah Norville, who's sitting in for Jane Pauley, who's on her way here. Good morning, Deborah.

Visual: Closeup of Bryant Gumbel at Toksu Palace with orange Seoul Olympic banner waving in the wind behind him.

As promised, the "Today Show" began broadcasting a number of feature and background stories on Korea. This pattern continued throughout NBC's Olympic telecast and became a major point of controversy in Korea, as discussed later in the chapter. Here, it will suffice to note that the theme of student unrest—the "radical student movement" referred to by Gumbel in his commentary—received early attention on NBC's "Today" broadcasts. In one remarkable report, a young stringer correspondent for NBC followed the life and daily routine of a student activist who happened to be the son of a Protestant clergyman. The spot juxtaposed scenes from the student's home and interviews with his parents, on the one hand, with video recorded in the midst of a violent confrontation between students and riot police near a university campus. The report was edited so that it appeared the NBC stringer had breathlessly questioned both students and riot police as a demonstration was unfolding, exposing himself to danger in the process. Visually, the report fit the pattern to which U.S. television viewers had long been accustomed. There were scenes of combat police with their padded uniforms, large shields, and masked, Darth Vader-like helmets. Also featured was the characteristic exchange of tear gas and Molotov cocktails.

More generally, network television's early evening news coverage from Seoul during September increased markedly, mostly because of NBC's presence there. A review of coverage during the first two weeks of the month is instructive. "NBC Nightly News" carried a total of eight items. Five of these were correspondent reports with video, four featuring particular U.S. athletes or teams and one 2-minute, 30-second report on the torch relay. The three others were short anchor reports dealing with student demonstrations in Korea. During the same two week period, the other two networks carried no news from Korea, except for a 20-second anchor report on ABC noting North Korea's announcement that it would boycott the Seoul Olympics. Over this same two week period, the 1988 Bush-Dukakis presidential campaign was rather consistently the dominant story, leading most of the newscasts and occupying a considerable amount of the available time. Other stories that led network telecasts during the period were forest fires in Yellowstone National Park, difficulties faced by two Soviet cosmonauts in returning to Earth after a stay in orbit, and Hurricane Gilbert's destruction and threat in Jamaica and the Caribbean. In terms of the Seoul Olympics, the most striking aspect of U.S. television coverage during this period was its lack of attention to the torch relay, which at the time received saturation levels of attention within Korea itself.

For seven weeknights, from Thursday, September 15, through Friday, September 23, anchor Tom Brokaw hosted the "NBC Nightly News" from Seoul, using the main Olympic stadium and scenes of the city as a backdrop for the news broadcast and with the Olympic rings prominently included in the newscast's logo at the beginning and end of the telecast. As would be expected, news of Korea and the Olympics increased greatly during this period, occupying from one-third to one-half of the approximately 22 minutes of available news time during each of the telecasts.

ABC and CBS took note of the Seoul Olympics on September 15, each airing reports from correspondents in Korea that touched on security arrangements for the games, preparations more generally, and the possible North Korean threat. On September 16, ABC broadcast a 3-minute report on Sohn Kee Chung as a possible anchor runner for the torch relay. The next day, CBS broadcast a report previewing the Olympics and noting the first medals awarded in Seoul, with emphasis on U.S. athletes. On September 18, several U.S medal winners were noted as part of a sports report on ABC, and one day later, both CBS and ABC carried reports that focused on medal results and profiles of particular Olympic athletes. On September 20, ABC carried a report by correspondent Mark Littke on counterfeit goods being sold to Olympic tourists and athletes. ABC focused on the medal count and U.S. runner Carl Lewis on September 21, and CBS aired a report on the winning of Olympic medals and the politics of national pride. On September 22, Peter Jennings mentioned the Olympic boxing incident, accompanied by a few seconds of videotape, in the introduction to a correspondent's report on a Danish yachtsman. Notably, CBS did not carry anything on the incident, and no more was said about the incident by either CBS or NBC in their regular early evening news broadcasts. On September 26, news of Canada's Ben Johnson testing positive for steroids led both the ABC and CBS broadcasts but not that of NBC, perhaps because the latter network was already carrying so much Olympic coverage throughout the day.

To this point, the review of how Korea was covered by mainstream U.S. media before and during the Olympics has focused largely on normal news stories and news telecasts. To answer the question of how the Seoul Olympics affected the image of Korea in the United States and, by implication, in certain other Western countries, the content of Olympic television—those 170 hours plus that NBC Television broadcast from Seoul—needs to be explored. Within the Olympic telecast, content dealing more or less explicitly with Korea as a nation and culture is of particular interest. For reasons already noted, the single most important broadcast of the Olympics is the opening ceremony telecast. Consequently, it receives extensive treatment in the following discussion. During the many hours that constitute the bulk of Olympic television, feature reports that deal more or less explicitly with Korea are of obvious importance. Also, during the sports coverage per se, the behavior of Korean athletes or fans, along with the transitional visual coverage of Korea used by NBC in connection with commercial or other breaks, could be expected to contribute to a viewer's overall impression of the nation. Although these materials do not exhaust NBC's coverage of Korea as a nation and culture, they do constitute its core and the vast majority of such content.

The Opening Ceremony Telecast

Television was integral to the theme and performance of the Seoul opening ceremony. Given South Korea's major foreign policy goals of improving its image in the international community, opening up to Socialist bloc nations, and reunifying with North Korea, no other communications medium was as important as television in moving toward those goals, and perhaps no other Olympic event was as important as the opening ceremony. The ceremony used television to convey its theme,"Beyond All Barriers," and suggest moving beyond such barriers as time, space, or the political and cultural gap between East and West. It included such spatially separated elements as the Han River boat parade, fireworks outside the main Olympic stadium, jets flying overhead trailing a jet stream in the Olympic colors, and the forming of the Olympic rings in the sky above Seoul and again on the stadium field by an international team of sports parachutists. Television visually symbolized the breaking of spatial barriers by bringing those elements together on a large screen within the Olympic stadium for spectators there and on millions of television screens in households around the world.

A study conducted with Nancy Rivenburgh compared the content of complete opening ceremony telecasts by NBC in the United States, Australia's Network TEN, and the BBC in Britain.[22] It analyzed both visual content and audio commentary from each of the twenty-five segments of the ceremony designated by Seoul Olympic planners and from the entry of each nation's athletes during that portion of the ceremony. All story units were categorized as (1) Olympic ritual, (2) cultural performance, or (3) broadcaster-added segments.[23] Major findings of the study are summarized below in terms of the four general research questions it addressed.

How do different editorial and production styles shape the presentation of Olympic and national images by broadcasters around the world?

The international feed provided by the host broadcaster, KBS/SORTO, covered all episodes of the ceremony in their entirety. Individual national broadcasters made selections from the international feed and interrupted

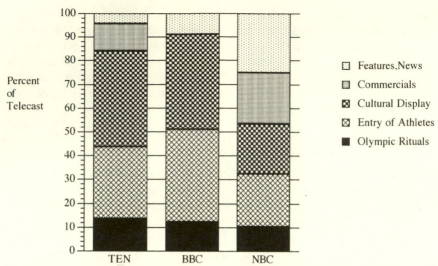

FIGURE 8.2   Time structure of opening ceremony telecasts. *Source:* James F. Larson and Nancy K. Rivenburgh, "A Comparative Analysis of Australian, US and British Telecasts of the Seoul Olympic Opening Ceremony," *Journal of Broadcasting and Electronic Media* 35 (Winter 1991): p. 81.

or supplemented them with broadcaster-generated segments consisting primarily of commercials, newsbreaks, and background reports or interviews to create their own narrative structures. Both NBC and BBC supplemented the KBS feed with footage from their own, unilateral cameras, and all broadcasters provided their own audio commentary.

The overall structure of each telecast is indicated in Figure 8.2, which shows the percentage of time each broadcaster devoted to the major types of stories, both broadcaster-supplied and from the ceremony itself. There were notable differences among the three broadcasts in the type, number, and pattern of departures from coverage of the actual ceremony as it unfolded. The major types of interruption were commercials, newsbreaks (NBC only), and interviews and background pieces. The latter two categories are grouped together in Figure 8.2 as "Features, news."

Generally, the departures and additions mirrored the commercial obligations of the three broadcast systems. The total BBC telecast, without commercial commitments, included only 5 breaks for interviews and commentary, averaging 3 minutes, 50 seconds in length. The TEN telecast included 13 commercial breaks averaging 1 minute, 47 seconds in duration and 4 breaks for interviews, which averaged 2 minutes, 10 seconds in length. NBC's telecast included 25 commercial breaks, with an average length of 2 minutes, 4 seconds, and 21 newsbreaks, "Olympic Chronicles," or other background pieces averaging 3 minutes, 3 seconds in length.

In the United States, the commercial and other interruptions in NBC's opening ceremony telecast drew considerable press criticism, as expressed in comments by Tom Shales of the *Washington Post*.

> Superstar Bryant Gumbel, the highly paid anchor for the whole shebang, tends toward pomposity and seems to lack a certain joie de anything. He and Dick Enberg were both pretty dreadful hosting the opening ceremonies Friday night, a four-hour broadcast of which a total of one entire hour consisted of commercials or cutaways to NBC affiliates for local news.
>
> The evening began with a technical goof, when coverage from Seoul was momentarily interrupted by a shot of NBC News correspondent Robert Bazell being harnessed with a microphone for an update on Hurricane Gilbert. Most of the evening's other intrusions were carefully and stupidly planned by NBC.
>
> NBC's perpetual promotional machinery cannot resist the urge to foist network anchor Tom Brokaw on viewers in the hope that more exposure will improve ratings for his third-place "NBC Nightly News." Brokaw was repeatedly shoehorned into the opening ceremonies with political analysis from Seoul that nobody needed to hear. He was hauled in to interrupt one of the most beautiful parts of the awe-inspiring ceremony, as hundreds of balloons rose into the sky over the stadium. More pageantry was ignored later so Brokaw could offer a humdrum and unillustrated report on security precautions in Seoul.
>
> Even the unforgettably spectacular display by precision parachutists zooming above and into the stadium was truncated. The parachutists formed into an airborne Olympic ring symbol 15,000 feet up and were supposed to do it again on the ground, but if they did, we never saw it.[24]

The predictable style and structure of NBC's coverage unwittingly contributed to the disorderly behavior of U.S. athletes during the entry of the athletes. Many members of the U.S. team fell out of formation onto the grassy inner area and other parts of the field during their entry into the stadium, gathering in groups around cameras in order to wave to friends and family at home. Their behavior was in stark contrast to the orderly procession of teams from the other 159 participating nations. While it occurred, NBC was conducting on-the-field interviews, including video close ups, with U.S. athletes Mary T. Meagher and Carl Lewis via remote microphones. NBC also televised glimpses of several homemade cloth signs carried by U.S. athletes (e.g., "Hi Mom! Send Won," "Hi Mom. I'm Here," and another mentioning "NBC" and the "USA"). In short, the U.S. athletes, by bringing signs and gravitating toward cameras, and television personnel, by obliging such maneuvers, showed that they shared certain cultural norms attendant to television broadcasting in the United States—norms that, if shared by those from other nations, were not considered appropriate to the Olympic opening ceremony. Moreover, by conveying a lack of respect for the ceremony, they violated the Korean cultural norm that the guest does not do anything to offend or insult the host. The opening ceremony behavior of the U.S. athletes was one factor contributing to increased anti-American sentiment among the Korean public during the Seoul Olympics.

How do national telecasts of the Olympic opening ceremony differ in the amount and nature of their attention to cultural and national versus Olympic characteristics and symbols?

To accommodate commercial, news, and other breaks, NBC cut heavily into its potential coverage of both cultural performances and the entry of the athletes. TEN made room for its breaks by cutting primarily from the entry of the athletes, and, as noted, the BBC carried virtually the entire 3-1/4-hour ceremony with just one 45-second break to interview a British athlete. Other BBC interviews took place before the ceremony began.

Figure 8.2 also shows the relative amount of time the broadcasters devoted to each of the three major components of the planned ceremony: Olympic ritual and gestures, the entry and exit of the athletes, and cultural performances (display). Only time devoted to coverage of the Olympic rituals common to every opening ceremony is consistent across broadcasts, ranging from 24 minutes, 9 seconds on NBC to 27 minutes, 19 seconds on TEN.

Visual symbols of nation and culture, ranging from national flags to traditional Korean costumes, were prominent in the opening ceremony telecasts. This corresponded to the emphasis in the audio commentary but was less pronounced. Symbols such as the Olympic rings, flag, or flame were shown to viewers far more than they were discussed by commentators; they were pervasive elements in the visual landscape, whether part of a performance, painted on the stadium, or towering in the sky. In fact, they provided a dominant visual motif throughout all three broadcasts.

Do the telecasts give clues to the international relationships of the broadcasting nation? Does the commentary focus more on allies, trading partners, or nations with similar political systems?

Analysis of the nations mentioned by commentators for each of the three broadcasters shows several patterns. First, South Korea was by far the most frequently mentioned country on all three telecasts, and though such mentions were slightly more frequent during the cultural performance segments of the ceremony, they pervaded all broadcasts. These data underscore the effectiveness of the opening ceremony as a vehicle for the Olympic host city and nation to assume its moment in the spotlight. Second, the three broadcasting organizations all referred to their nation of origin more frequently than to others in the world. Third, the fact that Japan and the USSR were among the most frequently mentioned nations is a reflection of geopolitical and economic power, athletic strength, and the long-standing rivalry between Japan and Korea. Finally, NBC spent less time on the entry of the athletes than did the other networks; consequently, the NBC telecast mentioned only 86 national teams entering the stadium, compared to 111 on TEN and 134 on the BBC, out of 160 participating nations.

In general, the frequency with which nations were mentioned was highly skewed toward a small group of athletically or economically powerful nations. Considering all three telecasts together, only 20 countries received 3 or more mentions.

In particular, how was Korea portrayed to the world, nationally and culturally, throughout the opening ceremony telecasts?

When considering Korea's national image, one significant difference was the amount of time NBC spent away from the cultural performances— most of which displayed Korean culture in music, dance, costume, and narrative. NBC devoted 49 minutes, 57 seconds of its telecast to cultural performances, compared with 81 minutes, 58 seconds for TEN and 85 minutes for the BBC. In fact, NBC skipped two cultural performance episodes altogether, the Han River Boat parade and the "Heaven, Earth and Man" segment. It could be said that NBC's frequent interruptions might have prevented television audiences from becoming engaged in the Korean cultural narrative that flowed through all the performances.

Seen in a more positive light, NBC offered a larger number of interviews and prepackaged segments to its viewers, airing 17 stories, compared to 5 by the BBC and 4 by TEN. NBC's "Olympic Chronicles" and "Olympics Past" were 3- to 4-minute segments shown throughout the Olympics. Topics ranged from close-ups on particular athletes to aspects of life in South Korea. Generally, the segments provided glimpses of Korea outside the Olympic stadium.

Dayan and Katz would describe such stories as offering television viewers cultural continuity or depth, a dimension of knowledge about the event not available to direct spectators.[25] NBC's "Olympics Past" segment tracing the experience of Sohn Kee Chung is an excellent example. Because Korea was under Japanese colonial rule at the time of the 1936 Berlin

Olympic Games, Sohn was forced to compete with a Japanese name and uniform, receiving his medal while the Japanese national anthem played. His victory was a bittersweet moment for Koreans, who have since tried, without success, to get his name and nationality corrected in the official Olympic annals.[26] Viewers of the NBC telecast were told this story, complete with film footage of Sohn's 1936 marathon victory and the medal ceremony and his comments and reminiscences. Hence, when he carried the torch into the Seoul Olympic stadium, they arguably had a more profound sense, along with Koreans, of the symbolic shattering of any traces of the earlier colonial-era experience.

Although visual content relating to Korea permeated all telecasts, it was most prominent during the various cultural performances and included such elements as traditional Korean musical instruments, costumes, the tiger cub mascot, "Hodori," and the Seoul Olympic emblem. The heaviest concentration of audio commentary on Korea also occurred during the cultural episodes of the ceremony.

The following audio themes were discussed by all broadcasters.

- the Korean War
- Korea's "economic miracle" accomplished in just thirty-five years
- Japanese occupation
- Korea's hospitality and courtesy as Olympic host
- Korea's desire for better international relations (specifically mentioning Hungary and China) as a result of the Olympics
- Korean national pride in staging such an event
- the time and money Korea spent preparing for the Seoul Olympics

Where the broadcasters departed from each other may be best described in terms of their attention to traditional or modern Korea. With more broadcasting on the cultural performances, BBC and TEN accordingly spent more time discussing traditional Korean culture and history, as described in their media guides. Both mentioned Korea's "rich appreciation for history" and "5,000-year history," although TEN commentators openly admitted it was sometimes "difficult to understand Korean culture."

NBC offered more glimpses of modern Korea, good and bad. It used brief, visual pans of Seoul as a transition into and out of many of its frequent commercial breaks, thereby placing the opening ceremony in the context of a city and its buildings, traffic, citizens, and surroundings. NBC also offered brief audio tidbits on current issues, including present-day North-South tensions, new trade relations, political changes, and the recent wave of anti-Americanism.

Korea Throughout NBC's Olympic Telecast

Easily the most comprehensive and thorough analysis of Korea's national image as portrayed in Olympic television was that undertaken by Rivenburgh.[27] She examined all feature reports about Korea that were broadcast by NBC during 170 1/2 hours of Olympic television coverage from Seoul, beginning with a preview show on September 15, 1988, and ending with an Olympics highlights show on October 4, 1988. These 41 feature segments were mostly pretaped for use in NBC telecasts, but on occasion, they were shown live, using either a roving reporter or an interviewer in a studio. Appendix A contains a complete listing of the segments and their main themes.

The overall focus of Rivenburgh's study was on how television as a medium is used to construct images of nations and their cultures. She conceptualized the process of producing television content about another nation as a "translation" process. In her words, "This 'translation process' is subject to many of the same influences as a direct intercultural interaction between people—simply because the producers of television *are* people."[28] However, unlike a personal intercultural encounter in which the purpose is normally to reduce uncertainty and increase understanding, the producers of commercial television operate under a mandate to provide entertainment and maintain high levels of audience interest.

To guide her analysis of the image of Korea presented in NBC's Olympic telecasts, Rivenburgh introduced the construct of *national image richness*, a multidimensional approach drawn from two bodies of scholarly literature that had previously been largely separate—one dealing with national images and the other pertaining to intercultural communication. The main dimensions of national image richness are *"image visibility*, or the amount and location of image exposure; *image valence*, or how favorably or unfavorably a nation is portrayed, *image breadth*, referring to the cognitive complexity and character of the aural and visual symbols associated with a national image, and finally *attribution*, which focuses on how another culture's behavior is being interpreted for home television audiences."[29]

Using the concept of national image richness, Rivenburgh addressed the following general research question: "What picture emerges of South Korea from the NBC broadcast of the 1988 Seoul Summer Games, and how might it be characterized in terms of national image richness?" She analyzed the visual characteristics of the 41 segments on Korea as well as the sound they carried and the verbal commentary that accompanied each. Although her research focus extended broadly to the actual and potential role of television in intercultural communication, some of the key findings carry direct implications for Korea's national image as political communication.

First, she found that the 41 Korea segments broadcast by NBC totaled 2 hours, 22 minutes, or just under 2 percent of its total Olympic broadcast time. In sheer quantitative terms, this amount of coverage appears, at first glance, to offer a low level of image visibility, as Rivenburgh herself noted, but it is a partial measure that can only hint at the total overall exposure of the host nation in all media. Furthermore, as the discussion of the boxing incident will show later in this chapter, even this level of attention to Korea's culture helped ignite a wave of public reaction in the Korean public, more because of the qualitative character of the coverage rather than its quantity.

Second, Rivenburgh found that, as an overall summary of image valence, 30 percent of the segment themes were negative, 58 percent were neutral, and 12 percent were positive, based on the value perspective of a U.S. audience.

> Positive themes referred to beautiful scenery, Korean pride, a move towards democracy, openness to different religions, modernization and Westernization, economic success, and the hosting of a successful Games. Negative themes focused around North/South issues (tension, threats, divided families), negative aspects of the Olympics (e.g. displaced residents, the hassle of tight security, lack of tourists), social issues (mixed marriages, the 'export' of orphans) anti-Americanism, personal and property devastation caused by the Korean War, urban congestion and pollution, and being 'less advanced' in some way (sports, economy). Neutral themes, the majority, carried no implicit or explicit evaluative association and included descriptions of the Korea education system, families and foods.

The third and most extensive set of findings by Rivenburgh had to do with image breadth. Here, she examined in detail both verbal and visual representations of Korea on NBC's telecasts. Political and social themes predominated, which helps explain the controversy that swirled around NBC in Seoul, along with those relating to the Olympics, architecture, and urban institutions. As the author put it,

> In considering image breadth, the verbal and visual associations with South Korea clustered primarily around security issues, social institutions (but not values), Olympics and urban characteristics—which clustered further into a handful of repeated themes. ... The image associations don't stretch out to cover more fundamental aspects of culture (e.g. communication patterns, conceptions of time or space, or gender roles) which might shed light on observed behavior. Accessibility of visual images plays an important role here, as well as an avoidance of that which is difficult to explain and understand.

In line with her central concern about the performance of television as a cross-cultural medium, she further noted that

> behaviors are not connected with an underlying and logical stream of cul-
> tural values. The only attempt at making a connection between belief and
> behaviour was to suggest that Confucianism somehow relates to ancestor
> worship. The result is that Korean activities—whether street markets or cel-
> ebratory ritual—seem different and odd; or possibly worse, visuals of Kore-
> ans eating at McDonalds or Kentucky Fried Chicken might make it seem
> that Koreans are becoming "just like us" to US audiences.

A final set of Rivenburgh's findings about attribution showed that NBC's team of U.S. media personalities, led by anchor Bryant Gumbel, dominated the narrative about South Korea. Each of the segments analyzed was introduced by a host anchor or 1 of the 6 NBC reporters assigned to provide such coverage. From a total of 97 people who were interviewed in the 41 feature segments, 46 percent were native Koreans. An analysis of all speakers in the segments, including the primary narrators, showed that nearly two-thirds were non-Koreans and just over one-third were Koreans. The overall cultural frame of reference was decidedly Western, in both topic and presentation.

In terms of Rivenburgh's focal research concern with national image richness and television as a medium for intercultural communication, NBC's telecasts "displayed a poverty of perspective, empathy, and knowledge." However, in the historical context of prior media coverage of Korea, as reviewed earlier, her data made it clear that NBC's coverage constituted a major increase in the amount and variety of information about Korea available to the U.S. public. Moreover, it was the sort of highly visual coverage that television viewers have come to expect around the Olympics, and the pictures from Seoul were a major part of what might linger in the minds of viewers around the world.

The Boxing Incident: News Events and International Relations in a Television Era

Early in the Seoul Olympics, an incident occurred in the boxing competition that served as a lightning rod for a surge of anti-NBC and anti-American sentiment in Korea involving the public, the press, politicians, and government officials. This coalescence of anti-Americanism, in turn, evoked a reaction from NBC and U.S. officials in Seoul and made the whole episode an international news story. This boxing incident, as it has come to be known, will be treated here in some detail because it sheds light on the central role of television and the other media in Olympic communication. It is a classic case study in the conflict of cultural norms about the proper behavior of athletes and the media in sports and news reporting. Furthermore, the manner in which the incident grew into such a firestorm of controversy within Korea and internationally cannot be fully understood apart from the communications and media environment in South Korea at the time, including the unprecedented television and media infrastructure that was created expressly to allow the domestic and international press to cover the Seoul Olympics.

The boxing incident per se involved a flare-up of anti-U.S. sentiment, but had it occurred in isolation, it could hardly have created such an uproar. Therefore, after describing the communications environment in South Korea, our treatment of the incident will place it in the historical context of changes in the U.S.-Korean relationship and a series of related events that occurred during or near the Olympic Games.

As noted in Chapter 1, television had been a universal phenomenon in South Korea for a number of years by the time of the Seoul Olympics, with most families owning color sets. The nation possessed the second largest advertising and media market in Asia. Although far smaller than Japan's market, it was also far larger than that of the other Asian economies. Given the highly literate public and increased leisure time accompanying the economic growth of the 1980s, Korean viewing patterns broadly approximated those in most other industrialized nations.

As discussed in Chapter 4, the amount of sports on Korean television channels had increased dramatically during the 1980s as part of the overall buildup toward the Olympics. During the Olympic competition itself, this attention reached a peak, with KBS-2 allocating 86.2 percent of its programming to sports, followed by KBS-1 with 76.5 percent and MBC-TV with 71.5 percent. In some cases, the networks simultaneously aired the same Olympic events, leading to audience complaints that they had no choice but to watch sports, regardless of their preferences. During the Olympics, the major Korean daily newspapers also devoted much of their space to news about the Olympics. Even after the papers increased the number of their pages from 16 to 24 or 32, a content analysis of two leading, large-circulation newspapers showed that the Dong-A Ilbo and the Chosun Ilbo devoted 80.3 percent and 83 percent of their news holes to the Olympics, respectively. On a more typical day, these papers might devote about 6 or 7 percent of their space to sports news.[30]

In terms of both media availability and usage, South Korea was, by any measure, a media-rich environment. However, there was one remarkable difference that helped to make the Seoul Olympics unique—indeed, unprecedented—in modern Olympic history: the Armed Forces Korea Network nationwide broadcasts on television (Channel 2) and radio throughout South Korea. Beginning earlier in the 1980s, AFKN relayed a range of network and cable television programming from the United States via satellite through the Armed Forces Radio and Television Service studios in Los Angeles. Notably, such programming routinely included network newscasts and CNN reports, along with entertainment programming, but with all commercial content excised. Officially, AFKN broadcasts in South Korea are a service to members of the U.S. military stationed there. Unofficially, the network is widely viewed by business and other international residents of Korea and by a substantial audience of highly-educated, English-speaking Koreans.

During the Seoul Olympics, AFKN had its own studio and set constructed in the NBC wing of the International Broadcast Center. It telecast all 179 and 1/2 hours of NBC's Olympic coverage in South Korea just as viewers in the United States would have seen it, with the exception of the commercials.

These circumstances meant that, for the first time in Olympic history, virtually the entire population of a country in which the Games were hosted could view or videotape the whole telecast of the Olympics from another nation. Of course, it is of particular import that the other nation was the United States, both because of its dominant involvement in Olympic television and because of Korea's special relationship with that nation. It is reasonable to expect that not only those Koreans fluent in English but also a substantially larger group of people took advantage of the opportunity—with the flip of a remote control button—to see how a foreign network was covering the Korean Olympics.

Also of importance is the role of AFKN, with its English-language NBC coverage, as a source for the large international press and broadcast contingent staying in hotels around Seoul. In many cases, members of this group also had access to an English audio channel that carried a translation of the Korean Broadcasting System's extensive coverage of the Olympics. Nevertheless, it would be expected that the NBC coverage on AFKN attracted a substantial part of what audience existed, especially once the boxing incident emerged as a news story.

If AFKN is the first unique aspect of Korea's media environment, the communications infrastructure created expressly for the large international broadcast and press contingent in Seoul is a second broad consideration essential to understanding the boxing incident and the Ben Johnson story that would come to overshadow it as an international news item. As described in detail in Chapter 5, the city of Seoul was figuratively "wired" or networked and had itself become a global village in miniature. The communications infrastructure, together with the large critical mass and proximity of so many news and sports reporters, helped to explain the rapid, almost instantaneous development of the boxing incident.

Even had a cluster of unfortunate events not taken place in Seoul during the Olympics, South Korea was ripe for such an outburst of anti-Americanism. Indeed, anti-Americanism had already taken a new and more public form over the preceding eight years as a growing number of Koreans questioned the U.S. role in the tragic Kwangju uprising in May 1980 and the Reagan administration's public support for the Fifth Republic under President Chun Doo Hwan during the ensuing seven years.

Broader considerations also form an important part of the context in which the boxing incident occurred. Korea had not only come to view the Olympics as a chance to enter the upper echelon of nations in the world but had also energetically seized every Olympic-related opportunity to pursue improved relations with the Socialist bloc nations.

During or immediately surrounding the Olympics, a set of events occurred that heightened the public and media reaction to the boxing incident.[31]

- During the opening ceremony, the behavior of U.S. athletes during their march into the main Olympic stadium was in stark contrast to that of the athletes from the 159 other national delegations. They waved, frolicked, carried handmade signs for the television cameras, and spilled off the track onto the grass field.
- Before the Olympics began, two teenage children of Americans stationed in Seoul beat a pregnant Korean in an incident that provoked outrage.[32]
- Two U.S. swimmers who won gold medals were caught and arrested with a stone lion mask they allegedly took from the Seoul Hyatt Hotel disco during a night of celebrating.[33]
- Three American servicemen were detained by police for allegedly refusing to pay a taxi fare of 15,000 won ($20); they also hit the driver in the head with a bag containing bottles of liquor.
- Unidentified NBC employees tried to have T-shirts made in Itaewon that read, "We're Boxing, We're Bad" on the front and "Chaos Tour '88" on the back, along with a sketch of two boxers superimposed on the South Korean flag. The shopkeeper refused to serve them and reported the incident to a Seoul newspaper, arguing that they had degraded the Korean flag and insulted the host country.[34]
- The boxing incident itself stemmed from a bout in which the losing Korean boxer, Byun Jong Il, was penalized by a referee from New Zealand. After the bout, several Korean boxing officials entered the ring and punched the referee. Chairs were thrown into the ring, and the boxer staged a 67-minute sit-in in the ring to protest the decision. Subsequently, Byun was suspended indefinitely by the International Amateur Boxing Association, five South Korean boxing officials

were thrown out of the Olympics, and Kim Chong Ha, the president of the South Korean Olympic Committee, resigned to take responsibility for the incident.[35] Initial reports in the Korean press expressed regret and shame over the occurrence. However, the focus swiftly changed to NBC's coverage of the episode, which became the central controversy and attracted attention not only in Korea and the United States but also internationally.

Because NBC Television's coverage of the boxing incident was so central to this entire episode, it will be described in some detail.[36] The network's initial report on the incident was broadcast in the United States on September 21, 1988, and consisted of the following 3-minute, 27-second segment. NBC Sports had been covering a long fourth game in a volleyball match between the United States and Argentina before switching back to cover the boxing incident.

Commentary: Marv Alpert: Alright Charlie … I should say Bob, it was quite a bit of action, Marv Alpert, with Ferdie Pacheko, Wally Matthews. It is some seventeen minutes since the ugly, scary scene in the ring that followed this man's defeat.

Visual: Close-up of Byun Jong Il sitting on the floor of the boxing ring.

Commentary: Alpert: This is Byong Jong Il of Korea. He lost on points to Alexander Hristov of Bulgaria, and then the crowd went wild on the announcement of the decision. The referee Keith Walker of New Zealand was jumped in the ring by the Korean coaches and then when the referee was escorted by the security staff, this is what took place. Wally Matthews was on hand. Wally, what happened?

Visual: Byun Jong Il. Camera zooms even closer.

Commentary: Matthews: Marv, it was one of the most amazing things, unbelievable things I've ever seen. They were trying to get at the referee and, uh, when he went for some sanctuary among these officials here in the yellow jackets who are supposed to be security guards, one of them actually tried to kick the referee in the face. I tried to get the referee to go on camera with us. All he would say to me was, "I'm taking the next plane back to New Zealand." The man was obviously scared out of his wits.

Visual: Referee being escorted away from the boxing rings amid security guards and others. Reporter Matthews attempting to get a comment from him.

Commentary: Alpert: And so that's the scene as the boxer, Byong Jong Il remains in the ring, obviously embarrassed by what has taken place.

Visual: Overhead shot of Byun Jong Il, zooming away to show ring with the Seoul Olympic Emblem in center of ring floor.

Commentary: Pacheko: I think he's humiliated, embarrassed, and the lucky thing is that this didn't happen in the evening when this place is packed with Koreans or we might have had a very ugly incident. One remarkable thing, it was a criminal activity on the part of that cornerman, and the lack of Korean police which surround this place, I mean there's some massive security here. Nobody was in the ring to stop this embarrassment, and you cannot escape from the fact that this should never take place in a sporting ring or a sporting event.

Visual: Closeup shot of Byun Jong Il's face.

Commentary: Alpert: What was most scary, the fact that chairs were being tossed into the ring following this controversial, foul-filled three rounds and the absurdity of it all, as the chairs were flying, as people were jumping into the ring, over at ring A, the boxing continued.

Visual: Long shot of both boxing rings. Camera pans to the other ring where a match is taking place.

Commentary: Pacheko: Let the games go on.

Visual: Close-up of Byun.

Commentary: Alpert: So, another controversial event here during the course of the boxing competition, but this time it did not involve an American. It involved instead, the host country, Korea. Let's get back to Bryant Gumbel.

Visual: Bryant Gumbel, then split screen with Gumbel and Byun Jong Il.

Commentary: Gumbel: Hey Marv, real quick, before we let you get away. This has now happened, I'd say about 17, 18 minutes ago. Has the security situation changed? Have they added people? Has it been beefed up?

Alpert: I don't think so, Bryant. But I think that things have now settled down. I would have a feeling that the particular security man who went at the referee Keith Walker, I would hope at least has seen his final days working here.

Pacheko: I think they removed the irritant, the referee. What's left is to remove the boxer. So far nobody's come out. I think they've sent for the movers to come move him, because he doesn't look like he's getting up and going anywhere.

Gumbel: Well, if history is the precedent, he could be there a while. We note that in 1964 back in Tokyo a Korean flyweight by the name of Cho Dong Kee staged a 51 minute sit down strike in the ring after he was disqualified, so I'd say young Byun Jong Il has a ways to go yet, he's … oh at least 40 minutes or so.

Visual: Alternates split screen and closeups of Byun.

Commentary: Alpert: Yeah, 18 minutes and counting, Bryant. We'll be standing by, though.

BG: (laughter) Put a clock on it. O.K. Marv and Ferdie, thanks very much. The U.S. men are all tied up with Argentina after four sets. We'll be getting back for the fifth and deciding set of volleyball in just a moment, right after this.

Visual: Close up of Byun Jong Il.

Following a commercial break, NBC returned to the boxing venue for 32 seconds as follows:

Commentary: Gumbel: Back here in Seoul, the picture from the Chamsil Students Gymnasium tells the whole story. Young Korean bantamweight Byun Jong Il continues to sit in the center of the ring, this following his controversial loss to Alexander Hristov of Bulgaria. He's been sitting there, holding this little personal strike now for oh, a little more than twenty minutes. It was a controversial decision that prompted a mini-riot inside the ring. We'll be getting more on that as we continue to report on throughout the day. Right now let's get back to volleyball. We're set for a fifth set.

Visual: Closeup shot of Byun Jong Il, shoulders and face.

NBC's coverage switched back to volleyball, then returned to the boxing after a few minutes, with the following commentary from anchor Bryant Gumbel:

Commentary: Gumbel: Back in Seoul as the Games continue, you can see the U.S.-Argentina volleyball game is continuing, and so is the sitdown strike of Byun Jong Il, the young Korean bantamweight who suffered a controversial loss, shall we say, to Alexander Hristov of Bulgaria. He lost on the card four to one, this after Keith Walker, New Zealand referee, had deducted two points from him for head-butting, or for rough treatment. We understand that his sitdown strike is continuing. There has so far been no attempt ... no attempt to remove him from the ring. He's been sitting there now for twenty-eight minutes. We'll be taking a look at his fight just a little bit later on. But for right now, let's get back to volleyball, where the U.S. and Argentina are tied at three in the final and deciding set. Let's go back to Bob Trumpey.

Visual: Split screen with U.S.-Argentina volleyball game in upper-left part of screen and closeup of Byun Jong Il in lower right quadrant.

Commentary: [Bob] Trumpey: Thank you Bryant. Anthony Hembrick couldn't get a second in that ring, and that young man, they can't get out.

Visual: Split screen with U.S.-Argentina volleyball game in upper-left part of screen and closeup of Byun Jong Il in lower right quadrant.

More volleyball competition. Next commercial break.

Commentary: Trumpey: There's the boxer still in the ring. Time elapsed, 32 minutes … in this volleyball match it's been two hours and thirteen minutes, game five.

Visual: Split screen with volleyball game and the boxer sitting in.

More volleyball.

Visual: Split screen with a "Live" graphic and a display of the duration of the sit-in. No mention by volleyball commentators.

Visual: Transition to station break with NBC Olympic logo superimposed on an overhead shot of the boxing ring with Byun Jong Il. The following commercial logos and messages superimposed sequentially over a medium shot of the boxer sitting in the ring: Lite Beer logo ("Miller Lite, sponsor of U.S. Olympic training centers") and Kodacolor Gold ("Show Your True Colors"), Visa ("It's Everywhere You Want to Be"), Isuzu ("the First Car Builders of Japan").

NBC's coverage continued in this vein until about 48 minutes into the boxer's sit-in, at which time the network replayed coverage of the bout and the ensuing fracas, which had not been telecast live to the United States. The following commentary accompanied NBC's visual coverage as the decision was announced.

Commentary: Pacheko: Back at Chamsil Student's Gymnasium, a look first at the third round according to count-a-punch, with Byun throwing the 82 and landing 17, so 21 percent proficiency as opposed to Hristov (graphic shows 16% proficiency). And the final card, as far as count-a-punch is concerned, would give the bout to the Korean, Byun Jong Il, over Alexander Hristov, but you must also factor in the two points that Byun will lose on the scorecard because of the warnings. You lose one point for a warning. Three cautions add up to a warning. And, we're ready now for the decision.

Visual: Long shot of boxing venue with count-a-punch graphics.

Commentary: Public Address Announcer: Ladies and Gentlemen. We will now announce the winner of Ring B. The winner is, on points 4-1, in the red corner, Alexander Hristov, Bulgaria.

Visual: Two boxers and referee in the ring.

Commentary: Alpert: A disappointed crowd, as they have seen another Korean lose, but those two points taken away because of the warnings. Look out! Here's the Korean coach challenging the referee, Keith Walker.

Visual: Man jumps into the ring after Walker.

Commentary: Pacheko: And physically challenging. That's ugly. That's not something ...

Visual: Security guard in ring. Chairs flung into the ring.

Commentary: Alpert: And now we have a very ugly scene ... chairs being thrown into the ring. Look out! This is most unfortunate, in particular that its [unclear] a Korean boxer, and they are trying to get ... Look out! The referee just took a punch from one of the Korean coaches.

Commentary: Pacheko: And these are the officials fighting. Now the security is coming in. It's ugly because the Korean coaches are punching the referee. Keith Walker is getting punched by the cornermen.

Visual: Melee in the ring.

Commentary: Alpert: This is ugly.

Return to live telecast, following Byun Jong Il's sit-in.

As the preceding passages make clear, NBC treated the boxing incident as a newsworthy event and an unusual occurrence in the context of Olympic sport. It was clearly thought to have high audience-holding or interest value, as shown by the network's regular return to it before or immediately after commercial breaks. This impression was further reinforced by the use of split screens and the manner in which the network clocked the duration of the boxer's sit-in and reminded viewers of it through both verbal commentary and on-screen graphics.

The reaction of the Korean press and public was strong, but the pattern in which it emerged said a great deal about the nature of the incident. Korean politicians, government officials, and representatives of the Seoul Olympic Organizing Committee also reacted, but they attempted to play a moderating role once the strength of the press and public response was apparent.

The *Dong-A Ilbo*, a leading Korean daily, wrote that "this is a bad omen for future Korean-American relations. The American press has to know that this kind of distorted reporting is hurting the dignity of Korean people who have been preparing for the Olympics for seven years and is fanning anti-American sentiment."[37] Most South Korean newspapers reported on foreign coverage of the boxing incident, and some of them carried strong editorials that, according to the Japanese news service Kyodo, singled out the U.S. and Japanese print media as being especially insensitive in their handling of the story.[38]

Such press commentary reflected and perhaps also contributed to a strong public response. In addition to the editorials and articles, there were letters to the editor and telephone calls.[39] At least one reporter wrote about anti-NBC comments made by medical personnel at the Main Press Center's first-aid center, and signs on some shops in Itaewon, a popular shopping area for Western tourists near the large U.S. Eighth Army base, read "NBC Not Welcome."[40] Notably, many owners of businesses in the Itaewon shopping area speak English and regularly view AFKN telecasts. As a result, they, perhaps more than any other subgroup of the Korean population, would have been likely to view the telecasts and contrast NBC's treatment of the boxing incident with the coverage on the Korean Broadcasting System.

The public response was eventually accompanied by high-level official commentary. In an interview with international journalists, Park Seh-Jik, president of the Seoul Olympic Organizing Committee, said, "When you look at the matter from a different point of view, you get different perceptions. Maybe some more consideration should have been given ... maybe NBC focused too long and hard on one aspect and gave the wrong impression. One instant and one moment should be representative of one instant and one moment. While the incident was regretful, maybe the situation needed some considerate thinking."[41]

The secretary-general of South Korea's ruling Democratic Justice Party (DJP) joined in criticism of NBC, calling its coverage biased and disparaging.[42] Another ruling party legislator, Son Chu Wan, accused NBC of showing too many "undesirable aspects" of South Korea. According to the *Washington Post*, "Although the network has aired many positive accounts of Koreans and Korean culture, many Koreans—who have been able to watch NBC's coverage on the U.S. Armed Forces network—resented reports on the black market, the mistreatment of Amerasian children and a few other negative aspects."[43]

Eventually the press, public, and official reaction reached such a level that both President Roh Tae Woo and the main opposition leader, Kim Dae Jung, addressed it publicly. President Roh told his cabinet that he believed anti-American feelings were damaging and were getting out of control. Government officials met with newspaper editors and publishers to ask for cooperation in calming public feelings. President Roh also made a brief tour of the Olympic Main Press Center, meeting with reporters there in what was viewed as a gesture of support for the foreign press. Opposition leader Kim Dae Jung also warned against the growing anti-Americanism, saying that "the present impatient fever toward the Soviet Union, and also some impatient anti-American sentiment, both are not mature attitudes."[44]

NBC responded to these developments in several ways. Kevin Monaghan, a spokesman for the network, apologized on Korean television.[45] Internally, NBC executives in Seoul warned their staff not to wear the NBC Olympic pin, a combination of the peacock logo and the Olympic rings, in public.[46] In addition, senior NBC executives publicly responded, and the network aired news and feature reports dealing with the controversy—

one on "NBC Nightly News" and others aired during Olympic coverage. Michael L. Eskridge, executive vice president of Olympics for NBC, said that "we thought it was part of a developing story. That the Korean team was involved was incidental. We gave the same kind of coverage to the U.S. boxer missing the bus and to the U.S. swimmers being thrown off the team."[47] Terry Ewert, coordinating producer for the Olympics for NBC Sports, said, "It was news and we covered it as news; it wasn't viewed as a condemnation of the Korean people. But they're very sensitive about their country. You say anything wrong about Korean society and it's like taking a swipe at their whole culture."[48]

One of NBC's most revealing responses to the incident was a decision to cut back on the nonsports coverage the network had planned to broadcast. According to the Kyodo News Service, "The network discontinued its non-sports coverage after being accused of scouring the back alleys of the capital in an effort to dig up negative aspects of the country such as student demonstrations, illicit trade and prostitution."[49] A report in the *New York Times* stated that it was not only the public outcry in Korea but also ratings reports that U.S. audiences were uninterested in coverage of South Korean society during the Games that "prompted NBC to drop a scheduled feature on Monday on Korean women."[50] Although NBC dropped some of its planned nonsports coverage because of the controversy, it also took the step of inviting two Korean journalists to its studios to be interviewed about the affair. The transcript of that interview, contained in Appendix B, offers some fascinating glimpses into the conflicting cultural norms that were at the heart of the entire NBC incident.

A report in the *New York Times* described NBC's coverage of South Korean society in the following terms:

> "In addition to some admiring portraits of South Korean economic and political progress, NBC has broadcast reports prepared by its news and sports divisions on Korean sweatshops, squatters forced from their homes as Seoul prepared for the Olympics, urban poor, prostitutes, and adoption of Korean children by foreigners. Bob Eaton, executive producer for the Olympics for NBC News and Michael Weisman, executive producer for NBC Sports, said they had received complaints about several of the broadcasts. Regarding the decision to shelve a planned program on Korean women that was scheduled Monday night, Kevin Monaghan, an NBC spokesman, said: 'We know people are very sensitive now about features involving Korea, and the piece wouldn't have been a positive piece. We also were hearing from the United States that people were saying they wanted to watch sports and not features about Korea.'"[51]

The report in the *New York Times* contained the following perceptive comment: "Koreans can watch NBC coverage live on the American military station here, although many of those questioned said their reaction was based on South Korean news reports and hearsay."[52] It was apparently not AFKN alone but rather the intense concentration of international and Korean media attention, along with the technical infrastructure to facilitate instant communication in Korea and globally, that conditioned public reaction.

NBC's executive producer, Michael Weisman, also commented on the NBC coverage of the boxing incident: "The Koreans obviously were very sensitive. When that brawl broke out, the Korean Broadcasting System pulled out to a wide shot. The KBS didn't even show it. It was good television, good drama. ... We don't think we've been one-sided or heavy-handed."[53]

In summary, several points can be made about the boxing incident as an episode in what Lee Sang-Chul termed "crossed-cultural communications."[54] First, it is apparent that the incident grew to such proportions because it was treated by both NBC Sports and NBC News reporters—and subsequently all international and Korean media—as a news event. It was not the coverage of the actual event as it occurred that aroused the ire of Koreans but rather the repetition of the occurrence.

Second, even if taken as a news event, the incident highlighted different cultural norms as to how the news media should cover an occurrence. The Korean cultural norm demands that the guest show respect to the host and refrain from hurting the host in any way. Furthermore, Koreans expected that because NBC was in Korea, its practices should tend toward the Korean, rather than the American, cultural norm.[55] The same principle applied to the manner in which most Koreans viewed the behavior of U.S. athletes during the opening ceremony.

Third, the present analysis indicates that the NBC production team viewed the boxing incident as attention-getting and, hence, audience-holding. The repeated use of split screen visuals and shots of Byung Jong Il in the ring leading into and out of commercial breaks shows this most clearly. The impact created by such repetition in a commercial format could hardly be equaled by a noncommercial broadcaster and must to be considered in interpreting the Korean press and public reaction.

Fourth, the boxing incident underscores the importance of interpreting major news events in light of audience predispositions. As shown here, the context of public opinion in South Korea was ripe for such an outburst of anti-Americanism. Indeed, at least since the 1980 Kwangju uprising, anti-American sentiment had been spreading and was expressed much more publicly.

Fifth, in a global context, the incident stands as an exemplar of how worldwide communication technology and travel, by allowing greater contact among cultures, accentuates and, in a political sense, exacerbates different cultural interpretations of the same event. The phenomenon of "parachute journalism" or the so-called firehouse model of covering the news has long been known. This appears to be the approach taken by NBC. As noted by Frank Deford in NBC's own exploration of the incident, "Well of course, the problem is that we've been trying to put on an Olympics at the same time that we've been trying to get to know you and I think maybe the next time we come back we'll get to know you a lot better."[56] It is precisely this lesson that should be taken away by the news and sports media. That the Olympics are a cultural and communication project, and as such, they require cross-cultural and language sensitivity. This may be an old lesson, but it is one that the Seoul Olympics strongly underscored.

The Ben Johnson Incident

By far the major news event of the Seoul Olympics was the incident in which Canadian sprinter Ben Johnson was stripped of his gold medal for the 100-meter race after steroids were detected in his urine in a postrace test. *Sports Illustrated*, in its first issue following the Seoul Olympics, wrote that "one must go back to 1964 and Tokyo to find the last Games without some kind of scandal or disruption. ... And now Seoul '88, the Games that will forever be remembered for drug busts."[57] Of course, the biggest of these busts was Ben Johnson's.

However, although the Ben Johnson incident overshadowed any other single incident as a news event, all evidence suggests that it did not reflect much at all on Korea as a nation. To the contrary, one of the major U.S. television networks, ABC, even awarded its "Person-of-the-Week" recognition to the Korean physician who supervised the doping control for the Seoul Olympics, it also telecast a story on him. Instead, the incident's ramifications were felt very broadly within the Olympic movement and the wider world of international sport. According to Thomas McPhail, the underlying problem that led to the Ben Johnson fiasco involved a subversion of de Coubertin's ideal of competing to the best of one's ability into the goal of winning at all cost, even if that cost included medical assistance or cheating in competition. It is noteworthy that McPhail's analysis pointed to the contribution of the media and corporate sponsorship to this "winning at all cost mentality." As he stated, "It's not only on the track or ice surface where athletes are competing. They are now also competing for extremely lucrative marketing/advertising sponsorships."[58] Moreover, he suggested that "this phenomenon of Olympic success meaning instant star status has been indirectly supported by Juan Antonio Samaranch of the IOC" through the pursuit of lucrative television contracts and an expanded program for the marketing of Olympic symbols. Thus, "drugs, media attention and endorsements are indirectly related to this winning at all cost mentality."[59]

The national repercussions of the Ben Johnson affair affected Canada most directly and immediately. As Bruce Kidd noted following Johnson's victory, "Few moments in our history have produced such a Durkheimian moment of pan-Canadian communion. But if victory was national affirmation, disqualification was national disgrace."[60]

Image Effects in Other Nations

As mentioned at the outset, the question of how global television and media coverage affected the image of Korea is of interest not only in the United States but in other nations as well. Research from several other countries bears directly on the nature of the more global experience.

An extensive study revealed that New Zealand's press coverage of Korea during 1988 closely mirrored the coverage of mainstream U.S. media. As Laurence Chalip summarized his findings, "For the media, Korea was a stage on which a drama was unfolding. That drama was a political one, with the narrative's conflict being built around two phenomena: international terrorism and local violence. Together, these generated dramatic tension by suggesting threats to the safety of the Games themselves, and, by extension, the participants."[61] As in the United States, the theme of "international terrorism" focused heavily on North Korea, with attention to the unfolding revelations about the bombing of the KAL jet in November 1987, reports of North Korean troops massing near the DMZ, U.S. State Department warnings about possible terrorism during the Olympics, and so forth. The "local violence" theme focused heavily on the confrontations between student demonstrators and South Korean combat police. In the press of New Zealand, as in that of the United States, these two themes dominated the narrative during the 8 and 1/2 months preceding the Seoul Olympics.[62] Such a finding is not surprising given a wealth of research evidence suggesting that Western news media follow similar practices and are heavily dependent on the same wire services for much of their news.[63]

In one of the most thorough image studies on the Seoul Olympics, Chalip also conducted both surveys and focus group discussions before and after the Games.[64] His findings were striking. Before the Olympics, only 47 percent of respondents gave an affirmative response to the question, "Do you think Seoul, Korea is a good place to host the Olympics?" as compared to 76 percent who responded favorably after the Games. Although 89 percent of respondents could identify Seoul and Korea prior to the Games, due to the pre-Olympic buildup of publicity, that proportion had risen to 95 percent following the actual Olympic coverage.

Nevertheless, when Chalip probed for details about Korea, only vague generalizations could be elicited, such as, "It was a big place"; "It was heavily guarded"; "The city looked pretty, green, well laid out"; or "All

the houses were squashed together." He concluded that "the Games enhanced New Zealanders' awareness of Korea, but only in vague terms. The
media narrative had concluded, leaving positive impressions about Korea's place as a nation among nations. But Korean society, history, culture
and politics had been presented merely as a scattered assortment of unre-
lated, decontextualized details."[65] It should also be noted that his research
measured a short-term response to Olympic television and media coverage. Over the long term, the presumption would be that New Zealanders'
image of Korea would depend on the nature of ongoing press attention to
that nation.

   Research reported by Wojceich Liponski in Poland is of particular interest because it suggests the nature of image effects in a Socialist bloc nation
with a government-controlled press system.[66] Moreover, Poland was second only to Hungary in the haste with which it moved to establish ties
with South Korea.

   In Poland, as was likely the case in the other nations of Eastern Europe,
the significance of communication emanating from the Seoul Olympics
was strengthened by the "information drought" about South Korea that
had existed since the Korean War era. As he put it, "In this context any portion of information on Korea which was eventually brought to Poland during and after the 1988 Olympics unquestionably did not simply play the
role of a proverbial drop in the bucket, but rather the role of magic crystal
ball carefully watched and passed to any and all."[67]

   Polish public opinion about Korea began to change in 1980, when initial resentments about the "restored order" of Gen. Chun Doo Hwan were
supplanted by a "hesitating esteem" based on economic considerations.
Support of Solidarity in Poland and resistance to the Warsaw government
coincided with developments in Korea, as Lech Walesa issued his famous
call for "Poland as the second Japan into the future."[68] However, it was not
until the months preceding the Seoul Olympics that a significant amount
of information about South Korea began to come through to the Polish
public.

   Liponski described the December 1987 broadcast of a 35-minute television program, *Seoul—Its Controversies and Hopes*, as a "battering ram" that
opened up the possibility of a broader range of press coverage. It had originally been conceived as an hour-long broadcast in October 1987, but plans
met with resistance from the director of television Channel II in Poland. In
its original length, the program included an 18-minute film titled *Seoul
Welcomes the World*, produced by KBS in Korea, and a 42-minute discussion
by Polish journalists on the problems faced by the forthcoming Olympics.

   Once the program was finally broadcast, it was received by a public eager for information about the realities of South Korea. In a particularly re-

vealing passage, Liponski described the public reaction to such television programming in Poland:

> In the case of the ROK even short TV clips showing strikes and street tur-
> moils provided Polish watchers with some quite positive observations de-
> spite intentions of official propagandists: Well dressed young people, Ko-
> rean cars, "Oh Lord, why they burn them!" impressive architecture of the
> city in the background etc., were visible enough to cause at least occasional
> reaction of the following type: "This country looks much better than we are
> officially informed." It is easy to understand then that the impact of almost
> 170 hours of TV transmission during the Olympics brought incomparably
> stronger and more lasting effects.[69]

In a telephone poll conducted in Poland following the 1988 Olympics, the following nonsport features of Korean reality were most frequently mentioned by respondents: (1) rich and beautiful folklore, (2) country pro-ducing good electronic equipment, (3) imposing architecture, (4) nice cars, and (5) cleanness of the city and people.

Liponski suggested that the contribution of television to shaping such a positive but simplified picture of South Korea was obvious. This oc-curred mainly through the opening and closing ceremonies, with their op-portunities to view Korean folklore, and through such athletic events as the marathon, which provided panoramic views of Seoul.

A research team from Moscow University examined coverage of the Seoul Olympic Games and Korea by nine Soviet newspapers and maga-zines between 1981 and 1991. Findings from that study, which included the three most influential daily newspapers—*Pravda, Izvestiya,* and the *Komsomolskaya Pravda*—offer a useful supplement to Liponski findings in Poland. In general, the study found that little attention was paid to South Korea during most of the period. From 1981 to 1988, it was portrayed in confrontational terms as a U.S. satellite dictatorship. For example, in an ar-ticle carried by *Pravda* on September 26, 1981, dealing with Chinese-South Korean trade relations, the author stated that by broadening trade and eco-nomic relations with a reactionist regime, China was assisting Washing-ton's growing efforts to build up the military-economic potential of South Korea.[70]

Quantitatively, there was very little news about South Korea in the So-viet press during the 1981–1988 period. For instance, only two stories were found in *Pravda* during 1981, and two in 1984. In 1988, the number of *Pravda* stories jumped to 31.[71] A similar pattern was found in *Izvestiya,* which carried three stories about South Korea in 1981, one in 1984, and sixty-four in 1988.

The coverage in 1988 largely centered on the Olympics and sports events, but the stories contained enough information to help readers imagine the everyday life of Seoul during that period. They touched on such topics as comfortable apartment housing, good European cuisine, rapid economic growth in South Korea, good medical service, the freedom to practice different religions, the friendliness of Korean people, and the expense of hosting the Olympic Games.[72]

The Moscow University researchers also interviewed journalists working for each of the publications in their study. Those interviews suggested that the experiences of Soviet journalists in Seoul during the Olympic Games promoted new social, economic, and cultural concepts, some of which were helpful to the development of the perestroika process in the Soviet Union and changes in the Soviet society. Overall, the authors concluded that the impact of the Seoul Olympics on Soviet public opinion went far beyond demonstrating the beauty and importance of sport and became an event of global importance in promoting new thinking and creative approaches in politics, economics, culture, and international affairs.[73]

Altogether, the evidence presented in this chapter is partial; it comes from disparate sources and deals largely with the symbolic suggestion component of televised images rather than their actual impact on audiences. Hence, the findings cannot be interpreted as a definitive answer to the question of how Olympic television affects national images, especially that of South Korea as host for the 1988 Games. However, there is good reason to believe that the overall impact of television surrounding the 1988 Olympics as an *event* not only helped to change South Korea's image around the world but also began to change it in a positive direction. The best support for such a proposition involves the nation's persistent "image problem" over the years leading up to the Seoul Olympics. Given years of sporadic media coverage highlighting political unrest and violence, as experienced in the United States, or even more limited coverage with similar emphases in Socialist nations, the pictures televised from Seoul in September 1988 could only contribute to a more positive view of the nation. Nevertheless, it should be remembered that Olympic television and press coverage, while massive in global reach, may not accomplish the same thing as steady repetition, over time, of a positive message.

These findings also direct attention to the central role of televised images in the politics of the Seoul Olympics and, by extension, in political processes more generally. There is ample evidence that television messages were taken seriously, however differently they may have been interpreted, by such interested parties as the Korean public, government officials in Seoul, leaders of the Seoul Olympic Organizing Committee, or the NBC Television staff. The information in this and earlier chapters suggests a rather broad consensus among those who make up the modern "Olympic family"—that the televised messages constitute a core aspect of the Olympic experience.

Notes

1. Hwang Kil-Woong, "Sports Federations and Host Broadcaster in the Games of the XXIV Olympiad," *SORTO Courier* 2 (December 1986): p. 20.

2. Daniel Dayan and Elihu Katz, *Media Events: The Live Broadcasting of History* (Cambridge, Mass.: Harvard University Press, 1992).

3. Park Seh-Jik, "Seoul Olympic Memorial Address," in *Toward One World Beyond All Barriers*, proceedings of the Seoul Olympiad Anniversary Conference, vol. 1. (Seoul, Korea: Poong Nam Publishing, 1990), p. 112.

4. W. Lance Bennett, *News: The Politics of Illusion* (New York: Longman, 1983), p. 37.

5. James F. Larson, "Quiet Diplomacy in a Television Era: The Media and U.S. Policy Toward the Republic of Korea," *Political Communication and Persuasion* 7 (1990): pp. 73–95.

6. John J. MacAloon, "Comparative Analysis of the Olympic Ceremonies, with Special Reference to Los Angeles, 1984" (Paper presented at the International Symposium on the Olympics, Communication and Intercultural Exchange, Centre for Olympic Studies, Barcelona, Spain, April 3–5, 1991).

7. This is a Korean Broadcasting System estimate. Also according to KBS, estimates of the cumulative audience—those who watched any part of the Olympic telecast on at least one occasion—exceeded three billion viewers.

8. Daniel Dayan and Elihu Katz, "Television Ceremonial Events," in A. Berger, ed., *Television in Society* (New Brunswick, N.J.: Transaction Books, 1987), pp. 41–53.

9. John J. MacAloon, "Olympic Games and the Theory of Spectacle in Modern Societies," in John J. MacAloon, ed., *Rite, Drama, Festival, Spectacle: Rehearsals Toward a Theory of Cultural Performance* (Philadelphia, Pa.: Institute for the Study of Human Issues, 1984), pp. 252–253.

10. Margaret Walker Dilling, "The Familiar and the Foreign: Music as Medium of Exchange in the Seoul Olympic Ceremonies," in *Toward One World Beyond All Barriers*, proceedings of the Seoul Olympiad Anniversary Conference (Seoul, Korea: Poong Nam Publishing, 1990), pp. 357–377.

11. Park Seh-Jik, "The Seoul Olympics: A People's Masterpiece," 1991, manuscript, pp. 79, 80.

12. Nancy K. Rivenburgh, "National Image Richness in NBC Television Coverage of the 1988 Seoul Olympics," Ph.D. diss. University of Washington, Seattle, Wash., July 1991, p. 125.

13. International Olympic Committee, *Olympic Charter '91* (Lausanne, Switzerland: International Olympic Committee, 1991), p. 58.

14. For a summary of this research and related considerations, see James F. Larson, *Television's Window on the World* (Norwood, N.J.: Ablex, 1984), pp. 7–12.

15. Harold D. Lasswell, "The Structure and Function of Communication in Society," in Wilbur Schramm and Donald F. Roberts, eds., *The Process and Effects of Mass Communication* (Urbana: University of Illinois Press, 1974), pp. 84–99.

16. Larson, *Television's Window on the World*, p. 56.

17. Larson, "Quiet Diplomacy in a Television Era," p. 80.

18. *Television News Index and Abstracts,* a guide to the videotape collection of the network evening news programs in the Vanderbilt Television News Archive, Vanderbilt University, Nashville, Tenn.

19. Ibid.

20. Fred Hiatt, "Seoul Frets over Olympics Security; S. Koreans Resent Others' Fears but Warn of Danger from North," *Washington Post,* June 27, 1988, p. A17.

21. Transcription from an off-the-air videotape of NBC's telecast, recorded in Seattle, Wash.

22. James F. Larson and Nancy K. Rivenburgh, "A Comparative Analysis of Australian, U.S. and British Telecasts of the Seoul Olympic Opening Ceremony," *Journal of Broadcasting and Electronic Media* 35 (Winter 1991): pp. 75–94.

23. For a more detailed description of methods, see Larson and Rivenburgh, "A Comparative Analysis."

24. Tom Shales, "NBC, Dropping the Torch; Olympic Coverage: Dull and Over-commercialized," *Washington Post,* September 19, 1988, p. B1.

25. Dayan and Katz, "Television Ceremonial Events."

26. Sohn Kee Chung participated in ceremonies in both Los Angeles and Berlin, and his name and nationality were corrected on Olympic monuments in those cities.

27. Rivenburgh, "National Image Richness in NBC Television Coverage of the 1988 Seoul Olympics."

28. Nancy K. Rivenburgh, "National Image Richness in US-Televised Coverage of South Korea During the 1988 Olympics," *Asian Journal of Communication* 2 (1992): p. 4.

29. Ibid., p. 5. Quotations and other information from Rivenburgh's study in the next six paragraphs are from pp. 5–30 of her work.

30. Sang-Chul Lee, "Seoul Olympics: Some Crossed Cultural Communications," *Media Asia* 16 (1989): p. 195.

31. For the most complete English-language study of the boxing incident to date, see Sang-Chul Lee, "Lessons and Achievements of the Seoul Olympics," in *Toward One World Beyond All Barriers,* proceedings of the Seoul Olympiad Anniversary Conference (Seoul, Korea: Poong Nam Publishing, 1990), pp. 200–213.

32. Susan Chira, "U.S. Olympic Reporting Hits a Raw Korean Nerve," *New York Times,* September 28, 1988, P. A1.

33. "Koreans Fan Anti-U.S. Feelings at Olympics," *Chicago Tribune,* September 29, 1988, p. 6.

34. Randy Harvey, "Seoul Notebook—Hosts Earn a Thumbs-up," *Los Angeles Times,* October 3, 1988, p. 1.

35. *New York Times,* September 24, 1988, sec. 1, p. 51.

36. All transcriptions of verbal commentary and descriptions of what television showed visually were taken from off-the-air videotapes of NBC's Olympic telecast, as recorded in Seattle, Wash.

37. As quoted in Chira, "U.S. Olympic Reporting."

38. "Seoul Gov't, Press Slam Foreign Media Olympic Coverage," Kyodo News Service (Seoul, Korea), September 24, 1988.

39. Chira, "U.S Olympic Reporting."

40. Harvey, "Seoul Notebook—Hosts Earn a Thumbs-up."

41. George Solomon, "Park Speaks Out About Melee; SLOOC President Disappointed by Coverage of Boxing Fiasco," *Washington Post*, September 26, 1988, p. B12.

42. "Seoul Gov't, Press Slam Foreign Media Olympic Coverage."

43. Fred Hiatt, "Seoul Tries to Counter Growing Anti-U.S. Mood," *Washington Post*, September 30, 1988, p. A18.

44. Ibid.

45. Harvey, "Seoul Notebook—Hosts Earn a Thumbs-up."

46. Chira, "U.S. Olympic Reporting."

47. Solomon, "Park Speaks Out About Melee."

48. Chira, "U.S. Olympic Reporting."

49. "South Korea Media Hits NBC Over T-Shirt Incident," Kyodo News Service (Seoul, Korea), September 29, 1988.

50. Chira, "U.S. Olympic Reporting."

51. Ibid.

52. Ibid.

53. Norman Chad, "Weisman, NBC Deserve Credit, Not Criticism for Telling Whole Olympic Story," *Washington Post*, September 27, 1988, p. D9.

54. Lee, "Seoul Olympics: Some Crossed Cultural Communications."

55. Ibid., p. 197.

56. Frank DeFord interview with Korean journalists Hee Yon Kook, from *Dong-A Ilbo*, and Park Sung Hee, from *Chosun Ilbo*, broadcast by NBC Television as part of its Olympics coverage.

57. William Oscar Johnson, "Take a Bow," *Sports Illustrated* 69 (October 10, 1988): p. 38.

58. Thomas L. McPhail, "Canadian Media: The Ben Johnson Saga Continues" (Paper presented at the 39th Annual Conference of the International Communication Association, San Francisco, Calif., May 25–29, 1989), p. 2.

59. Ibid., p. 3.

60. Bruce Kidd, "'Seoul to the World, the World to Seoul' ... and Ben Johnson: Canada at the 1988 Olympics," *Toward One World Beyond All Barriers*, proceedings of the Seoul Olympiad Anniversary Conference (Seoul, Korea: Poong Nam Publishing, 1990), p. 450.

61. Laurence Chalip, "The Politics of Olympic Theatre: New Zealand and Korean Cross-National Relations," *Toward One World Beyond All Barriers*, proceedings of the Seoul Olympiad Anniversary Conference (Seoul, Korea: Poong Nam Publishing, 1990), p. 415.

62. Ibid., pp. 414–419.

63. For a summary of research and concerns widely expressed during the 1970s, see *Many Voices, One World*, report by the International Commission for the Study of Communication Problems (New York: Unipub, 1980).

64. Chalip, "The Politics of Olympic Theatre," pp. 408–433.

65. Ibid., p. 427.

66. Wojceich Liponski, "The 1988 Olympics as Catalyst for Changes in the Attitude of Polish Society Toward the Republic of Korea," in *Toward One World Beyond*

All Barriers, proceedings of the Seoul Olympiad Anniversary Conference (Seoul, Korea: Poong Nam Publishing, 1990), pp. 249–310.

67. Ibid., p. 252.

68. Ibid., p. 256.

69. Ibid., p. 274.

70. Yassen N. Zassoursky, "The XXIV Olympic Games in Seoul and Their Impact on the Soviet Media and the Soviet Public," a report based on a study of the Soviet media in 1981–1991, Faculty of Journalism, Moscow University, 1991, p. 2.

71. Ibid. p. 6.

72. Ibid., p. 3.

73. Ibid., p. 1.

9

Toward a Media-Theoretic
Understanding of
Political Communication

The Olympics in Seoul, like other recent Summer and Winter Games, were intrinsically a television spectacle, albeit larger in their global reach and reflecting advances in the television industry and telecommunications generally. On this matter, there can be little debate, regardless of whether the Seoul Olympics are conceived of as a global television event or as a decade-long communication process. Consider that when the Games were awarded to Seoul in 1981, Cable News Network—now the leading global television news service—was but an upstart operation in the United States. Indeed, the rapid development of telecommunications worldwide during the 1980s coincided with South Korea's massive national effort to host the Olympics. The challenge of hosting the world's largest television event accelerated the nation's involvement with the new communications realities.

Along with the transformation in communications around the world, it was the changing political climate of the 1980s and Korea's distinctive place in relation to such changes that set Seoul apart from preceding Olympics. As cold war understandings crumbled internationally, South Korea was naturally eager to identify with and, if possible, expedite the transformation. Although the tragedy of national division served as a continuing reminder of the cold war, the Olympics provided an ideal vehicle for leaders in Seoul to push their Northern policy in foreign affairs, even as they helped progressive elements domestically to begin removing the heavy-handed influence of the military in government. The confluence of changes in communications and politics made Seoul an especially cogent

237

example of the role played by the Olympics as "actor and stage"in the world political system.[1]

An underlying premise of this book is that neither the Seoul Games themselves nor the broader global context in which they took place can be adequately understood without considering the changing relationship of politics to television and other media at national, international, and transnational levels. Beyond description and exploration, our intent is to contribute to a more media-theoretic understanding of political communication. Accordingly, this final chapter summarizes the major findings of the study in terms of the questions and issues posed in Chapters 1 and 2 and treated in each of the ensuing chapters.

The Olympics as Communication Event Versus Process

One important purpose of this study was to describe and explore both the numerous ways in which television influenced politics through the Seoul Olympics and also the multitude of ways in which political considerations shaped the global telecast from Seoul. This volume has approached the Seoul Games as an event-centered communication process, rather than simply a media event. Such a conceptual approach draws on many important insights from the recent study of media events, but it offers a somewhat different conception of Olympic communication. It sees the Seoul Olympics not only as a festive television spectacle, preplanned and largely integrative in its effects (as suggested in the slogan "Peace, Harmony, Progress") but also as a source of unplanned and, at least in the short term, divisive news events like the boxing incident. Moreover, if the Seoul Olympics are conceived of as a sixteen-day event, more or less bounded in space and time, the Games served as an important object of contention and point of reference in the longer-term political transformation within Korea during the 1980s. The central question is whether the Seoul Olympics would be viewed and remembered for their legitimation of a military government or, alternatively, as a triumph for the whole Korean people and a step on the way to democratization. This study suggests that the process of political change in South Korea progressed on its own momentum and literally enveloped the Seoul Olympics.

As stated in the opening chapter, few Olympic Games have entailed such a massive, lengthy, and national mobilization. For the Korean people, television and other communication about the Seoul Olympics spanned the better part of a decade, even provoking some resentment about the activities by the "Sports Republic" and the increasing amount of sports on television. Clearly, Koreans were exposed to more and varied messages about the Olympics—occurring more frequently and sustained over a longer period—than television viewers or consumers of other media anywhere else in the world. In most of the rest of the world, by contrast, the focus of attention peaked rather more quickly during the Games themselves and then just as quickly shifted elsewhere. Outside of Korea, it was correspondingly easier to think of the Olympics as an event, rather than a process.

The Olympic Movement as Transnational Actor

One major message throughout this study concerns changes within the Olympic movement and its arrival on the world stage as a major transnational actor, seemingly destined to play an even more important role in the post–cold war world. In Seoul, near-universal participation in the Games was achieved, and a major new source of financial support in the form of the TOP program for global sponsorship was introduced. However, the experience highlighted a series of persistent policy questions that continue to vex the actors or constituencies within the Olympic movement.

The Seoul Olympics once again posed the question of the basis on which the IOC acts in awarding the Games. In 1981, they were awarded to a military regime in Seoul that lacked broad popular support. During the early 1980s, it was the high visibility of the Olympics that legitimized the Chun government and made the Games such a bittersweet experience for many Koreans.

The Seoul Olympics were widely viewed as a beneficial influence in ousting a dictator, eventually allowing South Korea to come to grips with Kwangju and the misdeeds of the Fifth Republic. Consequently, the IOC may be tempted to draw parallels in considering Beijing's bid, in the wake of Tiananmen Square, to host the Olympics in the year 2000. On the other hand, the IOC played a positive role in the negotiations with North Korea over possible cohosting of certain events and in support of full participation by Socialist bloc countries more generally. In these, the transnational reach and power of the Olympic movement, epitomized by television, were significant factors. The relatively small television rights fees paid by Eastern European nations through OIRT carried the largest possible political significance for South Korea by signaling the definite intention of those nations to participate in the 1988 Games.

A number of the questions surround commercialism's dominance in the Olympics and its intrusion into the global telecast. The U.S. networks continue to provide such a large proportion of revenue to the Olympic movement that it becomes difficult to challenge the degree to which their numerous commercial interruptions change the very nature of Olympic television, at least in the large U.S. market. Moreover, because the U.S. rights fee constitutes such a large segment of the revenue for Olympic television, U.S. influence is correspondingly high in the planning and production of the global telecast.

The present study shows that NBC's coverage focused disproportionately on a small number of athletically or economically strong nations. There was also disquieting evidence of a continued difficulty for the Western-dominated television networks in the Asian setting. NBC approached its preparations for Seoul warily, concerned that its investment might be jeopardized by unrest in Korea. Although it succeeded in protecting its investment, a furor arose in Seoul over aspects of its coverage. Overall, the network's approach echoed the past record of commercial television in news and entertainment programming and did not offer hope that the Olympics will soon become a truly global and inclusive spectacle.

The anti-American sentiment sparked, in part, by NBC Television's coverage ran counter to the central themes of the Seoul Games—"Peace, Harmony, Progress." The entire Olympics process highlights the present and future challenge facing the IOC. The IOC exerted its control over television and sponsorship revenues, after being taken somewhat by surprise in Los Angeles. But it was apparent that the U.S. network still wielded enough power on its own to create other difficulties in an Olympics telecast, whether through an overcommercialized program that departed from the intent of Olympic organizers or through a lack of cultural sensitivity in the planning of that telecast.

In short, having secured a large and stable source of income through television and sponsorship rights, the IOC now faces the dual challenge of maintaining universal participation and continuing to exert some control over those corporations footing the bill for the Olympics. As President Samaranch himself has said, the key question is no longer one of commercialism in the Olympics but one of how funds might be directed back to the athletes and spread more equitably around the world.

An equally crucial question concerns the amount of attention paid in Olympic telecasts to the symbols and ceremony of the Games or to the culture of the host city and, by extension, the nation or region in which the Games take place. As the NBC telecast from Seoul clearly demonstrated, a large number of commercial departures from an Olympic opening ceremony does not automatically mean that the audience for commercial television receives less culture or history. Indeed, commercial broadcasters do have the resources, financial and otherwise, to provide material that is either not offered or offered only sparingly by other broadcast systems. Hence, U.S. television viewers were able to learn some of the political history and cultural background that made Sohn Kee Chung's entry into the main Olympic stadium with the torch such a powerful and moving statement.

These considerations exert a strong influence on the very meaning of the modern Olympic movement. The difficulty at present is that the International Olympic Committee and the other key actors have no overall policy to ensure that central symbols and meanings of the movement are telecast with adequate reach and frequency to guarantee their continued centrality.

An emerging policy question is that of introducing coproduction and pooling arrangements into Olympic television. The present arrangement, in which the largest rightsholding broadcasters unilaterally and exclusively telecast their own material and which requires a rights fee for access to the host broadcaster's international television signal, has obvious shortcomings. These were poignantly illustrated in Seoul by the situation of the Union of African Broadcasters, who wanted access to the entire international television signal but could only afford to pay a small and symbolic fee.

To place the question of possible coproduction or pooling arrangements in broader context, it may be helpful for those responsible for Olympic television to look at what has happened in commercial television news. Through the 1960s and 1970s, the three major U.S. commercial networks competed relentlessly, pushed for the exclusive "scoop," and resisted various suggestions for news pooling. Today, technological change and the realities of the more global competition in television news has forced them, like CNN, to move into cooperative arrangements.

Closely related to the range of questions about cooperation among world broadcasters is the increasing size of television's presence in the Olympic host city. Television and other media personnel constituted the largest single contingent to attend the Seoul Olympics. Although the infrastructures prepared to host them in Korea were sufficient, there was ample evidence of the pressures created when media representatives are present in such numbers. The future policy dilemma for the Olympic movement seems clear. As the technologies of global television continue to develop and mature, there will be an increasing number of broadcasting organizations at all levels—global, regional, and local—that wish to cover the Games. On the other hand, if the Olympic movement maintains its commitment to the "host city" concept, there will always be some clear limit to the number of broadcasting and media personnel who can be accommodated in a given city. In the context of the present research, it is important to realize that television is the catalyst for this policy challenge but also that the manner in which the dilemma is resolved is, at heart, a political question. In broad but very real terms, access and accreditation for the media are issues of control. Various levels of access translate rather directly into various forms of television and media coverage. When Dayan and Katz spoke of media events as being negotiated among the organizers of the event, the media, and audiences, they had this linkage in mind.[2] When the International Olympic Committee, in conjunction with leading television networks of the world, corporate sponsors, and other constituencies of the Olympic movement, issues a policy on the overall size of the media contingent for future Games and the various conditions under which media personnel will be able to work, they are balancing the competing interests of these various groups or publics.

Finally, through their opening ceremony, the Seoul Olympics offered a dramatic glimpse into how television can be used to break barriers of time and space. Viewers will long recall the sports parachutists who formed the Olympic rings in the air above Seoul and, moments later, on the ground within the main stadium. Television technology will make it possible for future ceremonies to break barriers of time by incorporating televised segments of a historical or cultural nature and to break barriers of space through the use of satellite "space bridges" linking different parts of the world.

The manner in which the preceding policy questions are addressed will have a great deal to do with how future Olympic television spectacles are constructed and, consequently, with their political effects nationally, internationally, and transnationally. Such questions are intrinsic to the cultural and political project of constructing and conveying the global Olympic spectacle. It seems certain that they will become more complex and persistent as a more completely global communications infrastructure is put in place.

Korea in the Global Communications Revolution

Korea experienced its own telecommunications revolution while it prepared to host the 1988 Olympics. Seoul became a wired city—and not only because of fiber-optic links among Olympic venues but also because of a fully modern telephone and telecommunications system. In general, the telecommunications infrastructure for communications within Korea and internationally was included in long-range governmental planning, and, hence, it is difficult to show that the Olympics per se affected its development.

However, there is stronger evidence that the Olympic experience stimulated development of the broadcast infrastructure, electronics equipment, and computer systems required to host the Games. In each of these areas, the requirements of the Olympics themselves spurred development. Today, visitors to Seoul can see tangible evidence in the complex of buildings, formerly the International Broadcast Center, that now house the greatly enlarged headquarters of the Korean Broadcasting System on Yoido Island. The growth of Korea's electronics industry offers similar evidence around the world, in the form of consumer electronics that have penetrated most major markets.

Perhaps the strongest influence of the Olympics on Korea's communications revolution is the most difficult to measure—its effect on the people who work in broadcasting, electronics, and telecommunications. Various production and design skills in those industries were upgraded significantly as South Korea strove to develop indigenously as much of the technology as possible and to meet as many of the requirements of the Games as it could.

Olympic Television and Korea's Political Transformation

Taken together, the evidence presented in this book suggests that the Olympics as a television spectacle had several strong effects on public opinion and politics in South Korea. First, there was the short-term spiking of anti-American sentiment during the sixteen days of the Games in Seoul during September 1988. The situation was ripe for such an outburst, given the recent history of relations between the United States and Korea and several preceding events in Seoul. However, there was also a positive element in that the expression indicated a growing sense of confidence and independence on the part of the Korean people.

A second effect of Olympic television and media coverage was on public awareness of and attitudes toward a variety of nations. Television not only conveyed an array of up-to-date images from South Korea to nations around the world, it also opened a large new window on the rest of the world for many South Koreans, especially the younger generations. It did so through a massive amount of television attention to the Olympic Games themselves and the many foreign participants and guests, preceded by six years of steadily increasing press and television attention to Olympic and Western sports as a whole. In a nation whose whole population is, demographically speaking, relatively youthful, this new view of the world may prove to be one of the strongest long-term effects of the television spectacle.

This role of television in opening a window on the world for the Korean public seems to confirm, on a broader scale, one of the major findings from a pioneering study of television's role in a media event. Kurt and Gladys Lang, in their study of the 1951 MacArthur Day parade in Chicago, noted the importance of "reciprocal effects, which modify the event itself by staging it in a way to make it more suitable for telecasting and creating among the actors the consciousness of acting for a larger audience."[3] All available evidence suggests that the Koreans were acutely conscious of being on a world stage through the global television coverage surrounding the Olympics. Accordingly, they sought to behave in a proper manner, as illustrated by public opinion polls before and after the 1986 Asian Games that showed dramatic increases, nearly a doubling, of the proportion of people who thought that sports spectators were "well behaved" during athletic contests.

A third effect of the Seoul Olympics as television spectacle relates to the central political debate and process under way in Korea during the 1980s. In general terms, it may be said that the Korean public and political institutions rendered a verdict on the role of the military in government, but they did so with a literal Olympic truce inserted into the process. Viewed as a political communication process, the Seoul Olympics offered ample evidence that global or "foreign" news and information coverage cannot be separated from domestic news in the modern information environment. At the same time, there is a blurring of the old conceptual distinction between "domestic" and "foreign" policy matters. Strong evidence of this came in June 1987, when the international media scrutiny that accompanied the Olympics became the major factor in a crucial political transformation. However, the transformation required a political accommodation that would allow a successful hosting of the Olympics. The eagerness with which Korea returned to its own uncompleted political business following the Olympic closing ceremony in October 1988 underscored the point. Moreover, although television was of central importance to the Olympic Games, it was equally important in Korea's politics, as the unprecedented size of viewing audiences for the televised hearings on Kwangju and the Fifth Republic showed.

This interpenetration of world and domestic opinion is not simply a deterministic effect of television and other new communication technologies; rather, it is a matter of Korean and world political change interacting with the technologies in a new communication environment. As a specific example, Korean policy and public opinion were ripe for a pro-Soviet and anti-American outburst because of historical circumstances during the preceding years. However, the actual manifestation of political sentiments surrounding the Olympics was heavily conditioned by the existence of the latest in communication technologies in Korea, in the form of a global village of journalists networked with each other and with their peers around the world.

The knowledge that Seoul was to be a focal point of worldwide attention that would reach its zenith in September 1988 conditioned the central political debate in South Korea during the late 1980s—the struggle to remove military influence from government and, in particular, to deal with the misdeeds of the Fifth Republic under President Chun Doo Hwan. From this perspective of Korea's domestic politics, the Seoul Games were an Olympic truce in what otherwise would certainly have been a raging political battle. In 1987, international scrutiny through television and other media was an important immediate factor in Roh Tae Woo's June 29 declaration and the associated truce with the opposition that postponed national hearings on the Kwangju uprising and activities of the Fifth Republic until after the Olympics. The importance of the Games as a global media spectacle in imposing this truce can be inferred from the rapidity and intensity with which the political process resumed once the closing ceremony of the Olympics had been completed.

Dayan and Katz conceptualized media events in a manner that allowed them to argue that these events are most often "salutes to the status quo, legitimations of elites, and reiterations of the national well being."[4] Korea's experience with the Olympics would seem to call into question this general conceptualization; at least, it was a notable exception to the rule. Political liberalization and democratization in South Korea quite literally framed or enveloped the Seoul Olympics. They appeared to signal change, rather than continuation of the status quo and delegitimation, rather than support, of a military dictatorship.

Media and Foreign Policy: Seoul and Image Politics

The Seoul Olympics provided many signs of the new power of image politics. This was especially so because Korea had been, in effect, hidden in the cold war shadows of the struggles between major powers, enduring years of military government and dictatorship in the process. Consequently, many realities of Korean culture were unknown to the world, and sadly, they were also unknown to younger generations of Koreans who knew nothing but the realities of internationally and military-based governments at home. This made the Seoul Olympics a powerful "coming out party" or presentation of the nation, both to the world and to the Korean people themselves.

Although South Korea had unquestionably experienced an image problem during the cold war years, it presented a historic first in Olympic television because of the presence of the U.S. Armed Forces Korea Network television and radio. Korea's ready access to a variety of U.S. news, public affairs, and entertainment television as it prepared for the Olympics undoubtedly sensitized Olympic planners to television's potential to improve the nation's image, especially through coverage in the world's largest commercial market by the dominant Olympic rightsholder.

Although available evidence from the United States and other countries suggests that the Seoul Olympic telecast accomplished what the Olympic planners had hoped, within South Korea, international television contributed to the wave of anti-American sentiment that swept the Korean public in September 1988. The Armed Forces Korea Network, with its rebroadcast of NBC Television's Olympic coverage (minus commercials), helped to fuel the frenzy of press and public comment surrounding the boxing incident in a manner that could not have been envisioned—at least not on the same scale and with the same speed—in a pretelevision era. The consciousness of scrutiny by a global television audience combined with the highly concentrated and efficient communications among media representatives in Seoul to produce this effect.

The study provides cogent support for the idea that the media themselves should be treated as a "third protagonist" or independent actor in politics. Most existing research on the Olympics, cultural exchange, and politics has failed to do this adequately. Although the boxing incident occurred in East Asia and had a genesis peculiar to the Korean setting, the more general pattern of conflict between hosts, athletes, or others who have a stake in Olympic images will likely continue and become even stronger in the future. The reason has to do fundamentally with the arrival of image politics on a global scale. In image terms, so many exposures and repetitions—with their moving, global reach—are at stake in such a short period of massive television attention that the nature of the image becomes a battleground of sorts. At this writing, one of the Olympic organizers for the Albertville, France, Winter Games was heard to remark that everything must be perfect because "there will be only sixteen days of television coverage, but we will have to live with the image for fifty years."[5]

If any single finding from our study should be underscored, it is that global media processes and new technologies are no panacea. The Seoul Olympics demonstrated that old habits die slowly for the Western-shaped international media. The phenomenon known as parachute or firehouse journalism in numerous studies of international affairs coverage in the 1970s, was revealed in how the media covered the Seoul Olympics. NBC's approach to its coverage stands in stark contrast to the contemporaneous efforts of Cable News Network to internationalize its offerings and provide a more truly global perspective. Along with other media, NBC exhibited a strong tendency to plan and frame its coverage of news and cultural affairs in terms of the existing story line about Korea in mainstream media: political unrest, crisis, and the threat from North Korea.

Overall, U.S. telecasts from Seoul demonstrated the manner in which global media events exacerbate conflicting cultural norms that govern virtually all forms of television coverage. Although this clearly involves culture, as in NBC's coverage of the boxing incident or the opening ceremony, it is equally a political struggle over control and shaping of the televised messages. Most Koreans thought their role as Olympic hosts entitled them to a certain kind of televised portrayal; NBC, proceeding on the basis of foreign cultural assumptions, obviously thought otherwise. The implications for a more adequate theory of the relationship between media, policy, and public opinion are clear: Any such theory must be culturally nuanced.

Not only journalists but also members of the public, government officials, and those involved in transnational movements like the Olympics operate according to cultural norms that define what television and the other media should or should not do.

The global reach of television appears to have been a key factor in changing images of Korea around the world. Prior to the Olympics, they were either nonexistent, as in Poland, or incomplete and inaccurate, as in the United States and New Zealand, where Korea was viewed in terms of such themes as military threat, student demonstrations, and related political violence. However dramatic the immediate impact of the Olympics was on Korea's image around the world, this study offers nothing to contradict the notion that long-term image and attitude change will depend on how Korea is consistently and repetitively portrayed in global media from now on.

Though television's global scope is important, an equally persuasive message from the Seoul Olympics has to do with its local impact. The findings presented here offer dramatic evidence of the political impact of the media feeding upon themselves in a "wired city" with the highly charged atmosphere of the Olympics. The boxing incident and eruption of anti-NBC feeling and the Ben Johnson story were the two primary examples of this dynamic.

The visibility of the Seoul Olympics through television and the other media must be taken into account in order to explain the Twenty-fourth Olympiad in political terms. This is the case whether one seeks to understand the annoyance of a Korean citizen at endless television coverage of unfamiliar sports, the spark that lit a fire under the boxing incident, or possible changes in South Korea's image around the world. The Seoul experience offers strong suggestions that an interpretation of televised images requires attention to the background as well as the foreground factors in the coverage. When television focused on street demonstrations, viewers in Poland (and presumably other Eastern bloc nations) saw not only the immediate action but also new cars, modern buildings, and the other outwardly visible trappings of a consumer society. In the United States, viewers were treated to numerous views of the city of Seoul, used as a backdrop for commercial sponsorship messages or to frame commercial breaks. Television is intrinsically and profoundly a visual medium, and the pictures of Seoul and of Korea likely had the strongest and most positive effect on Korea's national image, even if some elements of those pictures were only incidentally captured by broadcasters.

Although the preceding pages have emphasized repeatedly that the 1988 Olympics in Seoul were far more than a media event during September 1988, there can be no denying that the massive focus of worldwide attention and unprecedented levels of televised communication around the globe were the centerpiece of a long process. On multiple levels, it was a highly political process, focusing on a television-constructed reality that would bring "The World to Seoul" and "Seoul to the World." What matters now and for the future is what the millions of viewers around the world remember. In that collective memory, the Seoul Olympics must certainly stand as a monument of which not only Koreans but all those who participated with them can be justifiably proud.

Notes

1. Richard Espy, *The Politics of the Olympic Games* (Berkeley: University of California Press, 1979).

2. Daniel Dayan and Elihu Katz, *Media Events: The Live Broadcasting of History* (Cambridge, Mass.: Harvard University Press, 1992).

3. Kurt Lang and Gladys Engel Lang, "The Unique Perspective of Television and Its Effect: A Pilot Study," in Wilbur Schramm and Donald F. Roberts, eds., *The Process and Effects of Mass Communication* (Urbana: University of Illinois Press, 1971), p. 185.

4. Dayan and Katz, *Media Events*, p. 224.

5. Report on National Public Radio's "Morning Edition," monitored on KUOW, Seattle, Wash., February 7, 1992.

Appendix A:
Korea Segments in the NBC Telecast of the Seoul Olympics and Their Main Themes

The material in this appendix is reproduced from Nancy K. Rivenburgh, "National Image Richness in US-televised Coverage of South Korea During the 1988 Olympics," *Asian Journal of Communication* 2 (1992): pp. 34–39. It is used with the permission of the *Asian Journal of Communication*.

Segment Type:
C = Chronicle
VR = Video Report
LR = Live Report
I = Interview
SS = Seoul Searching
O = Other

Type/Number: Working Description/Primary Narrator
Themes (up to three)

C1: M*A*S*H TV Show/Pauley
M*A*S*H has been a popular and familiar television show in the US.
Korea is the setting for M*A*S*H.
M*A*S*H has had a negative impact on Korean tourism.

VR2: Security of Games/Miller
Security is very tight at the Games.
South Korea and the US have prepared for terrorist threat.
North Korea poses a threat to the Olympic Games.

VR3: Seoul Preparing for Olympics/Gardner
Far ranging changes have occurred in Seoul in preparation for the Games.

The new regulations have not all been popular with Seoul residents.
This is a very important 'coming out' for Korea.

C4: US Military in Korea/Shriver
US troops are trained and ready.
Americans are carving out their own places in Korea.
The Korea tour of duty solicits responses on the part of military personnel.

C5: Baseball in Korea/Costas
Baseball is a very popular spectator sport in Korea.
Baseball in Korea is not on the same level as US baseball.
Baseball players are celebrities and make more money than the average Korean.

VR6: Shopping in Seoul/Leonard
An unusual variety of goods are sold alongside each other in wholesale markets.
Bargains, because of counterfeiting and cheap labor, are to be had in Itaewon.

C7: Korea Outside of Seoul/Pauley
There is a more traditional Korea outside of Seoul.
There is plenty of natural beauty in Korea.
Tourists are not coming to Korea in the numbers expected.

VR8: Opening Ceremony Pin Artist/unknown
A 9-year-old girl won the Opening Ceremony pin design contest.
The girl has many interests and hobbies.

VR9: American Influences in Seoul/Lewis
Evidence of American influence can be found all over Seoul.
It comes from US military, business, and tourist presence in Seoul.
Koreans seem eager to embrace that which is American.

VR10: Adoption of Korean Babies Abroad/Diaz
Korean orphans are often 'exported' to America for adoption.
Korea prefers not to acknowledge that these 'social outcasts' must leave the country to find homes.

C11: Divided Families North, South/Pauley
A KBS television programme was a catalyst for reopening wounds of divided families.
Divided families remain a source of great anguish among Koreans.
Some still work and wait for reunification of families.

SS12: US Soldiers at DMZ/Rashad
US soldiers stationed at the DMZ use sports as stress release.
Constant tension and preparedness is necessary at the border between North and South Korea.

VR13: Olympics Security/Grey
Security for the Games is very tight.
Security is an unpleasant necessity.
Koreans are taking security very seriously.

VR14: Korean Ginseng/Grey
Ginseng is considered a traditional miracle cure in Korea.
Ginseng is also big business in Korea.
Whether it 'works' is not conclusive.

LR15: Korean Restaurant/Grey
Dae Won Gak restaurant used to be a house of ill repute.
It is now a very fine restaurant catering to foreigners and diplomats.
Korea has many unique traditional foods and musical instruments.

LR16: Korean Restaurant/Grey
Some dance and music performances in Korea come from Buddhist rituals.

SS17: Itaewon Shopping for a Suit/Rashad
You can get a tailored suit in Itaewon in less than 24 hours.

C18: Korean Boxer Duk Koo Kim/Gumbel
Duk Koo Kim, a boxer who died after a fight in the US, is infamous in Korea.
He attempted to use boxing as a route out of poverty.
The sport suffered in Korea, and the US, as a result of his death.

C19: Mixed Marriages/Pauley
Mixed marriages are not often accepted in Korea.
Couples feel isolated and often divorce.
It is most difficult for the children; they are complete outcasts in Korean society.

SR20: Student Pub/Grey
One way college students meet each other is to play 'pub' games which introduce them to each other.

I21: Jimmy the Tailor/Rashad
The tailored suit for Ahmad Rashad wasn't ready in 24 hours.

SS22: Korea's Favourite Soap Opera/Rashad
'Diary of a Farm Family' is a popular show in Korea; it reminds Koreans of their roots.
It is unusual in that the TV family has an adopted child.
The show's stars are well known throughout Korea.

C23: US Military in Korea/Pauley
Our military relationship has been our strongest link with South Korea and one that will probably remain.
The Kwangju incident was a turning point in creating a generation of negative Korean sentiment towards the US military presence.
Korea has a large and strong military of its own.

I24: Kim Dae Jung/Pauley
The primary goal of the investigation into Kwangju is to restore honor and get compensation.
Opposition leader Kim Dae Jung believes the US military failed to prevent the incident; it was in their power to do so.

Koreans disagree only with misguided US government policy which has supported military regimes, not with the idea of America as an ally.

VR25: Hiding the Poor in Seoul/Diaz
Tourist don't see the 'other', poor side of Seoul.
Urban congestion is pushing out traditional residential Seoul neighborhoods.
The Olympics is a matter of pride for all Koreans.

I26: Jimmy Brings in Suit/Rashad
The blazer was ready in 24 hours this time.

VR27: Anti-Americanism, Kwangju/Pauley
There seems to be a growing anti-Americanism in Korea.
The Kwangju incident was a turning point.

I28: Govt. Official/Pauley
Much about the Kwangju incident has been distorted.
According to a national assemblyman, the US did not have any jurisdiction over the troops in Kwangju.
The US presence in Korea shouldn't be linked with Kwangju.

C29: Origins of Shilla Dynasty/Pauley
The Kyongju valley was the centre of Korea's golden age, the Shilla Dynasty.
The Korean peninsula was united during this time, and the nation of Korea was born.
Buddhism and Confucianism were also both introduced during this period to have a lasting effect on Korean culture.

O30: Montage of Korean Children/Costas
Korea is moving towards democracy.

VR31: Chusok Holiday/Shriver
Chusok is the most important holiday of the year.
Chusok is a gathering of family to honor their ancestors.
Chusok is grounded in Confucianism.

SR32: Shilla Hotel, Chusok/Lewis
Chusok is similar to the US Thanksgiving.
The traditional foods of Korea are very different from American foods.
All holidays in Korea are tinged with a bit of sadness because of divided families.

C33: Education in Korea/Shriver
Education is very important in Korea.
The Ahn family went to the US so the daughters could pursue a music education.
Students in Korea study very hard to get into the right university.

I34: US Professor in Korea/Shriver
The importance of education in Korea is grounded in Confucianism.
Teachers are very well respected in Korea.
In a male dominated society, women have equal access to educational opportunities.

SR35: Han River Festival/Grey
The Olympics Han River Festival is very popular.
It's a carnival atmosphere with games.

C36: Confucianism and Tradition/Pauley
Seoul and Korea are becoming very Westernized.
Confucianism is very influential in Korean life in areas of work and family.
Korea must figure out how to embrace the new without losing touch with the traditional.

VR37: US Military in Korea/Shriver
US military presence is necessary to uphold the DMZ.
Military service is an honorable mission in an American man's life and can serve to bond fathers and sons.
Seoul was very grim during the Korean War; Korea needs the US.

C38: Christianity in Korea/Shriver
Christianity is popular and growing in Korea—in particular evangelical Christianity. Its success is rooted in both the US missionary movement and the trend towards urbanization.
Rev. Sung Yung Moon has few followers in Korea.

I39: US Missionary/Shriver
Koreans historically have been open to different religions and they co-exist fairly well in present day Korea.
Christian groups tend to be the most outspoken concerning political issues.
The US missionary movement is still active, although not necessary any longer in Korea.

I40: Korean Journalists/DeFord
An increasing number of Koreans are feeling anti-American.
American journalists don't have a very good grasp of Korean culture.
Koreans have a different view of the Olympic Games, so they are particularly sensitive to negative coverage by NBC.

C41: Korea as Olympic Host/Gumbel
The Seoul Olympics are very important to Korea in terms of global image.
The Koreans want everything to go well.
There is a parallel with 1964 Olympics in Japan.

Appendix B: Transcript of NBC's Televised Interview on the Topic of Anti-Americanism and NBC's Reporting

Report on Anti-Americanism and NBC's Reporting

Interviewer: Frank Deford (FD); interviewees: Yon Kook Hee (Yon), Sung Hee Park (Park)

FD: Welcome back [to] Seoul this morning. As perhaps many of you have read or know, there's been a certain amount of anti-American feeling here in Seoul about, particularly the way that the press and especially NBC has handled the Koreans themselves, and we have with us this morning in the studio two Korean journalists who will discuss this with us. On my far left is Mr. Yon Kook Hee who is with the Dong-A daily, the largest afternoon paper here in Seoul, and on my immediate left is Ms. Sung Hee Park who is with the Chosun Daily, which is the largest morning newspaper. Both of these journalists have studied in the United States of America and know our culture very well. So I think they are not coming to us as aliens from the moon, but they do appreciate America and can speak with a great deal of authority.

Mr. Yon, let me ask you first, do you think the feelings about the way the press has covered Korea ... do you think the negative feelings are confined to the journalist, or do you think it is widespread? Do you think many Koreans feel that we have mistreated you?

Yon: Yes, I think that the bad feeling about NBC's reporting is now just spreading, especially among the youth.

FD: The youth particularly think that NBC ...

Yon: Yes, like the students ...

FD: The students particularly. Are these the same ones who are particularly revolutionary, or is this a widespread youth feeling?

Yon: Well, …

FD: It's a general attitude among the young people?

Yon: I mean, the number of people is getting increased … getting increasing now days, now, I think.

FD: Ms. Park, you have watched the coverage of NBC. You have mentioned it for your newspaper. Do you have a specific complaint or do you think it's the general tenor of the coverage?

Park: I've watched, I've monitored the boxing coverage as well as the feature stories about Korea that NBC has made. And, about the boxing coverage, I have just a few points I would like to make.

FD: Go right ahead.

Park: Um, there was a scene that the reporter just pushed the microphone to the security guard who obviously did not speak a single word in English, and he just kept asking questions in English and he kept answering them himself, and that was … I thought that was against the journalistic ethic. If the interviewee doesn't speak English at all, he has to get an interpreter.

FD: I appreciate what you're saying. Do you think that is especially anti-Korean or was that just an American, in your terms, being rude? In other words, does this have anything specifically to do with Korea?

Park: It resulted in anti-Americanism in Korea, so but I don't think the motivation was that bad or intentional …

FD: It just came across that way …

Park: That's right. The reporter was just there and kept asking questions, because he has to obviously report something. He has to get something out of the interviewee, but …

FD: I know that the boxing episode, in particular, has caused a certain amount of anxiety. Do you think that NBC was wrong, Mr. Yon, in covering that and staying with it as long as the network did?

Yon: Partially that's true, I think, because when you cover the boxing brawl, you should have mentioned about the judgement, whether it was fair or not, but you didn't mention about that, you just focused on the boxing brawl. That's why the Korean people got angry.

FD: But …

Yon: I don't want to protect our Korean people, those who were involved in the boxing brawl, but I would like to point out that you should mention about the referee and his judgement.

FD: But don't you think that the news value was in the fact that this was a very unusual thing, that the security forces ...

Park: I agree with you.

FD: But then can you perhaps explain to the American audience, why is it that you feel we were insensitive or incorrect?

Park: Well, in general, I think the greatest factor that caused Koreans to be upset about NBC's coverage is the difference in viewing the Olympic games. Koreans have been preparing for this Olympics for seven years and they call it the biggest event in their history ever. Alright, then even politicians and students have issued a statement that they're gonna be calm during the Olympics because it is such a great national festival. But for NBC or for the United States NBC's here to broadcast for American viewers, to make money, to prove they are the good media, and American athletes are here to compete with Soviet Russians and athletes from other parts of the world. So ...

Yon: No, it's not only the problem with NBC reporting about boxing. So we have several deep rooted reasons why the Korean people have anti-Americanism. We don't differentiate ... between NBC and the American people. We regard them, all of them as Americans.

FD: Well, o.k. Let's take a break for just a minute, and we'll come back and we'll talk about the other segments that you've seen. More about the Korean culture, and the way we've treated the whole society. So we'll be back in just a moment.

COMMERCIAL BREAK

FD: Good morning again from Seoul. We're visited by two Korean journalists and we were going to talk about the cultural part of the NBC coverage, but quite before we get on to that, one question. Let's suppose that KBC ...

Park: KBS ...

FD: KBS was televising a boxing event in Los Angeles and the same sort of thing happened there with American officials that happened here with Korean officials. How do you think you would handle that, Ms. Park?

Park: I haven't been working with a broadcasting station, so I don't know professionally the technique of how it's going to work. But from what I perceive is that they're going to report about the same way, but I don't think they're going to repeat it like three or four times, and ... commentary ... and there was a saying that this is an ugly scene and that this is a criminal act, criminal activity. This is the host country. Where is the Korean guard? I don't think we're gonna go that sentiment about it because we care for, how the Americans would feel about it.

FD: Mr. Yon, do you agree with Ms. Park, it was the emphasis and the repetition that was so upsetting to the Korean people. They were not disturbed that we showed the incident. They were disturbed that we continued to talk about it.

Park: That wasn't news ...

Yon: That's right.

Park: You have every right to show, but what upset Korean people is you over-did it.

FD: Did you see the opening ceremonies on KBS?

Yon: Yes I did.

FD: Was there any comment made when the American team walked in?

Park: Uh hm.

Yon: Was uh, I don't think (unclear) but every Korean watcher they feel about that.

FD: Because many people felt, myself included, that the American team did not show itself to best ... uh ... they were almost disrespectful. I was wondering if that was covered on Korean television.

Park: That's another cultural difference. We're supposed to line up.

FD: That's not that much of a cultural difference. There were many Americans who got like that ...

Yon: You might think that they are free and they think that's natural, but we Koreans believe that that's too much free. I mean it's it was in disorder. That's the way we Koreans think about that.

FD: Was that written in the newspapers?

Yon: No, it was my own opinion.

FD: But was it written in any newspapers?

Yon: Not much about that.

FD: I see. Now let's talk about the cultural thing. NBC has been showing many segments, many features, talking about the Korean society and the Korean culture. Do you feel that they have been unfair?

Park: There has been many reports that NBC has been unfair in showing the Korean culture, and I've monitored myself about 90% of what actually ... the others I couldn't get it, but from what I've seen, they were OK, they were not biased, but there were obviously scenes showing the negative parts of Korea and then obviously this offended Korean feelings. It's not, um, I don't think NBC did it intentionally or they had bad intention to do it.

FD: Well surely there were many segments that were positive as well, weren't there?

Park: That's right.

FD: Was it balanced?

Park: Let's say, let's give you one example. Suppose there is a lady, right, and you can criticize her, you can judge her in any way you want. But let's say you went to her wedding ceremony. Then you don't easily come out and talk about her school grades and boyfriends … and that's the same situation in Korea. It's a special time for us. It is not a very good time to show the kind of image of Korea.

FD: We were perhaps, uh, a little too intrusive. We perhaps came in too closely and were too informal. Is that fair? I think you've got to keep in mind that, for many Americans, we're not that familiar with Korea, and we're trying to show a full Korea. But I'm quite sure that any country that we visited we would step over some of those boundaries. But I think, if you'd allow me just one brief final world. I think that all of the American press has leaned over backwards to find the real Korea, and I think most of us have liked the real Korea, and I think we've written very favorably of it, and I hope you get a chance to see some of the things that have been written, as well as the NBC coverage, because I think that most of us have truly loved our visit here and I think you all have been magnificent hosts. And I think almost all the journalists of the world believe that.

Park: We understand that NBC is here for American viewers, but what we want, resent is their failure to fully understand our culture and take that into their report.

Yon: Yes, that's right. So whenever I visit the United States, we try to adapt ourselves to American culture and way of thinking, but the Americans, when they visit our country, I don't think they really try hard to adapt themselves to a foreign culture.

FD: Well of course, the problem is that we've been trying to put on an Olympics at the same time that we've been trying to get to know you and I think maybe the next time we come back we'll get to know you a lot better. Thanks very much for coming and getting to know us just a little bit better. We appreciate it.

Park: Thank you.

FD: We'll be back with Seoul in just another minute.

About the Book and Authors

In this volume, James Larson and Heung-Soo Park contend that the modern Olympics have evolved into a worldwide media event with far-reaching political ramifications. Using the 1988 Seoul games as a case study, the authors explore the globalization of the media, the role of television and associated new media in the international political process, and media influence on South Korea's political and economic liberalization and on the country's emerging role in the post–cold war order.

The Seoul Olympics were a particularly cogent example of recent changes in media and politics. With the ultimate objective of fostering Korean reunification, South Korean policymakers used the games as an effective tool for nation-building—it was an effort that required sweeping economic, political, and social changes. In attempting to achieve its goals of "Northern Policy"—opening up trade, cultural, and official diplomatic relations with China, Eastern Europe, and the former Soviet Union—South Korea used Olympic communication and ceremonies powerfully to symbolize the breakdown of cold war barriers and the creation of a new world order characterized by peace, harmony, and progress.

This interdisciplinary text will be a valuable supplement in courses in East Asian Studies and international communications.

James F. Larson is senior lecturer in the Department of Mass Communication at the National University of Singapore. **Heung-Soo Park** is professor of mass communication at Yonsei University.

Index